Putting

Children

First

AVERY

a member of

Penguin Group (USA) Inc.

New York

. . . .

Putting

Children

First

Proven Parenting Strategies

for Helping Children

Thrive Through Divorce

JoAnne Pedro-Carroll, Ph.D.

Published by the Penguin Group
Penguin Group (USA) Inc., 375 Hudson Street, New York,
New York 10014, USA • Penguin Group (Canada), 90 Eglinton Avenue East,
Suite 700, Toronto, Ontario M4P 2Y3, Canada (a division of Pearson Penguin Canada Inc.) •
Penguin Books Ltd, 80 Strand, London WC2R 0RL, England • Penguin Ireland,
25 St Stephen's Green, Dublin 2, Ireland (a division of Penguin Books Ltd) • Penguin
Group (Australia), 250 Camberwell Road, Camberwell, Victoria 3124, Australia
(a division of Pearson Australia Group Pty Ltd) • Penguin Books India Pvt Ltd,
11 Community Centre, Panchsheel Park, New Delhi–110 017, India • Penguin
Group (NZ), 67 Apollo Drive, Rosedale, North Shore 0632, New Zealand
(a division of Pearson New Zealand Ltd) • Penguin Books (South Africa)
(Pty) Ltd, 24 Sturdee Avenue, Rosebank, Johannesburg 2196, South Africa

Penguin Books Ltd, Registered Offices: 80 Strand, London WC2R 0RL, England

Most Avery books are available at special quantity discounts for bulk purchase for sales promotions, premiums,
fund-raising, and educational needs. Special books or book excerpts also can be created to fit specific needs. For
details, write Penguin Group (USA) Inc. Special Markets, 375 Hudson Street, New York, NY 10014.

Library of Congress Cataloging-in-Publication Data

Pedro-Carroll, JoAnne, date.
Putting children first: proven parenting strategies for helping children thrive through divorce /
JoAnne Pedro-Carroll.
p.   cm.
ISBN 978-1-58333-401-0
1. Children of divorced parents—Psychology.   2. Divorced parents—Psychology.
3. Divorce—Psychological aspects.   I. Title.
HQ777 5.P43   2010   2009052681
306.89—dc22

Printed in the United States of America
5   7   9   10   8   6

Book design by Meighan Cavanaugh

Neither the publisher nor the author is engaged in rendering professional advice or services to the
individual reader. The ideas, procedures, and suggestions contained in this book are not intended as
a substitute for consulting with your physician. All matters regarding your health require medical
supervision. Neither the author nor the publisher shall be liable or responsible for any loss or
damage allegedly arising from any information or suggestion in this book.

All patients mentioned in this book are composites based on the author's real patients; however,
all details have been modified to protect those patients' privacy and confidentiality.

While the author has made every effort to provide accurate telephone numbers and Internet addresses at the
time of publication, neither the publisher nor the author assumes any responsibility for errors, or for
changes that occur after publication. Further, the publisher does not have any control over and does
not assume any responsibility for author or third-party websites or their content.

This book is dedicated to the children and families

who have trusted me with their stories.

Their courage, hope, and, ultimately, resilience

are the inspiration for this book.

❁

ACKNOWLEDGMENTS

This book would not have been possible without the help of many people along the way. Most notable among them is Laura McGrath, whose many talents include skilled writer, creative thinker, and collaborator par excellence. Laura's extraordinary professional skills, personal warmth, and integrity make me ever so grateful for her partnership in this endeavor. I thank my friend Cristine Chandler for connecting me with her.

Special thanks go to my agent, Brettne Bloom, who has provided energy and enthusiasm throughout this project and found a good home for it at Avery/Penguin. Lucia Watson, my clear-thinking editor, offered invaluable editorial guidance as well as compassionate understanding when I needed a deadline extension during my mother's final illness. Thanks to the rest of the wonderful team at Avery/Penguin, including Miriam Rich, Anne Kosmoski, Lisa Johnson, Jessica Chun, Megan Newman, and Bill Shinker.

I remain grateful to the William T. Grant Foundation, which supported my initial research on the development, implementation, and evaluation of the Children of Divorce Intervention Program. The foundation also supported my participation in the Consortium of Researchers on Children and Divorce, which gave me unparalleled opportunities to learn about cutting-edge research on children and divorce, and share ideas with some of the country's leading researchers.

My late mentor, Dr. Emory Cowen, a pioneer in prevention research and a professor of psychology at the University of Rochester, was a source of wisdom, support, and knowledge, and heavily influenced my commitment to prevention research and practice. I'm grateful to many colleagues at Children's Institute for their support of my work developing and conducting research on programs for children and families. Research on the Children of Divorce Intervention Program would not have been possible without the support and cooperation of several schools in the greater Rochester, New York, area, including the Allendale-Columbia and Harley schools, and school districts in Brighton, Churchville–Chili, East Irondequoit, East Rochester, Greece, Fairport, Ontario Center, Penfield, Pittsford, Rochester, Rush-Henrietta, Webster, West Irondequoit, and Williamson. Colleagues Drs. Linda Alpert-Gillis, Aaron Black, Sheryl Jones, Ellen Nakhnikian, Sharon Sterling, Sara Sutton, and Peter Wyman deserve special thanks for their contributions to the research and development of programs to help children and parents navigate the changes in their lives.

My work developing a parent education program would have been impossible without a collaborative partnership with the Honorable Evelyn Frazee, Justice, New York State Supreme Court, and the cooperation of New York State Unified Courts. Special thanks to Allison Osborn, Elizabeth Doyne, Lynn Delles, and Shannon Dortch for reading portions of this book and providing helpful comments, and to Peggy Brill for her thoughtful proofreading.

I am grateful to my late parents, Charles and Amelia Pedro, whose love and belief in me sustain me still. My beloved mother became ill and passed away during the writing of this book. I'm thankful that I was able to take time away to care for her, and I'm deeply grateful that my sisters, Donna Murphy and Carla Kania, were lovingly by my side throughout that process, in person or in spirit. My mother would often remind us to take care of ourselves, especially during stressful times. My message to parents is similar: We all need to care for ourselves and keep the balance in our lives so we can be our best, for ourselves and our children.

All children need someone who is their champion and always ready with a hug during the rough times in life, and my grandmother Philomena Pannunzio provided that loving presence in my life. It was she who taught me some of the most important life lessons, especially about love. Although she could neither read nor write and spoke very little English, she was truly literate in the art of loving family relationships. She had a profound influence on me, personally and professionally.

I have been blessed with a large and loving family of my own. My abiding gratitude goes to Roger, my husband and soul mate, for his unwavering support of my dreams and passion for my work and our family. What a gift it is to have a husband who is a best friend, confidant, and partner in every sense of the word. My profound thanks and love go to Chris, Shawn, Shannon, and Scott, for welcoming me into their family so many years ago, when I married their dad and got four wonderful children as part of the package. They and their families continue to bring us love and joy. And to our younger children, Kristen, David, and Michael, and our son-in-law Austin, I feel so lucky to have you all so near. Thank you for your support, encouragement, love, and laughter—and for getting me out to play when I needed it! I have been blessed in love and in work. I am truly grateful.

CONTENTS

To Begin . . .

Eight-year-old "Jessica" sat in my office one rainy November day, drawing pictures as we talked through her feelings about all the changes in her family. Her thin body was curled up in the chair, and as she spoke, I marveled at how this small child carried such big adult burdens. Her parents had been separated for ten months, and she and her sister shared their time between their two homes. Jessica was very worried about her mom, who cried a lot and spent a lot of time on the phone, talking about "all the bad things that are happening to our family."

Her parents, Carol and Paul, were embroiled in disputes over property and finances, and now they were contesting some of the custody arrangements. Jessica found a poster with facial expressions showing a wide variety of feelings and began to study it carefully. After a while she looked up and commented, "You're missing some feelings on this." When I asked her if she wanted to add to the poster, she wrote the word "miserable" and began to draw a stream of tears flowing down a deeply unhappy face. As she drew, she talked about how "all the good stuff has gone away" since her parents' separation, "like how they used to snuggle with me at night. Now they are always tired and grouchy and just talk about all the bad stuff." She described her sadness at the loss

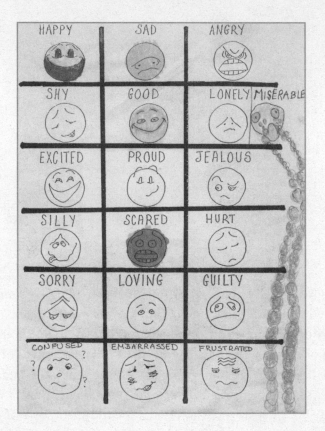

of family times together—simple routines like sitting with Dad in his special chair at night while he read the comics to her.

For Carol and Paul, divorce was the only solution to a marriage that had become increasingly bitter and unhappy. For Jessica, however, her parents' divorce felt more like a problem than a solution. The upheaval and acrimony of the divorce had compounded her losses, eroding her precious time with both of them. Like the majority of children in her circumstances, Jessica was afraid to fan the flames of conflict or burden her parents further, so she never told them how she felt.

Jessica is typical of so many children I see in my practice. They internalize their feelings, not wanting to complicate matters further. They take on a huge burden of responsibility and guilt for their parents' problems, often believing that if only they could be good enough, their parents would reconcile and their families would become whole and happy. As a way of protecting themselves from further disappointment and emotional pain when they lose secure family connections, many young people ultimately disengage from their parents, both emotionally and physically. Even as young children, they may withdraw from communication. As young adults, they may move out, sometimes putting hundreds or even thousands of miles between themselves and what was once their home.

Fortunately, Jessica's story has a happier outcome. Despite their own battles and the deep sense of guilt that had prevented them from recognizing their daughters' distress, Carol and Paul chose to make successfully raising their children their top priority. With help, they learned how to listen more attentively and empathically to Jessica and her sister and connect with them through positive activities and open communication. They also worked hard to develop and use parenting plans and practices that promoted their children's well-being and growth. Although ending their marriage still resulted in painful times for everyone in the family, Carol and Paul found ways to address the feelings, express their never-ending love for their children, and help them not only survive, but thrive. Through their child-focused, positive parenting, they helped Jessica and her sister to become the confident, capable, and loving young women they are today.

As Carol and Paul's story reveals, one of parents' toughest tasks is to allow themselves to recognize their children's pain, especially if they are likely to have caused it. Kindhearted people never intend to hurt those they love the most, so it is not surprising that divorcing parents may find it hard to acknowledge all the emotions their children grapple with, especially when parents, too, are going through one of the hardest times of their lives.

It is a lesson well documented in research and particularly important in healing from grief and painful emotions. It takes courage to acknowledge pain, but that acknowledgment allows healing to happen. In these situations children, like adults, need to know that their feelings matter—and that *they* matter. In the midst of their own pain, parents need to look beyond the surface of their children's "it's-no-big-deal" response and both recognize and acknowledge their deeper feelings. Only then can they begin to help them heal.

We hear a lot about the children who bear the brunt of their parents' divorce and the long-term consequences on their lives. We all know sad stories of children who have struggled through divorce, at great cost to them. But we don't hear enough about the success stories of children who come through the process with resilience, thanks to the support and guidance of loving, conscientious parents. This is not because these children don't exist, but because their stories have not been told yet—or often enough—with sufficient detail about the essential ingredients for their success. This book is about the Jessicas of the world and the parents who work hard so that their children come through divorce stronger on the other side. It is ultimately a book about success—and love.

Where It All Began . . . for Me

Early in my career, I worked in a school-based mental health program, providing early intervention and support to children with adjustment problems. Teachers referred children to me for several reasons: their difficulty concentrating, their anxiety-ridden withdrawn behavior that kept them from participating in class, or angry, disruptive behavior that kept them—and sometimes their classmates—from succeeding in school.

As I worked with these children, a recurring theme emerged. Many of their concerns were related to stress that stemmed from turmoil in their families. With nowhere to turn for support, this stress was spilling over into the classroom. With their parents' permission, I began to meet with children in small groups, to give them support and help them realize they were not alone in these experiences and emotions. Their relief was palpable. The sense of camaraderie and mutual support that began to develop in the groups made me realize that what these children needed was a safe, supportive environment to share experiences, discover they were not alone, and learn skills to cope effectively with the challenges they faced.

I was determined to learn more about how I could help children and families facing major life changes. So I undertook a doctoral program in clinical psychology. My mentor, the late Emory Cowen, was a pioneer in community psychology and the promotion of wellness in children. When it came time to develop a dissertation topic, my thoughts went immediately to the children I had worked with in the schools. Indeed, I remember their names, their faces, and their courage to this day. It was the early 1980s, divorce rates were skyrocketing, and millions of children were affected. Newly married with four stepchildren, I also had compelling personal reasons to help children who had undergone big transitions in the wake of their parents' divorce. What was needed, I reasoned, was a model that could be repeated with not just one group of children, but thousands. Schools would be the ideal setting for such preventive programs, first because children view them as a second home, and second because through schools, the program could reach large numbers of children in need, free of charge.

It all seemed like a good idea to a young, idealistic, "newbie" psychologist . . . but not so much to the first few school administrators to whom I proposed the idea. The concept was relatively untried; there were no programs like this in the area, and only one or two nationally. Some administrators feared, understandably, that parents might have negative reactions.

After a few rejections, my dissertation committee became concerned about whether I would ever get enough schools, children, parents, and teachers to cooperate. I, too, began to have doubts. After a particularly discouraging day of rejections and obstacles, I told my stepson Scott, "I just don't think this idea to start a support program for kids is going to work. I might as well just give it up and find an easier dissertation project." Our beloved son, only fifteen but wise beyond his years, still remembered the pain from his parents' divorce. "Don't give up, JoAnne," he said. "I wish there had been a program like that for me when I was a kid."

I still remember that day as vividly as if it were yesterday. Scott's words inspired me and fueled my determination to see obstacles as challenges to overcome and rejections as problems to solve. Soon after, five schools agreed to pioneer a new way to support children's healthy adjustment and participate in a research study to see whether the program made a difference. I am thankful for the teachers, administrators, and group leaders of those schools for their willingness to try a new approach. Since then, the program they piloted has served thousands of children in more than five hundred sites around the world.

I am also indebted to the parents who agreed to have their children participate in the program, for their faith in me and in their school personnel. Most of all, I am grateful to the children who trusted us enough to share their stories, their feelings, and their inner lives. Children continue to be my inspiration. They teach me about hope, courage, and determination, even when everything in their lives appears temporary and unpredictable at best, and painfully and permanently broken at worst.

This book reflects the experiences and inner feelings of these children and millions of others who, like Jessica, feel deeply about the changes in their families, but usually do not—and often simply cannot—share their stories with those they love most, their parents. It also provides proven ways for parents and other caring adults to help children survive their parents' divorce and thrive as individuals. I use the word "divorce" to define the termination of any family partnership. The implications for parents are equally profound, whether they are straight or gay, legally married or not.

What I have presented on these pages is based on my own more than twenty-five years of experience developing, directing, and researching the results of programs for children and parents, from my own clinical practice, and from a large and growing body of research undertaken by colleagues around the world. Collectively, these provide abundant evidence that parents can successfully adopt proven strategies and practices to reduce or prevent many of the negative effects of divorce on their children.

What's in This Book for You

Writing this book is an extension of my earlier goal to reach out to many more children and families. I have written it for parents, grandparents, loving family and friends, teachers, judges, attorneys, mediators, mental health professionals, and others who make a difference in children's lives. I have written it for you, and ultimately for the children you care about.

These are my three primary goals:

1. To enable you—especially if you are a parent—to hear what children feel but often cannot or will not say, and to gain insight into the enduring impact of divorce and the challenges of remarriage and stepfamily relationships.
2. To help you—especially if you are a parent—understand many ways you can minimize the damage from your divorce and guide your children to become as strong and resilient as possible. These strategies are sound, practical, and based on a depth of research and my experience with thousands of children and families.
3. To offer you understanding, compassion, and hope, so you can turn adversity into opportunity for healing, positive changes, and new beginnings.

Through these pages, you will learn:

• what children say in the safety of a therapeutic environment but seldom tell their divorcing or divorced parents, and how to understand their words and behaviors,
• how children express the stress of divorce at various developmental stages and what parents can do to defuse it,
• how to talk with children of different ages about separation, divorce, and family changes in ways that provide reassurance and stability and prepare them for big changes,

- how parents can reduce conflict between themselves, promote their own well-being, and protect children from ongoing animosity,
- what recent behavioral and brain research contributes to our understanding of how to help children through difficult times, and
- what emotionally intelligent parenting practices parents can adopt—especially consistently expressing abiding love yet also setting very clear limits on their behavior—to ensure that their children grow up strong and resilient.

Since other books on the market provide a variety of viewpoints and sometimes conflicting advice, let me offer some perspective. Some controversy exists among professionals about the impact of divorce on children. Most of their differences are about the magnitude of this impact.

Some researchers and clinicians believe divorce inevitably creates difficulties for offspring that last throughout their lives. Indeed, research demonstrates the negative impact on a significant number of children both during and long after a divorce. Several national surveys confirm that children with divorced parents experience between two and three times as many mental health problems as their peers from non-divorced families. In a study my colleagues and I undertook with second- and third-grade children, we found higher levels of anxiety and depression among those from divorced families. Compared with their peers from continuously married families, these children were rated by their teachers, parents, and themselves as having significantly more anxiety and often appeared depressed or unhappy.

Other research suggests that the vast majority of children are resilient and do well after a breakup. This perspective is supported by studies that reveal tremendous variation in how children fare over time, including sizable numbers who live productive lives without evidence of significant psychological problems. As some researchers have noted, what studies may miss are the underlying painful emotions that are more difficult to measure in standardized research protocols. It has also been shown, however, that when children have witnessed prolonged, intense conflict between their parents, divorce actually reduces their stress.

When divorce results in a more peaceful family life, the long-term outcomes for children are better, too, than for children who remain in high-conflict families.

My own view is that divorce is unquestionably painful for children, but long-term negative outcomes are not inevitable. The key is in understanding which factors put children at risk for problems and which ones help them grow resilient. Multiple factors shape the course of children's lives, many of which are based on the quality of relationships between parents and their children before, during, and after divorce. It has consistently been shown that when parents can contain their conflict, manage their own emotions, and do their job of parenting well, their children can grow up without being burdened by the legacies of divorce. Today, because of the depth and breadth of research in this area, we understand better the nature of the specific— and unquestionably real—risks and challenges that divorce poses for children. We know that divorce is second only to death in the degree of stress it creates and in the amount of time required to adjust to it. We understand that divorce is not just a single change, but a series of changes, and that parents need to help guide their children through all of them.

Fortunately, we also understand what kinds of parenting practices have proven effective in helping children to become resilient and avoid the "miserable" feelings that were beginning to influence the course of Jessica's life. We have documented the successes of parents like Carol and Paul, who learned how to share in providing loving, stable parenting over the long term. They are proof that positive, emotionally intelligent parenting is possible, even in painfully broken marital relationships.

A Note About Second Thoughts

It is commonly understood that the decision to divorce is filled with painful emotions. Less well understood are the misgivings and ambivalent feelings that often accompany the process. For a significant number of people, those mixed feelings extend to lingering regret. In her "Virginia Longitudinal Study of Divorce and Remarriage," psychologist E. Mavis Hetherington and colleagues followed divorcing adults over time to better understand their longer term changes and adjustments.

Among other things, this study revealed the enduring power of attachment that some former partners maintained over time. One year after the divorce, at least one partner in three-quarters of divorced couples had second thoughts about their decision to divorce. Former partners confided to the researchers, if not each other, that perhaps they should have worked harder at the marriage, and they expressed regret over the path they chose.

Data collected two months after divorce sheds additional light on couples' sustained affection and attachments. Three-quarters of the women and two-thirds of the men said that in an emergency they would call their former partner first. Fifteen percent of the couples reported having sex with each other at least once since the divorce. Another 15 percent of men were still helping their former wives with household repair and related chores. This study highlights the reality that we are hardwired for strong attachment in our relationships—even those that are complicated by seemingly irreconcilable differences, strong emotion, and conflict.

With this information, I want to suggest that it's worth asking just how irreconcilable your differences are. If you and your partner are engaged in intense conflict or violence, divorce offers greater safety and release from a situation that is toxic not only for you, but for your children.

Only a minority of all divorces are characterized by such high levels of conflict, however. And ironically, it is low-conflict divorces that appear to pose the greatest challenge for children's adjustment. Perhaps these are marriages that may also have the greatest potential for reconciliation, or at least the potential for managing the breakup in ways that reduce the stressful impact on children.

There may be an important window of opportunity for couples in the early stages of marital distress to address troublesome issues, deepen intimacy, and strengthen their relationship. Unfortunately, one of the major challenges to intervening early enough to salvage a marriage is the well-documented "delay" problem. Couples who realize that their marriage is in trouble wait an average of six years before seeking help. By that time, at least one partner often has already begun to disengage emotionally, and it may be too late to recapture the feelings that brought them together in the first place.

But here's what I want to say to you. If you are having misgivings about your separation or divorce, consider addressing those misgivings with a mental health professional, member of the clergy, or—perhaps most important—your partner. Even if you think it may be too late, you might achieve resolution through honest discussion and hard work. I have worked with couples who have done this, even after a divorce was finalized. With diligent work, good faith, and commitment, they found ways to renew and strengthen their relationship. A few have chosen to remarry each other; others were content to continue to be together without remarriage. Although it doesn't happen often, I know that for those who took the risk to address their regrets, the payoff was significant.

Please understand that I am not opposed to divorce. I am convinced that it is sometimes the best decision for all concerned, particularly when perpetual conflict makes everyone in the family tense and miserable. But as you learn more, through the pages of this book, about the impact of divorce on children, I do encourage you to consider whether yours is likely to become a divorce of lingering regrets, or whether you can rebuild your relationship and preserve your family.

Certainly marriage does not guarantee happiness. Tough times are inevitable in any relationship. The question is whether you will benefit most by investing the hard work to make this marriage stronger, or by leaving it behind and starting anew. Either way, you will breathe easier if you feel certain that you have given your marriage your very best effort, for your sake and your children's.

A Vision for Your Positive Future

Parenting is a lifelong process for all dedicated parents, divorced or not. While that may sound particularly daunting for those in the throes of divorce, the process of working through these hard times and painful adjustments together gives parents and children opportunities to develop strong, loving relationships that can deepen over time.

It is that vision of a positive future that I want to offer you. This book integrates a huge body of research with what I have learned through thousands of individual stories that reveal the fears, experiences, and wishes of those whose parents divorce. It also reflects my own experience as the wife of my beloved husband of thirty years and as mother of our seven children, including the four that Roger brought with him into our marriage. Our children have proven the possibilities of resilience, taught us both much about parenting, and today are leading fulfilling lives. They are also the source of immeasurable joy.

I am convinced that parents and children can weather the very real challenges of divorce and its aftermath. My heart goes out to parents who, in the midst of their own profound pain and vulnerability, must find the inner resources to take on their children's confusion, sadness, and fears. I know that, in the early stages of a breakup, nothing seems more difficult. But I also know that parents who can find ways to listen attentively and empathetically to what their children are experiencing and feeling, and make the commitment to positive parenting, will give their children the greatest gift of all. My hope is that this book will be both a helpful and a healing guide.

"My Divorce": What Children Say and What They Mean

Understanding Children's Deepest Emotions

The hardest thing about my divorce is seeing the empty chair at the kitchen table at my mom's house and missing my dad. Then, when I'm at my dad's, I miss my mom."

"For me, the worst thing about my divorce is all the fighting. I keep hearing them say my name over and over when they're arguing. It makes me worry that I'm the cause of all this trouble. I just want to plug my ears and scream."

"Yeah, my divorce is like that, too. I just run into my closet and hide when they argue."

Back in the early days of my work with children experiencing their parents' divorce, I asked the members of a children's support group what was hardest for them about the changes in their families. As I listened to them describe their feelings, I could not help noticing their use of the words "my divorce." Just minutes earlier, as these children had chattered happily about their favorite TV shows and foods, they had seemed like typical young school-age children. Now, as they talked about their parents' divorce and their feelings of loss, sadness, worry, hope, and yearning connected to it, they seemed somehow older, burdened by the new realities of family disruption.

For all of them, "my divorce" represented unwanted and unwelcome changes. For many, it was also a shock.

When I suggested that divorce was between their parents—not them—they described convincingly why the divorce really was theirs, too. These children's tales all had the same underlying story line: The two people they loved best and depended on most were parting ways, and life as they knew it had utterly, often bewilderingly, changed.

It was on days like this, many years ago, that I began listening with particular attentiveness to how children describe their inner experiences of divorce and to what additional meanings might lie beneath their words. In the safety of a therapist's office or a support group with other children whose parents are separated or divorced, children often reveal feelings and thoughts they share nowhere else. Through countless sessions, I have learned children's perspectives on what helped, what hurt, and ultimately what made a difference to them over a lifetime.

Building on research-based information about children's experience of divorce, this chapter will focus on two related subjects: what children say—and what they mean—about their parents' divorce, and how parents can listen carefully and communicate their understanding, empathy, love, and support.

Children's own words provide insight into the multitude of feelings that many experience in relation to their parents' divorce. My interpretation of their words is based on many years of careful listening and learning from the real experts on the impact of divorce—the children themselves. The reactions described here are well documented in my own clinical research and that of many colleagues.

The final portion of this chapter describes some specific practices that parents and others can use to encourage children to talk about their feelings and to listen with greater insight and understanding. It also includes recent brain research that helps to explain why putting words to feelings has a calming effect and develops capacity for managing strong emotions. It is my hope that, with this combination of skill and knowledge, parents will be better able to foster warm and enduring relationships with their children—relationships that continue to grow stronger and richer throughout their lives.

A Special Challenge: Understanding What Children Really Think and Feel

Parenting through divorce presents particular challenges because it is often very difficult for parents to know what their children really think or feel about the breakup. Most children talk very little about their parents' divorce and their own complex feelings surrounding it. There are a variety of reasons for this.

First, children may not always understand their own feelings or—depending on their developmental stage—they may not have the emotional vocabulary or ability to explain them. The anxiety they feel may make it even harder for them to sort out and describe complex emotions.

Second, some children are so worried and anxious about family circumstances that they shut down all their emotions. Keeping silent is a coping mechanism children sometimes use to lock up their painful feelings and protect themselves from some of the hurt.

Third, children may maintain silence when they see that one or both parents are angry, depressed, vulnerable, or preoccupied with their own issues. Many children seem to have built-in emotional barometers. When storm clouds gather around their parents, they take cover and try to stay out of the emotionally charged atmosphere. If the situation appears volatile, children instinctively fear mentioning what they observe. Instead, they often go out of their way to maintain the status quo and avoid causing even the slightest ripple.

Fourth, they often feel both protective and worried, and they remain silent in an effort to shield the parents they love deeply from additional unhappiness and worry. In such circumstances, children do not want to add to their parents' burdens, especially if they believe there is already very little time or energy left for them. As the little girl who kept hearing her own name in her parents' arguments said so poignantly, "It makes me worry that I'm the cause of all this trouble."

Finally, children long for their parents' reconciliation or at least a truce. In this case, saying nothing seems to them the safest response— one that has no possibility of interfering with their wish for a reunited family.

Outside the family, school-age children who feel embarrassed and worried about how their friends will react to news of the divorce often keep their feelings to themselves, compounding their isolation. Surprisingly, in an era when about half of all marriages end in divorce, many children feel a sense of stigma, embarrassed and worried about what others will think of them and their family. At a time when they most need to share and explore their feelings and receive reassurance and support, they may instead become increasingly alone.

Despite their deliberate silence, children desperately need for their parents to understand what is going on beneath the surface and com-municate without barriers. They yearn for their parents to hear and understand their innermost feelings as well as to be part of their daily activities. Most of all, they want their parents to notice their pain and fears and alleviate them as much as possible.

It is important for you as parents to understand the meaning of your children's silence and avoid trying to forcefully break through this protective shield. Instead, you can best help your children by making them feel safe, secure, and protected. When children are confident that you will respond with understanding and empathy, they become more comfortable letting their feelings surface and sharing them.

Saying Versus Meaning

The late child psychologist Dr. Haim Ginott introduced new ways of communicating with children. He coined the term "childrenese" to define the unique language that children use—different from that of adults—to describe their feelings and motivations. In my training as a clinical psychologist, I learned about this language and how to listen for the unspoken meaning in children's questions and comments. Taking children's words at face value sometimes results in missing a larger meaning that has greater emotional importance. Very often, children's comments and questions are actually pleas for reassurance of their parents' continuing love and concern.

You can apply the concept of childrenese to your daily parenting by realizing that what your children say or ask may have unspoken meanings. It may be difficult for you to listen to your children with such a filter, especially when you may be concerned that your own decisions and actions are the source of your children's pain. As you gently probe for underlying feelings, however, you will soon find that such listening opens more meaningful and healing communication.

Developing the ability to listen for meaning is essential to achieving two critical goals: to help children feel understood and accepted, and to ensure that that they feel safe in expressing all their emotions. Such communication strengthens the all-important parent-child emotional bonds that have been proven to help children to thrive and grow.

Here is a fairly typical example of a child's apparently simple question and the kind of wise response that enabled her parent to uncover and help to allay her real concerns. Five-year-old Emily asked her father, "Are you going to get a new wife?" This sounded like a straightforward question to Dan, but he wisely anticipated that it might mask some worries. He responded by voicing some concerns that he thought she might have and soon discovered that Emily was, indeed, asking about more serious issues.

This was Dan's insightful response as he gently put his arm around his daughter: "Emmy, maybe you're wondering about what might happen if I got married again or maybe if your mom did, too? Maybe you're also wondering about what else might change in our family. I don't plan to get married again anytime soon, but if I did, I would be very sure to tell you in advance, so you would know. But here's the really important thing I want you to always remember. If I do get married again someday, I will still always be your dad, and your mom will always be your mom—no one will take her place. Both of us will continue to love and care for you. You will always be my special Emmy—nothing will ever change that. The kind of love I have for you is the kind that never stops or goes away, even if I love other people, too."

In fact, Emily had worried that if her dad got a "new mom," she might not be able to see and love her "real" mom as much. Added to this anxiety was her underlying fear that if her mom and dad got new partners, they might "get new kids, too." Would she then be replaced? Even if she did not lose her "official" position as Dan's daughter, she worried that she might lose her special place in his heart, or her usual spot beside him on the couch when they watched TV. These concerns were based on her misconception that if people stop loving each other, they just "get rid of them" and replace them with someone new—not an illogical concept for someone of her age and life experience.

Emily's question is very typical of what children in her circumstances ask, and her underlying concerns are also much like those of her peers. The challenge for her father was to translate her simple question into what it really was—an urgent need for clarification about what would and would not change in her family and for reassurance about her place in a loving family.

In addition to asking deceptively simple questions, children also may answer adults' questions in ways that mask their inner experiences. For example, if children are asked how they feel about their parents' divorce, they often say, "I don't know" or "It's not that big a deal" or even "This is boring to talk about." "Boring" is a hallmark protective response children use when they are confronted with topics that provoke anxiety or are threatening or uncomfortable for them.

These shorthand responses protect children from painful emotions, but it is important for parents to understand that beneath such comments often lie deeper feelings. When the climate is right and children and adolescents feel safe, they will let you in on their real concerns and feelings. The key is for you to help your children realize that their feelings will be heard without judgment, and even more important, without rejection. This may seem obvious, but it is quite an accomplishment to listen openly and calmly to your children's painful emotions while simultaneously immersed in your own.

Here is an example of the kind of gentle reassurance that you can offer at the same time that you open the door for future communication. "Right now you don't feel much like talking about your feelings. It can be hard to talk about things that are upsetting. But we've had some pretty big changes in our family—changes that cause a lot of feelings for all of us. All those feelings are normal for anybody who is going through the kinds of changes we are experiencing. So just know that when you're feeling sad or angry or worried or frustrated about these things, or even when you are having more comfortable feelings, I always want to hear how you're doing."

What Children Worry About

Several studies, including one my colleagues and I undertook with seven- and eight-year-olds, reveal higher levels of anxiety among children whose parents are divorced than those from continuously married families. There are a great many concerns that contribute to their anxiety.

These concerns are revealed quite regularly in the safety of a therapist's office or support groups. In our groups we begin by asking, "What are the first words that come to your mind when you hear the word 'divorce'?" For children from kindergarten through adolescence, this activity always generates emotional and insightful discussion of feelings they seldom mention outside the safety of the group. While responses vary with the age of the child, the words that are universally expressed include: *sad, scared, shocked, angry, depressed, frustrated, confused, worried, weird, different, fights, caught in the middle, lonely, leaving, broken, stomachaches, split, back and forth, lost, why, hopeless, helpless,* and sometimes simply, *oh, no!* Children who have had more time and experience in the long process of adjusting to family changes offer some positives such as: *relieved, hopeful, peaceful,* or *no more fighting*—if they are lucky.

A survey of children in our support groups over the years revealed their most frequent worries and sources of stress. Here are their responses to the question: "What is the hardest part of your parents' divorce for you?"

- When I'm with my mom I miss my dad—98 percent
- When I'm with my dad I miss my mom—98 percent
- I worry about what will happen to me—94 percent
- My parents fight about me—92 percent
- My parents argue a lot—86 percent
- I worry that family problems are my fault—79 percent
- Going back and forth between homes—78 percent
- I have a hard time in school—72 percent
- I don't get enough time with my dad—72 percent
- I don't get enough time with my mom—64 percent
- I worry about what kids will think if they know my parents are divorced—65 percent
- I worry about my family—65 percent
- I worry that we don't have enough money—56 percent
- Sometimes I feel like I don't have a family—29 percent

These responses convey the range of worries that children often keep to themselves. By recognizing and understanding these concerns and the emotional toll they can take on your children, you may be better able to reach out and provide them with much needed reassurance. Your empathic support provides your children with a sense of relief and comfort, helping them to realize they are not forgotten in the turmoil of family changes, and reassuring them that they are understood.

Children's initial concern: "What's going to happen to me?" In the early stages of the separation, this is the immediate and overriding concern for children of all ages. Young children worry about who will take care of them, and older ones are concerned about a number of ways the divorce may affect them. They may also worry about further divisions in the family: *"What if my brother wants to live with Dad and I want to stay with Mom?"*

Children from infancy to early school age do not yet have the ability to understand complex family circumstances, and they lack the verbal skills to express their vulnerability. They simply do not know what will happen to them or their family. These children worry about the immediate, day-to-day matters of being cared for—parents giving them their meals, taking them to day care or school, reading to them, putting them to bed, and being nearby if they wake at night. Sometimes they imagine dire situations that seem very possible and real to them.

Divorcing parents often are overwhelmed by the frequency with which their young children ask, *"Where are you going? Why do you have to go? When are you coming back?"* Every trip to the supermarket, every departure for work, even going to a different part of the house may be met with great anxiety. Young children often worry that they may be completely forgotten if they cannot stay right beside a parent all the time.

If their parents are unable to explain what is happening in ways they can understand, young children often fill in the blanks with their own fears and fantasies, which are often far worse than the reality. For example, they may think that if Mom and Dad could stop loving each other, then maybe they will stop loving and taking care of them, too. This leaves them vulnerable to a host of anxieties and worries that often contribute to regression in their behavior, difficulty sleeping, nightmares, increased clinginess or demanding behavior, unpredictable meltdowns, difficulty separating from parents, and other signs of stress.

School-age children often worry about where they'll live, when they'll see both parents, and how the divorce will impact their friendships, school activities, and other practical aspects of their lives. They, too, sometimes project worse scenarios for their lives than they will likely experience when they lack concrete information.

Anxiety that parents will "disappear"—physically or psychologically—and parenting will end. Often young children become afraid that since one parent "disappeared" from the only home they know, the other one might, too. Their anxieties generally increase when their own living situation changes. No wonder young children in these circumstances often have nightmares, cling anxiously to their parents, make increased demands, refuse to sleep in their own beds, resist separating from a parent when it is time for preschool, day care, or a transition to the other parent, and exhibit a wide variety of anxious behaviors.

Children also worry that even if their parents don't disappear physically, their divorce may mean that they will not remain involved in parenting. Six-year-old Justin told me, *"I'm afraid Mom and Dad won't know each other anymore."* When I asked him what he thought would happen if his parents did not see each other, he explained himself more directly. He was worried that if his parents did not see or speak to each other after they divorced, they would stop being his parents. His words express how deeply children recognize their own need for parents to take care of them and guide them. Children feel a sense of security when they are aware that their parents work together at parenting and provide a structure of love and caring. When faced with their parents' divorce, children fear greatly that they will lose the kind of attention that makes them feel loved and secure.

Adolescents may be able to express their big fears more directly, although usually not to their parents: *"What if they both leave? Who will be there for me?"* For them, the potential of "losing" one or both parents—or their attentive parenting—can be a rocky prospect at the very time in their lives when they are beginning to break away. They understand, deep down, that they need the structure and the guidance that keep them on a positive path. When loving but firm boundaries fall apart in the wake of divorce, they may seize the opportunity to live by their own rules—or none at all.

Older youths and teens may cover their fears with bravado or fierce, defiant displays of independence, or they may simply withdraw. Good students may do poorly in school, athletes may quit the team, and friends may abandon even their closest companions. All of these can signify an unmanageable amount of stress.

For children of all ages, worries are magnified when their parents are enmeshed in conflict or appear unstable or overwhelmed, leaving their children to wonder about who will be able to take care of them, set boundaries, and keep them safe. By understanding the fears that produce this range of behaviors, parents are better able to alleviate their children's worries and take important steps that help to provide support and stability.

Feelings of invisibility. Fourteen-year-old Sarah's poignant comment in a group session met with many nods of agreement: *"Sometimes I feel invisible, like no one even notices me . . . there are not as many hugs."* It's a theme repeated often. In the turmoil that often surrounds divorce and in the aftermath of grieving and adjusting to change, children often feel that no one truly "sees" them or is aware of their feelings and needs. I am sad to report that in too many situations, that perception is very close to reality.

Parents are often overwhelmed by their own emotions surrounding the breakup—pain, sadness, disbelief, anger, frustration, fear, abandonment, guilt, loneliness, and the deeply wounded sense of feeling unloved and perhaps betrayed. In addition to the emotional overload that many divorcing parents experience, their new situation demands that they spend time on innumerable practical and legal arrangements. Who will live where? How will they share parenting? How will they manage the tasks of parenting alone in a completely reconfigured household? What changes must they make to their work situations as a result of the divorce? These issues are almost always influenced by the reduced financial circumstances that a divorce creates for everyone. How will the money be divided? How will they make ends meet? What sacrifices must be made?

When parents are deeply absorbed by serious emotional and practical issues like these, they must spend time and energy dealing with them. If their children do not appear to be having difficulties, parents sometimes assume everything is fine and remain focused on other critical matters. Even when children are essentially "fine," they still need to have their parents present in their lives—checking in with them about how they're doing, providing reassurance and a secure structure of family life.

Is it any wonder that children feel—and sometimes essentially become—invisible? Their feeling of invisibility often erodes children's own self-concept. They reason that if they are not important to their parents, then maybe they are not important at all, to anyone, and they experience a very real sense of loss and isolation. Some children who feel this way simply become quiet and withdrawn. Some hide their feelings and pretend that everything is fine. Others may act out, trying to become important enough to get attention. All of these reactions can mask a depression that, if not identified and addressed, can threaten children's current and future well-being.

Emotional bonding is an essential human need, as important as food and shelter for children. Parents can fortify secure emotional attachments with their children by providing safe, loving physical affection, engaging in active listening, affirming their strengths and unique qualities, and providing limits and guidance. Rather than feeling invisible, children who regularly experience such loving emotional and physical contact with their parents receive the gift of a solid foundation for their own future relationships.

Worries about the future. Children are also concerned about many of these same matters. By early school age, they are better able to understand the concept of the future. Even with increased cognitive ability, however, they worry and wonder about what will happen to them and their family if their parents do not provide them with accurate information that is appropriate to their age and level of understanding. Thus the future—beginning on the day children learn of the breakup—can become a source of great anxiety. Children have a hard time envisioning a different reality than the one they know, so they are vulnerable to their own worst fears. They may cling to hopes of reconciliation and employ the kind of "magical thinking"—in which children believe their wishes can cause real results—that feeds both their guilt and the unrealistic expectations that they can engineer their parents' reunion. Both beliefs derail children from their most important developmental task—simply being children.

Middle- and high-school students worry about how their lives will change, and whether both parents will be involved in their important decisions and support their activities and special occasions. They often find it unsettling when their expectations about the future—whether their parents will support their high school activities, whether they'll be able to go to college as planned—are in jeopardy.

Worries about money. "*They're wrecking the house and there's no food,*" cried four-year-old Cassandra in a play therapy session. She reinforced every word, using the parent dolls to smash the dollhouse. As we talked about what was going on with the doll family, she was able to find words that got to the core of what was troubling her so deeply: "*They're afraid they're going to be poor and there won't be enough food to eat.*" She had repeatedly heard her parents argue so bitterly about money that she was afraid they would not be able to buy food, and she would go hungry.

As older children and adolescents witness the changes in lifestyle that accompany their parents' divorce, they often worry about money. They are often able to articulate their concerns, asking about the things that affect them directly. "*Are we going to have enough money to live on?*" "*Will I be able to continue my guitar lessons?*" "*Will I be able to go to college?*" "*Do I need to get a job?*" Underlying the literal meanings of these questions are likely to be their deep concerns about their parents' and siblings' well-being, as well as their own. Often they hide these deeper concerns, not wanting to add to the burdens their parents are already carrying.

Anxiety about loyalties. Concerns about their parents become a particular source of anxiety when children are caught in the middle of parents' conflicts and feel pressured to decide which parent is "right" and to whom they should remain loyal. They worry about whether to share with one parent any of their experiences with the other, and they sometimes agonize over whether to allow themselves to like a parent's new partner for fear of being disloyal to their other parent.

"Dad asks me about who Mom was with, but I don't think Mom would want me to tell him." "Mom said I should tell Dad that he needs to pick me up early, and I'm afraid to ask him." Children often feel trapped in the middle when they are asked to be informants or messengers between estranged parents. They are terribly uncomfortable being put in the role of a spy, and even being a messenger causes them to feel anxious. *"What if Dad can't change his schedule?" "What if he gets mad at me for asking to be picked up early?"* What if this request just makes them angrier at each other?

Some children are able to predict that their parents will fight over such questions, based on a history of conflict. Others simply do not know how their parents will react, but that very uncertainty ties them in emotional knots. Research is clear on this point: Unresolved conflict that involves children and puts them in the middle of their parents' discord has profoundly negative effects on them.

I frequently hear children say, *"I know they both want me on their side."* Often children worry that their parents want them to take sides in their dispute. Unfortunately, sometimes this does happen. In their bitterness, some parents try to win their children away from their spouse or use the children's words as ammunition in their conflicts.

Often, however, children simply react to the confusing situation in which they find themselves. Both parents love them, but each parent is angry with the other. The children want to be "on both sides." They love both parents and often live what feels like double lives— burdened by the feeling that they must keep secrets, not talk about one parent with the other, and assume the enormous responsibility of trying to make both of these sad, beloved adults happy again.

Children also may begin to behave differently with each parent, taking on characteristics and habits that mirror the parent they are with at the time. They sometimes worry that if they look or act too much like one parent, they risk invoking the other's anger or perceived rejection. Many children express how different their parents are and how hard it is for them to feel a part of two entirely separate worlds, whether they are hundreds of miles apart or just a few blocks away. Elizabeth Marquardt poignantly describes this phenomenon at length in *Between Two Worlds: The Inner Lives of Children of Divorce.* This book summarizes her research into the feelings of young adults whose parents divorced when they were children. The perspectives of these adults looking back on the changes that occurred in their childhood are remarkably similar to those of children I've worked with who are in the midst of family transitions.

Concerns about parents' well-being. Even without any pressure to share information, children worry about one or both parents after a separation, especially if a parent is struggling with depression or has other physical or emotional difficulties. Often, children worry that saying anything at all about one parent will make the other feel sad or angry or hurt. *"Will Mom feel bad if I tell her I had a good time with Dad?"* Most children understand how much their parents are suffering, and they often hide any information that they think might cause any additional pain. Even when one parent calmly asks about the other, children may agonize over what and how much to tell, especially if they sense conflict or animosity between their parents.

"Mom spends a lot of time in her bed, crying," seven-year-old Stephanie, whose mother was very depressed, told me in the privacy of my office. *"I worry about leaving her when I go to school or to spend time with my dad."*

Another asked, *"Do you think Dad's going to be okay in his apartment? He's going to be so lonely, and besides, he can't cook."* Worries about parents' well-being are especially burdensome to children who may feel responsible for keeping them safe and healthy, often at the expense of their own greatest need: to be a child. When children see that their parents are taking good care of themselves physically and emotionally, they feel far more secure and confident about their own needs being met.

Fear of losing parents' love entirely. *"Do you still love me?"* Children may not ask their parents this question directly; even saying these words out loud seems too risky. But they do worry and wonder about their secure place in their parents' hearts. Like Emily, whose real fear was unspoken as she asked her father whether he would get a new wife, they reason that if Mommy and Daddy could stop loving each other, then perhaps they will stop loving and taking care of their children, too.

The fear of losing a parent's love is a source of anxiety for children of all ages. Such fears are often magnified if one or both parents move out of the family home without adequately preparing their children for the changes. Sometimes this fear is the reason behind meltdowns and clingy behavior.

How Children Express Anger, Hurt, Betrayal, and Guilt

Anger. Older children understand that, unlike death, divorce is not inevitable. They realize that someone has made this decision that is disrupting their lives, and they are often angry, resentful, and ready to blame one or both parents. They may be very vocal, and although it may be difficult for parents to deal with the feelings they express, at least they are not left with the task of figuring out what the words mean.

Older children and teens are generally able to articulate why they are angry, even though many specific causes may be tangled together. Fourteen-year-old Melissa made a drawing with a very bold, black caption: *"Divorce sucks!"* As she handed it to her father, she said, "This is how it feels." Wisely, he answered, "Yeah, it does feel like that right now, doesn't it?" I often hear Melissa's words echoed by other children and teens. Other expressions that typify their anger are *"Divorce is dumb!"* and *"Why can't they just stop fighting? They tell us not to fight; why can't they?"*

Sometimes, anxieties about their parents' divorce, coupled with teenage angst, produce angry outbursts. *"If you hadn't gotten divorced, we'd have enough money to go on vacation." "You're just so selfish! You think it's all about you—well it's not! You have children, you know. Don't we count?"* Even the most bitter accusations often manifest worries that trouble teens deeply. All too often, their fears are based in a new reality that prevents their earlier hopes and dreams for their lives from coming true.

Younger children often have less perspective, but in their anxiety and frustration about the changes in their lives, they may display behaviors that can test the patience of even the most understanding parent. When change and other stresses upset them, young children often respond in the only ways they know to express their innermost fears—with anger and other out-of-control emotions, words, and behaviors. They may simply melt down, have tantrums, and scream at whoever is present at the moment. *"I hate you!" "Go away!"* Such outbursts, as well as prolonged crying and sobbing, can reasonably be translated to, "I'm scared and sad, and I feel like my world is spinning out of control."

Betrayal. "How could you do this?" Particularly when infidelity contributes to a divorce, children often feel deeply hurt and betrayed. Even fairly young children may have a sense of their own lost innocence when a parent has an affair. Adolescents, already struggling with their own developing sense of morality and sexuality, are especially vulnerable to feelings of anger, betrayal, and broken trust. They may become deeply wary of allowing themselves to trust completely in anyone.

Children's feelings are especially complicated when parents separate because of one's infidelity with a trusted family friend. Fourteen-year-old Brandi, devastated by her father's affair with her best friend's mother, sat across from him in my office, the tears pouring down her cheeks. *"I have just one question,"* she said. *"Why? Why, Dad?"* She handed him a poem she had written about this once trusted neighbor and family friend.

I believed in you,
You had my trust.
But the hurt you cause is deep and new,
and the tears pour through my heart.

Now that trust is gone,
my heart is sad,
but I also feel
angry, furious, mad.

Once, over cookies and milk,
you listened to my hurts, my hopes.
Little did I dream
you would take us all for dopes.

You sneaked into our home
and stole my dad
just like a thief.
You left our home empty and sad.

Well let me tell you this:
I am stronger than you know.
I will keep my chin held high
wherever I go.

Discovering that a parent in whom they had placed their trust breached it with another trusted adult is painfully traumatic for young people and may have profound, long-term implications for their ability to trust in their own future intimate relationships. Children reason: If they cannot trust their parents, whom can they trust? Although injured parents may feel vindicated by their children's shared sense of betrayal and anger, when children of any age are caught in the middle, these conflicts come with a huge emotional cost for them.

Some children respond with a determination never to allow anyone else to hurt them so badly. I've heard far too many say, *"I won't be able to trust anyone ever again,"* and live by that unhappy decision. The result is that they isolate themselves from friends and family and are wary about forming and sustaining long-term, loving relationships.

Guilt. This is another emotion that can wreak havoc with children following a divorce. Although young children express guilt about their parents' divorce more readily than older youths and teens, all are subject to the deeply painful sense that they have somehow been responsible for the destruction of their parents' marriage—or have been unable to do anything to stop it. *"It was because of me. I kept hearing my name over and over again,"* cried seven-year-old Matthew. Indeed, he had heard his name repeatedly as he lay in bed at night while his parents argued about the one issue that mattered to both of them more than anything else—the welfare of their son.

More specific "information" sometimes makes children certain that the divorce is their fault. *"They got divorced because I wet the bed, and they always fought over who had to get up and help me change the sheets,"* said humiliated five-year-old Tanya. The connection between her "bad" behavior and their fighting seemed obvious to her: If only she had been able to control her bladder at night, she could have prevented her parents' arguments and divorce. Other variations on this theme are bad grades and report cards, sibling fights, and other common childhood behaviors that may well be issues of disagreement between parents, but certainly not causes for divorce.

In extreme cases, children may show signs of depression, such as regression, loss of interest in normal childhood activities, persistent sadness, or changes in mood and behavior. These situations warrant qualified professional help. Studies show that children have far more adjustment difficulties when they blame themselves and internalize guilt or responsibility for their parents' divorce.

Equally painful is children's guilt when their wishes or magical thinking come true. *"When I got mad at my Dad, I used to wish he would disappear, and now he's gone,"* said Jeremy, whose hot temper was, in fact, much like his father's. Even at seven years of age, Jeremy was not quite able to believe that his wishes did not cause his father's move away from home.

Children's Wishful Thinking and Courageous Efforts to Cope

Hopes for reconciliation. "Maybe they'll get back together again." Of all the themes that recur when young children talk about their parents' divorce, this is one of the most heartfelt. Occasionally, children feel relieved when an abusive or severely unstable parent leaves the household. But most often they want, more than anything else, to bring their parents together again and have things back the way they were. They are tentative about expressing this wish openly, well aware of the limits of their control over any divorce-related decisions. Still, this hope for reconciliation may endure over many years. It is often at the root of sudden bouts of anger or sadness when a parent remarries, even many years after their divorce.

There are many variations on this theme. *"If I try extra hard to be good, maybe they'll stay together."* Because they often believe that the divorce is their fault, children may make extraordinary efforts to behave well. Their wish to have the family reunited is so strong that they will do anything in their power to make it happen. But children do not have control over their parents' differences, and it is important for them to understand this.

In one of our sessions, a group of second- and third-graders was engaged in a board game that posed questions about children, divorce, and effective ways of coping. Seven-year-old Allison picked a card that asked, "Can kids get their parents back together after a divorce? Is that a problem kids can solve?" Instantly she responded, "I wish my parents would!" and told a story about how someone she knew actually got her parents back together. The whole group immediately chorused, "That's a miracle, Allison! That's amazing!" These children understood how fervent and heartfelt were these secret wishes.

"Maybe if something really bad happens, Dad will come back." Children's hopes and wishes for a reconciliation can endure, even among older children whose parents divorced a number of years earlier. One very intelligent fifteen-year-old confided to me that when his mother had an attack of appendicitis and was taken to the hospital, he felt hopeful because his other mother—a physician—was on call that day, and he wanted to believe this emergency would be the catalyst for their reconciliation. Even for this bright, well-adjusted young man, the desire to have the two people he loved most love each other was an enduring dream he had never shared with anyone.

Such wishes lie hidden beneath the surface for many children and are part of their lifelong attachment to their parents. Parents and other adults can help children differentiate between their desire for their parents' reconciliation and their expectation that it will occur, or their belief that they can make it happen.

Shielding parents from troubled feelings. *"I just act like I'm having a good time and everything's okay so I don't add to all the trouble."* When ten-year-old Rob mentioned this in a support group with other children of divorce, many heads nodded. Like him, so many others at times masked their true feelings of worry, sadness, and fear. By the middle of their elementary school years, children notice how others feel, and they are often remarkably thoughtful and tenderhearted. At this age and beyond, children generally feel very protective of both their parents—so much so, that they often subvert their own feelings, as Jack did, to spare their parents any additional sadness or worry. Many children take on greater responsibility and maturity beyond their years. They often seem like little adults as they travel alone great distances, ache with concern for the parent they're not with, and become cautious and protective about the welfare of one or both parents.

Although such behavior reflects some admirable qualities of compassion and concern, it is unhealthy for children to shoulder the entire emotional responsibility for one or both of their parents. Despite their generous gestures, children still need to feel that their parents can and will protect and care for them. They benefit when their parents demonstrate that even in the midst of their own difficulties, the grown-ups can handle them and will also provide plenty of time, love, empathy, and good parenting.

Mental health professionals agree that taking on prematurely adult roles comes at a cost for children. They risk the consequence of a lost childhood in which they become burdened with adult concerns and worries and get derailed from the normal developmental tasks and pursuits that enable them to grow.

"My parents keep bugging me to talk to them about all this stuff. There's no way I can tell them how I really feel. I just wish things could go back to the way they used to be." Conscientious parents realize that their divorce, no matter how civil, does have a strong impact on their children. Understanding this, they encourage them to talk about their feelings and fears. The timing for such talks needs to fit with each child's readiness.

Young people often feel so overwhelmed that they cannot begin to sort out their feelings, particularly with their parents, who are at the center of their confusing emotions. They long for the happiness and security of a family life that is irrevocably changed, and they yearn for its return. Older children realize they are powerless to change the situation, which sometimes deepens their unwillingness to try to talk about their feelings. At the same time, they often feel protective of their parents and want to spare them hearing of their own deep sadness, anger, frustration, or sense of loss.

Advice to parents. Children's inner experiences are often reflected in the advice they offer to parents, expressed in the safety of a support group. Here are some of the things they have said:

- *When things keep changing, it's harder for us.*
- *Don't be so stressed and mad that you snap at us. It makes us feel like you want to divorce us, too.*
- *Treat each other right even if you're mad at each other. All the fighting makes my stomach hurt.*
- *Don't say things unless you're sure. Kids get their hopes up.*
- *Be careful if you start a new relationship. If you're going to get married again, we hope you won't get another divorce. We don't want to lose more people from our lives.*
- *Be there for us. Getting a divorce from each other is one thing. Be a good parent whether or not your marriage works out. Don't divorce us, too.*

The Possibility of Happiness

With the passage of time and the formation of new life patterns, many children feel calmer and less sad. *"I guess things are better now; there's not so much fighting,"* said one young teen. Even though she was still sad that the family life she had once enjoyed with both parents at home was never again to exist, she realized that things had improved, and this understanding tempered her sadness. She saw that positive change was possible and that the future could be brighter. Research has shown that when children have realistic positive expectations that caring adults will help and support them in the future, they are likely to demonstrate greater resilience and make more positive adjustments.

"Divorce is like a kidney stone. It's painful, but when it's treated right, it passes." What a wise young woman made this remark as our work together was coming to a close. Seventeen-year-old Samantha had been through her parents' divorce and gained perspective with the passing of time. She certainly had painful feelings and memories, but with good support and thoughtful parenting, she felt secure and

confident, and she was able to be happy again. Her life was coming together in a new way, with a new family configuration, and both of her parents remained a strong and loving presence in her life. Samantha understood, deep within, that she would never be abandoned, that her parents' differences were their own and not hers, and that life would go on. For too many children, the pain of divorce lasts a lifetime, waxing and waning at various points along the way, but with an enduring yearning for how things might have been.

How You Can Communicate Your Understanding, Empathy, and Love

"What is mentionable is manageable." The late Mr. Rogers's wise words convey the importance of learning how to identify, describe, and manage strong and sometimes painful emotions. As parents, you give your children an important life skill when you help them learn ways of expressing, understanding, and managing their emotions in healthy, productive ways. As you help them cope with the full range of their feelings, you also learn how to support, reassure, and comfort them during difficult times.

Uncovering and talking about painful emotions may seem like adding still more stress to your life when you may already feel deeply worried about the effects of your divorce on your children. But the reverse is actually the case. Understanding and putting words to these emotions is in itself a critical first step in healing, and I've found that parents generally have an enormous sense of relief when they feel better prepared to take this step. My own experience vividly demonstrates why talking about feelings strengthens and deepens relationships. Moreover, neuroscience research has shown that labeling emotions has powerful therapeutic effects in the brain. Thus, through frequent, open dialogue, you can help your children establish patterns for managing emotions that have critical lifelong benefits.

The first challenge is to help children feel safe enough to talk about what they are feeling. The second is to understand the meanings within their words. The third, of course, is to find the most effective ways of providing the help, healing, reassurance, and abiding love so that children can hear and absorb them.

The rest of this chapter is devoted to specific practices that you can use to encourage meaningful two-way communication with your children, and to provide the reassurance that helps them feel more confident. These practices aim to make all of children's feelings both mentionable and manageable.

Make the time. Children frequently talk about their parents' "busyness." When, they wonder, will they become important enough to have appointments on Mom's or Dad's calendar? In today's whirlwind lifestyle filled with jobs, appointments, chores, children's activities, social events, and many other commitments, there is sometimes precious little time for parents to just *be* with their children. In order to help your children feel connected and sufficiently safe to want to share their feelings, however, you need to create opportunities for such unstructured quiet times to occur. Often, that means taking deliberate steps to simplify your lifestyle and create more free time with your children. It also means creating a habit of paying attention—noticing what your children are saying, what expressions cross their faces, and what may be hidden beneath their assurances that everything is fine. Children are almost always watching to see if their parents notice the "real stuff."

Listen without judgment. Being able to predict how you will respond strongly influences what children will tell you as their parent. When they feel reasonably certain that you will remain neutral and listen to what they have to say without passing judgment, criticizing, or becoming upset, they are much more likely to reveal all of their worries and feelings, and to ask the questions that are churning inside them. You can convey your empathy by acknowledging how they feel and then letting them know you will be involved in finding solutions to their problems. "I understand, Ethan. You're really angry and disappointed. I know we promised you a big vacation trip this year, and now that your father and I are separating, we cannot keep that promise because of the expense. It's hard and upsetting to have all these changes. We are so sorry about that. But we can still have some special times and take some trips that aren't so expensive, and we'll work on figuring out how to make those happen for you with your father and with me."

It is relatively easy to listen without judgment when a child says, "I missed you while I was at Dad's," or "I need a hug." But it can be trying to set aside criticism when your children use language that violates family rules, or they express hurtful or negative thoughts and feelings. When a child explodes with, "Divorce sucks!" or "I hate your new girlfriend!" your immediate reaction may be to tell him, "We don't use that language in our house!" or "You don't even know Carol; you can't possibly hate her," completely rejecting both the statement and the underlying feelings. Unfortunately, such responses do not address the depth of the feelings your children are probably expressing. On the contrary, the pain, fear, and anger that underlie such comments may very well linger and fester, creating more serious problems over time.

Although you may find it very difficult to react calmly, when you respond to such comments by listening seriously and express-ing empathy, you actually promote healing over time. Here is one example of such a response:

"I understand that all the changes in our family have been really hard for you. You didn't want them and you're angry that they hap-pened. Right now things are really tough for you. Let's talk about the things that are especially hard and what we can do to make them better. There are solutions that can help; let's take some time to figure them out together."

As long as no destructive behavior has occurred, this sensitive, healing, problem-solving approach will yield a better long-term out-come than criticizing, arguing, or perpetuating anger.

Reflect understanding and connect words to feelings. You can encour-age children's open communication by letting them know that all of their feelings are understood and acceptable. (This is one half of a pair of principles: All feelings are okay. All behaviors are not okay. This and other aspects of discipline will be discussed in chapter 7.) Equally important is helping them develop an emotional vocabulary that allows them to express their feelings in words.

Abundant behavioral research has demonstrated that labeling emotions promotes calmer feelings and greater control over related behavior. This connection was intuitively understood long before it was proven. Individuals who practice mindfulness meditation, which originated in early Buddhist teachings dating back some 2,500 years, similarly produce calm by identifying their present emotions, thoughts, and sensations without passing judgment. The benefits of psychotherapy have long been thought to relate to the benefits of verbally expressing a range of emotions—and having them understood and accepted.

Recently, using functional magnetic resonance imaging (fMRI) scans of the brain, neuroscientists have added important new information to our understanding of why labeling emotions produces greater tranquility. In the study, individuals were shown drawings of faces that expressed a variety of emotions. When they observed angry or fearful faces, the MRI detected high levels of activity in the amygdala, a region of the brain that acts as an alarm center and is activated by perceived danger or threat. When these same individuals matched a descriptive word to each of these pictures, correctly labeling the emotions shown, the brain scan detected a markedly decreased response in the amygdala.

At the same time, the process of "affect labeling"—identifying emotions with words—was found to cause an increase in activity in another area of the brain. This area, the right ventrolateral prefrontal cortex (RVLPFC) located behind the right eye, is associated with thinking in words about emotional experiences, processing emotions, and inhibiting behavior. The combination of proportionately increased activity in the RVLPFC and decreased activity of the amygdala acts like an internal braking system to slow emotional responses and helps to soothe and make painful emotions less intense.

This fascinating research reveals the likely neurological pathway between the RVLPFC and the amygdala and provides a physiological understanding for why labeling powerful emotions helps us feel better and enhances our ability to regulate our behavior. The new neural pathways created by affect labeling may be linked to greater emotional adjustment over a lifetime. This new knowledge reinforces the importance of helping children, adolescents, and parents themselves find the words to express their feelings.

In doing so, the goal is neither to take children's painful feelings away nor to try to fix them, but rather to hear, accept, and acknowledge them. As you talk openly with your children about their feelings, you are giving them some descriptive language and also encouraging them to explore and describe these emotions in their own words. In so doing, you can help your children see that while painful emotions are a part of divorce, their understanding and acceptance of these feelings actually allows them to make room for joy, love, hope, and positive experiences. As ten-year-old Aaron said after expressing a lot of his painful feelings in words and drawings, "It seems like the bad feelings have to come out first before the good ones can come in."

The practice of observation and reflection can be helpful when a child acts angry or upset. You can usually read the signals of these feelings, and sometimes children open up when these are acknowledged without judgment. For example, you might say to a young child, "Wow, right now you seem pretty upset and angry. Maybe you'd like to draw some pictures to show me how you're feeling." Or with an older child who responds with clipped, one-word answers to efforts to draw him out, "Sounds like you're pretty frustrated and upset, John. The big changes in our family cause a lot of feelings in all of us, and it can be tough to carry them around. Let's talk about how you're feeling and find some ways to get through this that work for all of us."

Match responses to observed behaviors. You can encourage communication by responding to unspoken signals as well as verbal ones. An invitation to say more sometimes opens the floodgates and at other times gets no immediate results. Even in the latter situation, however, children store away their parents' willingness to hear the whole story.

The key to encouraging open communication is to be tuned in to your children's behavior and expressions and reflect your understanding by matching your words to the attitudes you observe. For example, if a child comes bouncing into the house, you can nurture a stronger connection with her by reflecting her mood: "Wow! You sure look happy. I can see you're feeling pretty good right now." On the other hand, if she comes back from time spent with her other parent upset and complaining that she did not have a book she really needed for school, a response that acknowledges her strong feelings helps her feel understood: "Oh, how frustrating not to have what you needed! Let's see if we can figure out some solutions so that doesn't keep happening." Such a response does not place blame on the other parent, criticize the child, nor try to fix or dismiss her upset feelings. It simply acknowledges the emotion and sets the stage for problem solving.

You can encourage more communication with simple, direct invitations that imply no criticism or judgment. In general, it is better to avoid asking, "Why do you feel that way?" This question can leave children feeling defensive and unable to explain their feelings. Even adults often have difficulty explaining the reason for their feelings; they simply are what they are. On the other hand, simple, low-key expressions of encouragement often elicit communication: "Tell me more. This sounds important; let's talk about it."

Allow silence and provide space. Sometimes parents' patient waiting gives children the time they need to begin to process their feelings. For example, when children return from the other parent's house withdrawn, quiet, and moody, it can be helpful to allow them some time and space to make the transition. Then gently, without pressure, you can provide an opening for conversation: "This was the weekend you and Dad were going to go fishing. How did it go?" So many children wonder whether it is okay to talk with one parent about their time with the other. You can help to ease that concern by consistently sending them the message that it is always acceptable—and important—to talk about all of their feelings, even those they think might not please you.

Sometimes it is helpful for parents to mention and show empathy for a child's silence. For example, when your child has been withdrawn for most of an evening, you might say, "You're pretty quiet tonight, pal. Sometimes we are very quiet when we have a lot on our minds. You know, when you're ready, I'd sure like to hear how you're feeling and what's going on." Then, without pressing the child to respond, you may provide some emotional space by engaging your child in some pleasant activity.

Using the information presented earlier in this chapter about how children react to divorce, why they often hide their true feelings, and what they say and mean, you may be better able to interpret what lies beneath your children's words and actions. There will inevitably be times, however, when their thoughts and feelings remain deeply hidden or they are unable to express them. At those times, you may be able to help your children talk about what concerns them by setting aside quiet moments to suggest gently and calmly, "Tell me about you. How are you doing?"

Accept ambivalent feelings. Mixed emotions are a part of all human relationships, and children's are no exception. Children who travel between their parents' homes must constantly disengage from one parent and reengage with the other, adapting to an entirely different situation. These ongoing transitions amount to enormous emotional tasks as they say good-bye to one parent at the same time that they experience a mixture of feelings about returning to the other. These transitions are even more complex when leaving one home also means parting with beloved pets and neighborhood friends.

When you can understand and accept these deeply mixed emotions and offer empathy and understanding, you may be able to open up communication, even if you make the wrong guess about the underlying cause. "It looks like you're feeling kind of sad right now, Julia. Maybe you feel two ways about coming home—happy to see me but sad to leave Dad. I can understand how hard that would be. You wish you

could have both of us in the same house, instead of going back and forth between our houses. Let's think about what might help right now."

Parents sometimes worry that talking so candidly with children about their feelings might prompt them to have painful emotions that might not have developed otherwise. You need not be concerned; research and years of clinical experience show that children have fears and anxieties about their families and their future, often unbeknown to their parents. Children often keep difficult feelings related to divorce to themselves, and they find it very comforting when you express understanding and acceptance. Even if children's sadness or worries come from another source, they are still reassured by their parents' concern. When you provide quiet, loving sensitivity, you make it possible for your children to bring other issues to the surface and continue to do so in the future.

Create context and normalize daily life. Children are often distressed when powerful, unruly emotions unexpectedly overwhelm them. The strength of their feelings and the surprise of being unable to control them often make children feel quite vulnerable. Very young children who absorb the stress surrounding them may cry uncontrollably, have tantrums, or become physically ill with far greater frequency than in more tranquil times. Older children are accustomed to exercising some control over their own behavior, and they may discover that the new range and intensity of their emotions interferes with their ability to productively manage their feelings and behavior.

Seldom are children of any age able to tell their parents, "It scares me to have these huge emotions and feel so out of control." Detecting this layer of additional inner turmoil is not always easy for them or for you. But by listening thoughtfully and observing changes in your children's behavior, you will probably develop a reasonably reliable sense about when there is more going on beneath their words.

Along with acknowledging your children's feelings, you can reassure your children greatly by helping them to understand that their feelings are normal for the current situation. When children feel overwhelmed, or struggle with what they believe to be "wrong" feelings, the knowledge that other people in the same circumstances feel the same way can be a huge relief. You can help put feelings in a normal context, even when your children have not expressed that specific concern. "We've had a lot of big changes in our family—changes that cause all kinds of feelings in all of us. Divorce is hard, even when it makes things better in the long run, and right now you have a lot of feelings about it. That's normal and understandable. It helps to talk about how you're feeling and questions you may have."

Specific examples of other people who have shared experiences and feelings can also be helpful. "You know, sometimes I have some of those same feelings you do. And remember when your friend Andy first found out about his parents' divorce? He felt a lot like you do right now. When his parents separated he felt sad and angry, too. Most kids do. It helps to know you're not the only one who feels the way you do, and it also helps to talk about it, and to know that those feelings can change."

Create one-on-one time. Making time with each child alone is essential to strengthening emotional bonds between parents and children. These relaxing times filled with simple pleasures create situations that allow conversation to flow freely and safely, and at the same time add to the emotional bank account of goodwill parents build with their children. Expressions that parents can use to get the process started may include: "I'd really like to have time together, just the two of us, to do something fun. What would you like to do?" Or, with a young child—"Let's have a snuggle and think about something fun we can do together. We could paint, play a game, or kick the soccer ball. What would you like? You decide." These are not times for parents to pressure, question, or scold children, but rather to simply enjoy being with them. Such times are precious to children and often become fertile ground for good memories.

Envision a happier future. Intensely painful times are often so overwhelming that it is difficult for any of us—adults or children—to realize that they will not always feel so miserable. As you listen and comfort your children in such times, it can be very helpful to engage them in thinking about a different kind of future—one that is realistic and positive, but not overly romanticized. Gaining a perspective on their own lives, and also those of yours and those of other family members they worry about, makes the present pain more bearable and provides hope for healing and a brighter future. I often think of hope as the "travel" virtue that transports us through dark days and helps us envision positive changes and new beginnings.

Reassure of steadfast love. Of all the messages that you as parents need to communicate to your children when you are in the midst of separation or divorce, the most important is the reassurance that your love for them is the kind that will last forever. Even if they never ask that most terrifying question—"Will you stop loving me?"—children need to hear repeatedly and often that you will always love and take care of them.

Since divorce is often a prolonged process in which the breaking of your marital relationship occurs over time, children may have many experiences that reinforce the notion that love can end. Thus, you need to reassure them of the permanence of your love for them over and over again through your words and, most important, through your behavior over a lifetime.

Keep on keeping on. As a parent as well as a psychologist, I am keenly aware that when we witness and absorb our children's pain and distress, we yearn for some magic words we can use to touch the right, healing spot. Sometimes, however, even our best words and most tender expressions of love and understanding are deflected from the walls our children build around themselves. Particularly when they are overwhelmed by painful emotions, children may erect strong barriers that keep out anything with the potential to touch a raw spot.

I know how very discouraging it can be to have loving words and intended hugs bounce off those walls, seemingly unheard and unfelt. During those times, I remind myself that communication is an ongoing process, not a one-time fix. What I have learned is that patient, steadfast, persistent efforts nearly always pay off. Eventually, the passage of time and concerted effort take the sharp edges off children's hurt, and when they are ready, they do open up. Then they share their innermost thoughts and feelings because we have, by continuing to reach out during those long periods of their silence, earned their trust. They have learned that we are ready, willing, and available to love and listen to them. And so the very best we can do is to keep on keeping on.

TWO

Risk and Resilience:
The Potential Impact of
Divorce over Time

Poised and confident, twenty-two-year-old Ben sits across from me talking about his recent year abroad. An excellent student at an Ivy League university, he vividly describes his encounters with people of diverse cultures, and I marvel at his intelligence and maturity. Yet he still occasionally feels some lingering emotional pain from his parents' bitter arguments and divorce fifteen years earlier, and surprisingly strong emotions overcome him even now. When he anticipates going to family events with both parents present, he feels inexplicably "kind of stressed out," even though his parents are now on better terms.

I've known Ben since he was seven. Then, his parents initiated an acrimonious divorce, resulting in a very turbulent time for the entire family. I worked with every member of Ben's family periodically over the years as transitions occurred and new stresses emerged, and I have come to respect and admire all of them. They weathered some extraordinarily tough times during which both parents sought help to contain their conflict and manage their own personal issues so that they could make their three children's needs their top priority. Today, it is evident that Ben has been shaped by multiple factors that fall into two categories—those that led to lingering painful emotions and the risk of long-term problems, and those that helped him to heal and grow with resilience.

This chapter examines the research into just such factors—those that put children in jeopardy of enduring problems, and those that help them to thrive in the face of divorce and major family changes. Findings based on robust research provide important guideposts for parenting after divorce.

Although the research on risks for children is very sobering, I present it here because so much is at stake, and because, as multiple studies confirm, parents do have a profound impact—for better or worse—on their children's adjustment over time. The decisions and actions that parents take put their children on pathways toward the risk of more problems, or to their own resilience and healthy adjustment.

I realize this chapter may be painful to read if you are in the throes of separation or divorce. But as you read it, I hope you will see the information as empowering because it reveals how you can make a profound positive difference in your children's lives. Ultimately, it confirms that the negative consequences of divorce are *not inevitable*. By understanding what can help and hurt your children in both the short- and long-term, you will be better able to reduce the risks for them, promote their resilience, and take steps that yield lifelong positive outcomes.

The other "warning" I want to offer is that this chapter is densely packed with research. By no means do I want you to feel like you or your children are in danger of becoming a statistic. Quite the opposite! I want you to be able to take as much control as you possibly can over the factors that influence your children's well-being now and for the rest of their lives. So this chapter gives you the benefit of knowing the results of some of the most important research: what has happened to many thousands of children whose parents divorced, and what has influenced their outcomes, for better or worse. Future chapters will offer specific guidance in what you can do to give your children the best possible foundation to weather these major life changes, and to use the most effective means to foster your children's resilience.

What Research Reveals About the Risks of Divorce for Children

Every caring parent wants to know, "How will divorce affect my children? Will they be okay? Or will our divorce harm them in ways we can't even imagine?" From my perspective, grounded in both research and my extensive professional experience with children and families, there are both risks of enduring problems for children, and very real opportunities for their resilience and healthy development. The major factors that increase the risks of long-term problems or promote resilience will be described later in this chapter.

For many years, professionals in the field of divorce held widely differing views about its long-term impact. Some believed nearly all children would experience enduring effects, while others felt that—at least in low-conflict situations—children adjusted fairly easily over time. Considerable evidence from numerous studies shows that children in divorced and remarried families do have an increased risk of psychological, behavioral, academic, and social problems, when compared with children in continuously married families. There is less agreement among researchers and practitioners, however, about the magnitude of the differences in adjustment between children from divorced and non-divorced families.

To better understand the extent to which children are affected by family changes and the duration of the consequences, researchers have turned to meta-analyses, which use sophisticated statistical methods to combine the results of numerous studies that address a set of related research questions. These meta-analyses provide a more accurate understanding of a topic than can be gained from any single study. They are particularly helpful in identifying the most reliable and significant findings when a large body of research includes contradictory evidence.

One such meta-analysis of ninety-five studies involving more than 13,000 children confirmed that divorce poses specific risks for children socially, emotionally, and academically. Children and adolescents were found to be at increased risk for a variety of problems, including their conduct (following rules and behaving in socially acceptable ways), psychological adjustment, academic failure, peer relationships, depression, and low self-esteem. One study found that the risk of psychological and social problems was at least twice as high for children whose parents were divorced than for those in continuously married families. Other large-scale studies using sensitive psychological measures assessed the severity of the problems. These revealed that while 10 percent of children in non-divorced families had severe psychological and social problems, the rate climbed to between 20 and 25 percent—more than double—for children in divorced families.

The greatest number of serious problems fell in the categories of academic achievement, hyperactivity, and "externalizing" behaviors—disorders that include "acting-out" behaviors, conduct problems, aggression, and other antisocial or disruptive behaviors. On average, preadolescent children from divorced families had higher rates of aggressive behavior, disobedience, and conduct disorders, as well as poorer school adjustment and academic performance, and more school suspensions.

Although not as common as behavior problems, significantly higher rates of anxiety and depression and lower self-esteem also characterized children from divorced families. In my experience, these quiet, more internalized difficulties in children and teens often go unnoticed in the midst of so many competing demands for the attention of even the most loving parents. Most children experience strong emotional reactions and show behavioral signs of stress immediately after a divorce, including sadness, anger, resentment, anxiety, and confusion as they grapple with the changes in their lives. These reactions begin to diminish in the second year after a divorce and during the third to fifth year following remarriage.

Unfortunately, the risks associated with parents' divorce do not end with childhood. For a significant minority of youth, the consequences are long-term, and difficulties may endure into adulthood.

Children from divorced families are two to three times more likely to drop out of school, and the risk of teen pregnancy is double that of youth from non-divorced families. Young adults from divorced families marry earlier, report more dissatisfaction with their marriages, and are more likely to divorce than their peers from continuously married families.

Studies reveal that adults whose parents divorced when they were children report more unhappiness, anxiety, and depression; less life satisfaction; and a reduced sense of personal control over their lives than those whose parents remain continuously married. Adults whose parents divorced also experience diminished quality and stability of their own intimate relationships, and they are twice as likely to have their own marriages end in divorce. Not surprisingly, given these problems, they also make more use of mental health services. The consequences affect a great deal more than social and emotional difficulties; a significant minority of individuals from divorced homes is also at heightened risk for measurably lower socioeconomic status over the long term.

One study explores the cluster of factors that affect these outcomes. Using longitudinal data from two generations spanning seventeen years, researchers found that the quality of the relationships between children and their parents influenced the link between divorce and children's psychological outcomes over time. The emotional bonds between children and their mothers were weakened by marital discord and conflict, while the emotional bonds between children and their fathers were weakened by marital discord and by divorce itself.

This study replicated previous research linking children and divorce with lower levels of psychological well-being in adulthood. Testing different explanations for this outcome, researchers found that parents' marital problems weakened the bonds between them and their children. In turn, these weak parent-child bonds put children at risk for distress, low self-esteem, and general unhappiness in adulthood. These studies and numerous others show conclusively that marital conflict and divorce impact children by disrupting the quality of parenting and the emotional bonds between children and parents.

It may be surprising to some that relationships with parents continue to be so important to children when they reach adulthood. Yet numerous studies show that children's emotional ties to their parents continue to be important to their psychological adjustment throughout their adult years. People appear to be hardwired for emotional connection. No matter what their age, children have an intense yearning to love and be loved by caring parents. This information can be empowering for parents because it points out the profound difference a loving relationship makes in children's well-being over a lifetime—a loving relationship that is within parents' ability to nurture and maintain.

Taken as a whole, the large body of research on the long-term effects of divorce yields an important perspective: that divorce is not a single event but a series of family transitions, all of which impact children. Divorce results in multiple changes in children's lives. It almost always means they lose one parent from their primary home, have less contact with the parent who lives elsewhere, and experience changes in the whole structure of their relationships with their parents and extended family. For some children it means loss of contact with a parent for extended periods of time—even years. Often, it also means less money in the family budget, ongoing tensions between their parents, living part or all of the time in either one or two new homes, adjustments to parents' new partners and their families, and sometimes a repeat of the entire overwhelming experience as subsequent divorces occur. What an enormous number of major life changes children are expected to manage!

Understandably, children's psychological adjustment is hampered by the number and severity of transitions they face. The number of stressful life transitions that children experience has a cumulative negative impact. The greater the number of stressful changes experienced in childhood, the greater the likelihood of a decline in psychological adjustment. Three or more major changes, such as divorce, remarriage, and another divorce, result in a significant increase in the risk that young adults' own marriages will end in divorce.

The risks of divorce have no national boundaries. A large body of research is based on populations in the United States, but studies in Canada, Australia, New Zealand, England, Germany, the Netherlands, and other European countries have yielded similar results. Collectively, these reveal that the stresses for children associated with their parents' divorce extend across many countries and cultures, and to families in every economic bracket. Most show a link between the family structure that children experience and their psychological adjustment as adults.

Parents benefit from a realistic understanding of the risks associated with divorce. Too often, these are either exaggerated or minimized. While the bad news is that more than twice the number of children from divorced families experience serious, enduring problems than do children from continuously married households, the good news is that the vast majority of children function reasonably well after a divorce.

Regardless of whether the statistics are interpreted as bad news or good, even one child who suffers serious problems or functions only "reasonably well" instead of "very well" is one too many. Although millions of children are at high risk because of their parents' marital problems, I am convinced they do not have to be. Research—with all those statistics—can help us better understand what parents can do to reduce or eliminate those risks. There are many largely untold stories of children who do remarkably well after their parents' divorce. Their success is not random luck or just the passage of time, but rather the cumulative impact of choices and actions to promote resilience that parents have pursued over the course of their children's lives. This book is about how to help more children live that reality.

What Is Resilience?

How often we hear people say, "They're young and resilient—they'll get over it." The belief that resilience is an intrinsic trait that all children have is widely—but mistakenly—held. Many assume that children are able to handle myriad family changes and challenges in stride simply because they are young. Although innate temperament does play a role in children's resilience, there is no psychological elastic built into children's makeup that gives them a greater ability to bounce back from stressful life experiences automatically, without support. This is not to say that children are never resilient; they certainly can be, but only with the right combination of temperament, quality parenting, strong relationships, support, and skills.

Here are some prevalent myths about resilience, and the corresponding facts.

> *Myth:* Children are automatically resilient.
> *Fact:* Children are not resilient merely because they are young. Rather, they become resilient through a combination of social and emotional skills that can be taught and learned, and through the consistent support of authoritative parents, families, schools, communities, and the social systems and people who touch their lives.

> *Myth:* Children become resilient fairly quickly.
> *Fact:* The process of fostering children's resilience happens over the course of children's development, day after day, month after month, year after year. This growth and maturation is not a quick fix.

> *Myth:* Resilience is a single "yes-no," "either-or" trait in children.
> *Fact*: Resilience is not a single "magic bullet," but rather an accumulation of multiple resources and competencies in varying degrees at various times in children's lives. Children and adults can develop a repertoire of social and emotional skills that enable them to deal with challenges as successfully as possible throughout their lives. That does not mean, however, that children will be 100 percent resilient or nonresilient, just as none of us is ever 100 percent healthy or unhealthy, or 100 percent smart or not smart.

- *Myth*: Resilience means that children no longer have painful memories and emotions.
Fact: Resilience does not mean invulnerability. Painful emotions and distressing memories are a natural part of encountering a major loss or stressful life changes. Being able to understand and address those emotions and experiences contributes to healing and resilience.

So what, exactly, is resilience? It is demonstrated competence in the face of significant challenges, the ability to bounce back from tough times. It is developed through a variety of pathways. Children who are naturally more easygoing may be less responsive to discord and stress, but temperament alone does not create resilience. Among the most important pathways are parenting practices, supportive relationships, and safeguards that buffer children from the jolt of adverse life experiences—all from the efforts of responsible adults who actively take the initiative and maintain watchful care.

Although children may learn to be resilient and cope successfully with challenges, resilience does not make them invulnerable to distress. They may come through difficult times with remarkable ability to succeed in school or activities, yet still have lingering painful memories and feelings.

Resilience and healthy development are nurtured by heavy doses of protective factors and by preventing children's exposure to the risk factors. This chapter focuses primarily on family risk and protective factors, especially those that parents can have a major role in controlling. Individual child factors will be considered in more detail in chapter 6, "Building Children's Resilience Skills," and some of the extrafamilial factors are incorporated in chapter 4, "Parenting Plans."

The following table summarizes outcomes from hundreds of studies. These identify specific factors that contribute to children's risk of problems, and those that provide a protective buffer against those negative outcomes during and after divorce.

RISK AND PROTECTIVE FACTORS IDENTIFIED IN RESEARCH ON CHILDREN AND DIVORCE

Risk Factors		
INDIVIDUAL	FAMILY	EXTRAFAMILIAL
• "Difficult" temperament • Pre-divorce adjustment problems • Fears of abandonment • Misconceptions, guilt, self-blame • Lack of coping skills, avoidant coping style • Caught in middle of conflict, aligned with one parent against the other	• Ongoing parent conflict • Poor parenting • Troubled parent-child relationships • Lack of monitoring children's behaviors and activities • Multiple family transitions (divorce, remarriage, another divorce) • Parent mental health problems • Chaotic, unstable household • Economic decline	• Legal processes and policies that fuel parent conflict • Lack of adult role models • Loss of positive relationships with extended family, friends • Lack of support network • Chaotic schooling • Unsafe schools and/or neighborhoods • Lack of healthy after-school activities • Lack of effective treatment for mental health problems

Protective Factors		
INDIVIDUAL	FAMILY	EXTRAFAMILIAL
• "Easy" temperament • Awareness and ability to manage own emotions • Empathy for others • Understanding what is solvable, not solvable • Accurate understanding of divorce as parents' problem; not self-blame • Problem-solving skills • Effective coping skills • Seeking support when needed	• Protection from conflict between parents • Parents' psychological well-being • Cooperative parenting (except in situations of domestic violence or abuse) • Healthy relationships between child and both parents • Quality, authoritative parenting	• Supportive relationship with positive adult models • Support network: family, school, faith, community • Evidence-based preventive interventions for children and parents • Legal procedures that promote resolution of conflict • Supportive, authoritative schools

(continued)

Protective Factors		
INDIVIDUAL	FAMILY	EXTRAFAMILIAL
• Self-confidence • Actively engaged in school and healthy activities • Hope, positive outlook	• Household structure and stability • Supportive sibling relations • Economic stability • Supportive relationships with extended family	• Healthy peer relationships • Safe neighborhoods • Involvement in healthy activities

There is general consensus among researchers that the most important factors that consistently have been shown to influence children's risk or resilience after divorce are the amount and intensity of conflict they are exposed to, the quality of parent-child relationships, and the quality of parenting they experience. Other factors that influence children over the long term are the family's economic circumstances, parents' psychological well-being, the number of additional stresses, household structure and stability, cooperative parenting, and children's understanding and sense of control over what is happening to them, and their effective coping skills.

The Importance of Containing Conflict

Children's adjustment before the breakup, the quality of parenting before and after the divorce, and the amount and intensity of conflict they experience before, during, and after the divorce all factor into how they fare over time. In every controlled study, ongoing conflict between parents is consistently linked to children's psychological problems.

Conflict is inevitable in any intimate relationship, and it is almost always a part of ending a relationship with a spouse, a lover, or even a friend. Conflict occurs in many forms, however, and not all have the same impact on children.

Nonaggressive conflicts that are resolved tend not to distress children any more than ordinary discussions without conflict. In fact, if children are told that a conflict has been resolved, the negative impact on them is reduced. So the key for parents is not to deny that anger and painful emotions exist, but rather to manage how and when they express them, so their children will not be caught in the crossfire.

In contrast, conflicts between parents that are especially dangerous for children are those that are verbally or physically hostile, frequent, intense, unresolved, or focused on the children. Unresolved ongoing conflict disrupts parenting, makes children more attuned to further animosity, and is linked to a great many more behavior problems. Child-focused conflict is the worst for children, putting them at risk for a host of behavioral and psychological problems.

This was a particular danger for Ben when his parents divorced. When his father discovered that his mother was having an affair, he was devastated. Jack felt betrayed, deeply hurt, and furious. When he first came to my office, he had filed for sole custody of their three children. In his own mind, he had made the case that the children would be better off with Nancy out of the picture. Nancy, too, had retained a lawyer to file for sole custody, and the battle was beginning to escalate.

Jack argued that he should "tell the kids the truth" about their mother's unfaithfulness and make it clear that she had left them, too. It was clear that beneath Jack's anger was enormous pain at feeling rejected, and I was fairly certain that it probably felt safer for him to hang on to his fury than to risk all the feelings of loss and sadness that would rush in to fill its void if he were to let it go. For her part, Nancy felt wounded, too. Their marriage had deteriorated well before her affair, and she, too, had resorted to anger to protect herself.

All of this rage was leaking out, and particularly because Jack and Nancy were battling over the children, they were caught in the crossfire. When I first saw seven-year-old Ben, he told me about some of the angry exchanges he had overheard between his parents. "It hurts my heart when they fight like that," he said.

As I worked with Jack and Nancy, it became evident that for both of them, beneath their anger was great pain and vulnerability. In one agonizing session, Jack's eyes filled with tears as he demanded explanations for Nancy's behavior—including her decision to file for custody of their children. "I never intended to hurt you, Jack," she said. "We both made mistakes in our marriage. We both put work ahead of anything else, and we put our relationship on the back burner. I don't want to take the kids away from you, but when I saw how furious and vindictive you were becoming, I got scared and decided I needed to protect myself." They both acknowledged that their actions were largely out of fear and vulnerability, and that they were trying to gain control in a situation in which they both felt powerless.

For both Jack and Nancy, although hanging on to the anger was easier than dealing with their more painful feelings, there was danger in staying stuck in anger. In so doing, they were actually building a strong, long-lasting attachment to each other based on negative emotions. Even worse, they were pulling their children into the maelstrom along with them. With help, Jack eventually realized that a custody dispute was not in the children's best interest. Deep down, Nancy, too, understood that. Because both Jack and Nancy were loving, conscientious parents who realized that their children needed both of them in their lives, they eventually dropped their motions for sole custody, and sought out collaborative attorneys to help with their legal agreement.

But in order for them to be able to share parenting, a lot of change was needed. We worked to negotiate a new kind of relationship in which they would become partners in protecting the most precious part of their marriage—their children. In individual sessions, they learned effective ways to manage strong emotions so they could plan for joint meetings to facilitate cooperative parenting. Jack and I began to work on separating his feelings for Nancy as wife and lover from her role as the children's mother and set new boundaries in their relationship. At the same time, Nancy worked on managing her feelings and recasting her relationship with Jack as a valued coparent. This was a lengthy and difficult process for both of them. The disappointment, sadness, loss, anger, and guilt they both felt did not dissipate easily.

At the same time, over several months, they worked hard at learning to communicate in ways that reduced conflict and making sure their children would not get caught in the middle. That meant keeping communication respectful, with a specific agenda that was related to the children, not to personal, marital issues. Over time, after some of the painful emotions had subsided, they were able to discuss parenting issues in person, sometimes meeting in a coffee shop to work out schedules or concerns about their children.

When I last saw Ben, I asked about his parents. He smiled and said they had both remarried and were doing well. He still has some painful memories of those "dark days" when they were fighting. But by now he has a growing storehouse of good memories, too. He feels "good inside" about having heard his parents comment on a happy, funny family memory, and say positive things about each other. "Just the other day, my dad commented that I have such a deep respect for people of different cultures—just like my mom." Their hard work clearly had paid off. Jack and Nancy had learned to genuinely appreciate each other as parents and as individuals, and developing the ability to reflect that with Ben and his siblings was enormously important to all of the children.

The story of how Jack and Nancy both determined to put their children first, sought the help they needed for themselves and their children, learned to renegotiate their relationship, communicate effectively, and ultimately provide loving, authoritative parenting for all their children is one of true dedication to their children and courage in the face of very real pain. The fact that Ben has become such a successful scholar and thoughtful young man, pursuing his own goals, is a testament to his parents' efforts and effectiveness in dramatically reducing the risks and promoting his resilience. Although Ben still has a few lingering emotional scars, he is largely whole, happy, and functioning well.

Some children are not as fortunate as Ben, however. Unfortunately, the impact of parent conflict on children's adjustment may be long lasting for some. High rates of parental discord have been shown to predict young adults' psychological distress twelve years later. Adults who recall high levels of conflict between their parents while they were growing up report higher rates of psychological and marital problems in their own lives.

The impact of conflict is not only psychological, but also physical. The biopsychosocial model of wellness reveals a direct link between parents' conflict and their children's levels of stress and anxiety. Research links children's exposure to parent conflict with actual physical illness, revealing that children who were exposed to parent conflicts showed higher levels of cortisol, the "stress hormone." Recent studies add further support, showing that children who were "very distressed" and very involved in responding to parents' arguments had especially high levels of cortisol. Produced in the adrenal gland, cortisol increases blood pressure and blood sugar and suppresses the body's immune responses.

Children with significant stress have more frequent headaches and stomachaches. After exposure to parents' angry arguments, children were three times more likely to become ill. Another study suggests that the stress children experience with their parents' conflict impacts not only their general health, but also their physical growth.

Because conflict can have such a profound impact on children, divorce has positive consequences for children from high-conflict and violent marriages by removing them from a hostile home environment. Research has shown that children of parents in high-conflict marriages which end in divorce fare better over time than those whose high-conflict parents remain married. An unequivocal finding of these studies is clear: when conflict between parents is chronic and intense, divorce provides an effective release from a harmful home environment and opportunities for a more stable family life.

Chapter 5 provides concrete, specific guidance on strategies you can use to manage conflict and protect your children from its corrosive effects.

The Quality of Parenting and Parent-Child Relationships

Among the most significant influences on children's resilience are two areas over which parents can have a great deal of control—the quality of their parenting, and their relationships with their children. Research on children whose parents divorce shares some recurring themes with research on children in other stressful circumstances. In all of these situations, the quality of the relationship between children and at least one parent or caregiver, and the quality of parenting children experience have been proven critically important for their long-term well-being, contributing to their resilience and healthy development.

In any difficult life situation, it is helpful to differentiate what is within our control and what is not; to figure out what we have the power to change, and what we cannot change. During or after a divorce, parents often feel powerless over how their former partner deals with them or their children. Trying to change a former partner is a recipe for frustration and often leads to depression. The research on parent-child relationships and parenting is especially important because it spells out the power that parents have when they focus their energy on what they *can* control.

Research confirms that children need and want two responsive parents in their lives. One of the best predictors of children's well-being in a marriage, and after divorce, is the psychological adjustment of their parents and the quality of parenting they provide.

The quality of parent-child relationships and the quality of parenting are deeply intertwined. I use the terms "quality parenting" and "authoritative parenting" to define a parent-child relationship characterized both by warmth and caring, and by consistent, effective discipline. The combination of giving one-on-one loving attention to children, while also providing structure, establishing positive expectations, and defining clear limits gives them the foundation they need to grow. Chapter 7 provides specific guidance on emotionally intelligent parenting that helps children to feel secure and come through challenging times with resilience.

The power of effective parenting is highlighted in a rigorous study of a research-based program that taught quality parenting practices to divorced custodial mothers who had primary responsibility for their children. The program focused on effective discipline (including setting and maintaining clear and appropriate rules and limits), and on supportive, nurturing behavior (including listening responsively, reinforcing positive behavior, expressing love, and spending one-on-one time with each child). Six years later, the children of those parents showed profoundly positive outcomes, compared with other adolescents with divorced parents. These included lower rates of diagnosed mental disorders and behavior problems, less use of alcohol, marijuana, or other drugs, better grade-point averages, less risky sexual behavior, higher self-esteem, greater involvement in positive activities, and greater success in coping with family changes. Better parenting was shown to be especially effective for those children who suffered the most severe problems. This research provides compelling evidence of the important role that quality parenting plays in helping children thrive after divorce.

Unfortunately, studies show that parent-child relationships erode significantly after divorce, especially in high-conflict situations. This erosion occurs not just in childhood but later on, as well. Data from the National Survey of Children reveals striking effects of divorce in young adults. Among eighteen- to twenty-two-year-olds from disrupted families, 65 percent had poor relationships with their fathers, versus 29 percent from non-divorced families, and 30 percent with divorced parents had poor relationships with their mothers, compared with 16 percent from non-divorced families. Other long-term studies have shown deterioration of the relationship between adult children of divorce and their parents, too.

Many researchers have found that the quality of parenting that both mothers and fathers provide diminishes prior to and after divorce. This is not surprising, since they are often struggling with their own very difficult emotions and feeling overwhelmed by the demands of parenting at the same time that they are also struggling to manage household, financial, and work responsibilities.

For children, the combination of high conflict and ineffective parenting can be very damaging, and, unfortunately, conflict and diminished quality of parenting often go hand-in-hand. Several studies of mothers in high-conflict marriages have shown them to be less warm, more rejecting, and harsher in their discipline and other interactions with their children than mothers who are not engaged in conflict. Research on fathers in high-conflict marriages has shown that they often withdraw from their children, but when they do interact their exchanges may be intrusive, pulling children into the middle of their parents' conflict. Problems in parenting may intensify for both mothers and fathers during the first few years after a separation. A significant negative effect of divorce has been found on mother-child relationships in adulthood, even though none had existed in adolescence, suggesting that for some, these relationships deteriorate over time.

The patterns of adjustment following divorce are different for boys and girls. Studies using direct observation of interactions show more angry exchanges and conflict between boys and their custodial mothers than between girls and their custodial mothers. A downward spiral can ensue, particularly with boys who feel angry and deprived. They often react with uncooperative behavior, making interactions between distressed single parents and their sons even more difficult and unsatisfying.

While it is painful to consider all the potential negatives of a poor or diminishing relationship between divorced parents and their children, it is heartening to realize that this is not an inevitable outcome. As Jack and Nancy's story shows, it is possible to halt and reverse a downward spiral. When parents take control of conflict and put their efforts into providing the best parenting possible in their own homes, a major positive change occurs in their children's lives. An end to bitter conflict and violence is not just a relief for most children and families, but the beginning of better discipline and warmer, better focused, and more authoritative parenting.

Increasing numbers of studies demonstrate that high-quality parenting by both mothers and fathers contributes powerfully to children's resilience. High-quality relationships protect children from divorce-related stress, enhance their feelings of security, and reduce their fears. Studies of resilience in children and youth consistently produce similar results; they show that a healthy attachment relationship between a child and at least one parent or caregiver is a critical link to children's competence and resilience.

In a study my colleague Aaron Black and I conducted on the long-term adjustment of college-age students whose parents had divorced eleven years earlier, we found that the effects of their parents' conflict on the young adults' psychological well-being were ameliorated for those who had emotionally secure relationships with their parents. There was a direct correlation between strong parent-child relationships and young people's feelings of personal effectiveness, greater ability to trust others, more independence in interpersonal relationships, and less likelihood of depression.

Unfortunately, for all too many children, divorce means either an abrupt or the gradual ending of a relationship with their fathers. Two to three years after a divorce, approximately 18 to 25 percent of children have no contact with their fathers. Even if their fathers do not disappear from their lives, many young people suffer the consequences if they are less actively engaged in parenting. Research shows that, compared with young adults in continuously married families, young adults of divorced parents have less contact with their fathers, are less trusting of and less affectionate with their fathers, and have fewer intergenerational exchanges of financial and emotional support.

The importance of quality parenting by fathers has been the topic of numerous recent studies. In a meta-analysis of sixty-three different studies of fathers, researchers found that noncustodial fathers' engaged and effective parenting is clearly and consistently correlated

with children's school and academic success and every measure of
healthy adjustment.

Strong emotional bonds and feelings of mutual benefits character-
ize the relationships in which children fare best. Specifically, children benefit when their fathers provide guidance and discipline and
are actively involved in their children's schoolwork and projects—not
just their recreational activities. Not surprisingly, fathers' timely pay-
ment of child support significantly improves children's economic and
general well-being and enhances their health status and educational
attainment.

Increased contact alone, however, does not improve children's
well-being if fathers fail to be authoritative parents. The consensus
from studies on this topic is that both girls and boys benefit from the
involvement of fathers who consistently provide emotional support,
praise accomplishments, discipline misbehavior, and support children's schoolwork and activities.

All of this research has important implications for parents and professionals who help children and families. Understanding the important role that authoritative fathers have in shaping children's healthy
development may influence more fathers to remain actively involved
in parenting and encourage professionals to promote both parents' full
participation in parenting. It may also help in establishing schedules
that allow fathers adequate time for meaningful involvement in their
children's schooling and related activities. Beyond this reasonable time

threshold, the manner in which fathers relate to their children is more important than the specific number of hours or weekly contacts they have. Thus, encouraging fathers to provide loving, authoritative parenting and helping them to further develop the skills that promote strong parent-child relationships result in important benefits for children.

Lingering Painful Memories and Emotions

I wish I could promise you that doing everything "right" in your divorce and parenting practices would result in lifelong happiness for you and your children. But that is not realistic for any individual or family, divorced or not. For all of us, life will include some hard times and painful experiences, and what ultimately matters is how we deal with them. This section is intended to help you understand what research reveals about painful memories and emotions so that you can anticipate them, understand the depth of your child's feelings, listen without judgment, and provide support.

The research is abundant, and it all points to the same conclusion. Some distress and painful emotions are lasting outcomes of divorce for even the most accomplished and apparently resilient young adults. Some factors do influence the degree of distress they feel, however, and how they handle it.

Ten years after their parents' divorce, well-functioning college students at a prestigious university were asked about their experiences when their parents divorced. Many reported that painful memories and emotions endured. Feelings of loss were prevalent, with the majority reporting that they missed having their father around. Many even wondered whether their fathers loved them. These students' pain and their continuing focus on the experience of their parents' divorce were related to the type of custody they had experienced. Those who had been raised in sole physical custody arrangements reported more painful memories and feelings of loss than those whose parents had shared in providing homes and parenting for them. Those in sole physical custody also were more likely to view their lives through the vantage point of divorce than those in shared physical custody.

Reports of emotional pain and distress were greatest among those students whose parents had engaged in higher levels of conflict. Despite these painful memories and beliefs, however, these students did not differ on standardized measures of depression or anxiety. This suggests that these young adults were quite resilient and functioning very well in important areas of their lives, yet they still had painful feelings and memories that continued to affect their relationships with their parents.

Resilience does not mean invulnerability. Painful memories and experiences often go hand-in-hand with emotional growth and resilience. So much depends on how painful experiences are handled and the support available to help children through them. This research underscores the importance of separating feelings of distress from actual psychological disorders when considering the long-term consequences of divorce.

Providing Support to Nurture Children's Resilience

Given the painful emotions that children experience with divorce, having a safe haven to address their concerns, discover they are not alone, and learn skills to help them cope is another supportive bridge to children's resilience. Carefully designed, well-run group intervention programs for children of divorce, such as the Children of Divorce Intervention Program that I developed, have proven very beneficial to children.

Numerous studies clearly demonstrate that such preventive interventions that combine support and skills training have a positive impact on children of all ages. Their healthy adjustment extends beyond their immediate divorce-related concerns to enhanced well-being at home, at school, in peer relationships, and even in their physical health. Evidence from our studies suggests that the benefits children receive from participation in this program endure in time, too, well beyond the end of the program. The support and skills that children learn in these interventions help to build a foundation of emotional intelligence and the ability to deal with the inevitable challenges and changes of life. Chapter 6 provides more specific information about these programs and the specific skills involved in fostering children's resilience.

Children's Understanding and Control

As described in chapter 1, children who do not have factual explanations about their parents' divorce and the changes in their own lives often fill the void with fears, worries, and very disturbing fantasies and misconceptions. Young children are especially vulnerable to fears of abandonment, worries about their basic needs being unmet, and terrifying fears about their safety and security. Numerous studies underscore the importance of parenting with consistency, reassurance, and warmth to create stability in the lives of young children. Protective factors for young children include helping them have an age-appropriate, accurate understanding of family changes, reassurance that they did not cause the problems, and confidence in their parents' unending love for them.

For young adults, the sense that they had no control over their lives following the divorce has been shown to be a source of pain and distress. The majority of children and adolescents are not adequately informed or prepared for the divorce and its impact on their lives. Even when it comes to planning their schedules and how they will get to spend time with both parents, children are rarely asked for their ideas. Transitions between households are matters in which children seldom feel they have a sufficient voice and input, especially as they move into adolescence. Once schedules have been set, they are rarely asked how these affect them emotionally and practically, but they want to be asked.

Studies have found a link between children's positive feelings about transitions and being given a role or a voice in some of the decision making, with the caveat that too much responsibility for the final decision can burden them unnecessarily. If accomplished with sensitivity and care, giving children the rights to be heard and to have input into the structure for their lives helps to decrease their stress over time.

One of the troubling matters that surfaced in this research was how the lack of communication and control influenced children's feelings about their fathers, in particular. The young adults in these studies longed to spend more time with their fathers but felt that they had little or no control over doing so. In lacking a voice on such important matters, not only did they miss their fathers over time, but they were left with lingering doubts about whether their fathers even loved them. Allowing children's voices to be heard and giving them some appropriate control over aspects of their lives ultimately contributes to their feeling valued by and connected to both parents and to their own sense of well-being. Chapter 3 focuses on the ways that parents can tell their children about family changes and open the door for important two-way communication.

The Impact of Parents' Psychological Well-Being on Children

It is especially hard to be the kind of parents we aspire to be during times of enormous stress and major changes in our lives. From a personal perspective, I realize that when I am under a lot of stress, I find it harder to be as patient and compassionate as I want to be and to provide my children with the kind of quality parenting that I believe in so strongly.

Among the other reliable predictors of children's healthy adjustment is the health and well-being of their parents. If parents are well physically and emotionally, their children tend to be well, too. Unfortunately, the opposite is also true.

At a time when children are grappling with stressful family changes and feeling vulnerable and worried about their future, they especially need at least one well-functioning parent to guide them and help them adjust and feel secure. Unfortunately—but not surprisingly—they often encounter parents who are unable to provide the emotional stability and support they so urgently need.

Divorce is an undeniably stressful process that can leave adults vulnerable not only to psychological problems, but also to physical ones. Marital disruption has been shown to be related to suppressed immune system function. In turn, this increases parents' susceptibility to disease and chronic and acute medical conditions. Stress is also linked to increased likelihood of accidents. Thus one of your most important challenges as a parent is to take good care of yourself, so you will be able to provide quality parenting for your children and foster healthy relationships with them. Chapter 5 provides some concrete guidance on a variety of things you can do to stay healthy and actively address problems as they arise.

The Bright Side

After all this information about what can cause lasting problems for children whose parents divorce, I want to remind you again—and again and again!—that although too many children have suffered less than optimal outcomes, your children do not need to be among them. As we saw in the story of Ben and his parents, creating a healthy new family structure after divorce is not always a smooth process (it may be more accurate to say it is *rarely smooth*!), but you and your former partner have the opportunity to help your children not only survive but thrive through your effective parenting, contained conflict, and warm, loving relationships.

Knowledge can be a source of power. This chapter gives you solid, well-researched knowledge about the factors that most strongly influence your children's future well-being. Armed with that understanding, you are now in a better position to take the steps that can help ensure the best outcome for them. The chapters to follow will give you some strategies and specific guidance that you can use to strongly increase the likelihood that the future will be filled with hope, healing, and resilience for you and your children.

. . . .

THREE

Telling the Children and Preparing Them for Changes

Jerry and Suzanne are like so many divorcing parents I have come to admire for their wholehearted commitment to putting their children's well-being first, despite the painful ending of their marriage. They had begun their life together just out of high school. Suzanne worked to help put Jerry through college and then an MBA. Their original plan was for her to go to college when Jerry finished, but by then they had two babies, and when Jerry went to work, Suzanne quit her job to stay home and raise the children.

Driven to succeed, Jerry worked long hours and was rewarded with increasing positions of responsibility in his corporation—and still longer hours and extensive travel. Meanwhile, Suzanne settled into a life of child-rearing, assuming more and more of the parenting responsibility. She spent her days with other young mothers, actively involved in the children's activities and developing friendships separate from Jerry. Unattended, Jerry and Suzanne's marriage had disintegrated by the time the children were in middle school. While they still respected each other, they had little in common except the children, and they found it hard to find friends as a couple. They sought couples therapy to help bridge the distance between them. Ultimately, however, Jerry confronted the empty shell of their marriage and initiated a divorce.

Suzanne felt deeply hurt and betrayed, but at the same time realized that she had been equally responsible for allowing their relationship to drift into a series of reports on the children and financial transactions, rather than a loving and intimate marriage.

As they struggled with how to tell their children about their divorce and how to plan for the new structure of life ahead, both Jerry and Suzanne were overcome with guilt and remorse. Telling the children was symbolic of all that they feared about how their decision would impact the rest of their children's lives. Jerry fought back tears as he said, "I just can't help thinking that the moment we tell the kids is the exact moment that we begin to ruin their lives. Rationally, I know that is not entirely true, but it sure feels that way."

Telling children about the decision to divorce is usually fraught with just such fears and feelings. Fortunately, Jerry, Suzanne, and I were able to work through how and when to tell their children and how to develop and maintain ongoing open communication with them. Together, we talked about their fears, anticipated their children's reactions, and planned what each of them would say. We also talked about an initial parenting schedule, working out when each of them would spend time with and have primary responsibility for their children.

Because they had a preliminary plan, Jerry and Suzanne were able to tell their children not just what would soon change in their lives, but also what would remain constant, and how their needs would be met in the days and weeks ahead. Although the plan did not diminish their children's sadness, it did reassure them that they were their parents' top priority and that both parents would continue to love and care for them, even though their marriage was ending.

A year later, the family's progress was evident. Jerry and Suzanne still struggled with their own feelings and worried about their children, but they continued to work hard at parenting. Their efforts were reflected in their children's behaviors, feelings, and overall adjustment. Jerry and Suzanne continued to improve their ability to communicate effectively with each other and with their children, and the children, too, learned how better to express their feelings and communicate their needs. Although there were still many tearful and sometimes angry moments, these became less frequent within two years after the separation. As the family members worked hard to manage the changes in their lives, they all understood that the road ahead—while changed and sometimes riddled with bumps—was the road to the future, not the road to disaster.

As Jerry and Suzanne's story suggests, my message in this chapter is one of hope and reassurance. Nothing will completely remove your distress as you undertake the major step of divorce and anticipate telling your children. Nevertheless, I hope you will find solace in knowing there is a proven process for preparing your children for this change that contributes to their immediate sense of security and to their long-term well-being.

While the decision to end a marriage is often accompanied by a range of emotions—sometimes including a sense of relief—parents are almost universally worried about its impact on their children. Their anxiety often increases as they anticipate having to break the news to them. Most parents dread causing their children distress and fervently hope to shield them from pain. Some hope that if they avoid the subject of their divorce, they will spare their children some of the hurt. Some worry that if they encourage their children to talk about their feelings and worries, they will put ideas in their heads that would not otherwise occur to them.

As a parent myself, I, too, am concerned about causing my children distress, and I dread the prospect of telling them things that may be painful for them to hear. But my training and long experience as a psychologist have proven repeatedly the healing power of talking with our children about the painful experiences and emotions that are a part of major life changes and loss. Likewise, providing children with clear, age-appropriate information before, during, and after big changes in their lives has proven equally beneficial.

The decision to divorce is certainly a high-impact change for children as well as for parents. Yet research reveals that the majority of

children and adolescents are not adequately informed about a divorce
and its implications for their lives. Their world is turned upside down
and changed dramatically, often with little or no warning, explanation, or preparation. Sometimes what information they do get is not
appropriate for their age, or it is insufficient for them to understand
the magnitude of the changes that will impact them. In one study of
parent-child communication about divorce, 23 percent of children
said that no one had talked with them in advance of a parent's departure, and 45 percent said they were given only one- or two-sentence
explanations such as, "Your father's leaving." Indeed, only 5 percent
of children said they were prepared in advance and were encouraged to ask questions. While these statistics may seem astonishing at
first glance, they are likely influenced by the desire to spare those we
love—especially our children—from pain.

As difficult as it may be for parents to talk with their children
about their divorce, children frequently are aware that something is
amiss. Children are deeply perceptive about their parents' emotions.

The example of four-year-old Ashley reveals how young children
internalize what goes on between their parents and why thoughtful, positive communication makes such a difference. Donna and Al
brought Ashley to see me because they were very worried about the
dramatic changes in her behavior. Formerly sunny-natured and easygoing, she now woke up nearly every night shrieking with night terrors, unable to catch her breath, her eyes glazed. During the day, she
relapsed in her toileting and had lots of meltdowns. These behavioral
changes began to occur just after her parents separated.

As I soon discovered, Donna and Al had gotten into volatile arguments that sometimes progressed to pushing and hitting each other.
They separated abruptly and drew battle lines. Both moved to different homes. Ashley's time was now split between two completely
new households, and as she was passed back and forth, she absorbed
her parents' glares and hostile exchanges. When I asked how they had
prepared Ashley for the changes, and how they were communicating with her about her new schedule, it became evident Donna and

Al had told her very little. Immersed in their own pain and anger, they had simply said that Mommy and Daddy now both had new homes. So Ashley was going back and forth between them without any understanding of what had happened or any clear expectation about when she would next see each of her parents.

Together, we worked on ways to help Ashley adjust to the changes in her life. The first step was to help her understand what had happened. In a loving way, her parents told her they had grown-up problems, and they were very sorry she had seen and heard their terrible fights. They explained that they would not live together anymore, and that's why they now had two different houses. They told her how much they both loved her, and that they both would always love and take care of her—and that the kind of love they had for her is the kind that never ends. I suggested that Donna and Al read books about divorce with her such as Mr. Rogers's *Let's Talk About It: Divorce* and Vicki Lansky's *It's Not Your Fault, KoKo Bear*, encouraging her questions and conversation about all the changes in their family. They bought a big block calendar for their schedule, and Ashley got to pick colors for each parent and color in "Mom blocks" and "Dad blocks" for the days she would be with each of them. With their consistent reassurance and communication, Ashley's world began to feel more secure, and she calmed down.

We also worked on a parallel parenting approach (see chapter 5) that would allow both Donna and Al to remain fully engaged with Ashley, but would prevent many of the hostile conversations between them. Because they realized how their angry exchanges hurt their beloved daughter, they found ways to control their emotions, especially when they were in Ashley's presence. Very soon, Ashley's night terrors ended. With time and loving attention, her toileting accidents stopped, and eventually she became more self-assured and sunny-natured once again.

The way in which children are told about a pending divorce shapes their perceptions and sets the tone for family life in the future. Their emotional associations and memories of how the message was conveyed often linger and set the stage for how family relationships will evolve over time. If the message is one of bitterness and blame, painful emotions may linger for years and damage relationships between parents and children. On the other hand, if parents express genuine regret about the end of the marriage, commitment to their children, hope for the future, and a plan for healing, they set the stage for more positive outcomes and strong relationships between themselves and their children.

You are already taking a positive step by reading this chapter and putting its concepts into practice. Your children will surely benefit from your courage in approaching this painful topic thoughtfully, with concern for their well-being.

Telling the children is not a one-time event, however, but the beginning of ongoing communication about their relationship with you and their other parent, the organization of their own lives, and all of the feelings that are part of the fabric of their most important relationships.

While the initial explanation and plans are very important, children are truly reassured only when these words and plans are backed up with parenting behaviors that demonstrate that they are a priority. Many children express frustration that their parents are "always busy"—often on the phone, e-mailing, or texting—and do not appear to have time for them anymore. Paying close attention to your children's need for your time and giving them your attention delivers the clear message that they will not be abandoned, physically or emotionally.

In this chapter, I will provide some general guidelines on how and when to tell your children and how to prepare them for the changes that lie ahead. Then, because children's ages influence both their needs and their ability to process and understand information, I will offer specific guidance on what to tell—and, equally important, *not* tell—children at all the developmental stages. Included are a list of messages and some sample scripts with language that may be helpful. Chapter 7, "Emotionally Intelligent Parenting," will include

more practical, proven strategies for developing strong and enduring relationships with children and effective ways to communicate
with them—even when they may be afraid to ask questions or do not
know what to ask.

Preparing Children for Changes: Some Broad Guidelines

Preparing children for the emotional and logistical changes that lie
ahead is important for two reasons. First, it gives them the information about what is happening in their lives—information that helps
to assuage many of the fears and worries that accompany this major
change in their lives. Second, this preparation helps to shape future
events in a positive way.

When to tell. Deciding *when* to tell children can be as difficult a
decision as *what* to tell them. One factor to consider is how certain
you are about your decision to end your marriage. The process of
reaching the decision to divorce is often filled with overwhelming
and sometimes conflicting emotions. So it is best to tell the children
after your decision to separate is final, rather than while you are in the
throes of an argument or still determining how to solve your marital
problems.

Once your decision to divorce is final and you have worked out
what you will say to your children, plan a family meeting for a time
when you, their other parent, and all the children can sit down
together without limits imposed by meetings, school activities, or
other commitments, and when no one is too tired, sick, or hungry.
Some children may react immediately, with questions, fears, tears,
or anger. Others—particularly when there has been little conflict in
their presence and the divorce comes as a complete shock—may say
little or nothing at first, as they are often stunned and disbelieving.
Their questions and reactions may tumble out over a period of time.
Even if you anticipate the latter, allowing plenty of time for this family

meeting communicates to children that this all-important decision is being treated with seriousness and that you want and expect them to talk about their feelings, concerns, and questions. If it is possible to have this important family meeting at home, children then have the option of spending some time alone in their own rooms later on, if they wish.

It is helpful for children if you plan this family meeting for a time when both parents will be available to talk with each child one-on-one later that day and for several days afterward. Each conversation provides an opportunity for parents to reassure the children and express unending love for them. If one parent immediately moves out of the house or departs for a business trip, children often fear that parent is leaving them, too.

In addition to the logistics of the schedule, it is wise—although often difficult—to plan for a time when you both have the emotional wherewithal to provide reassurance and encouragement for your children. This is not to suggest that you hold your tears in check, but that you are emotionally able to focus your full attention on your children and respond to their needs.

The age of the children influences the time frame for telling them, too, and ranges from about two weeks to a month or two. For young children of preschool and primary school age, it is generally best to tell them about two to three weeks before a parent moves out of the home. Older children and adolescents may need more time to plan and process how the changes will affect them, and telling them a month or two before a parent leaves gives them the opportunity to ask questions and plan for whatever changes will occur.

In planning the timing of this emotional conversation, you give your children a real gift by avoiding special occasions like birthdays and major holidays. The memories of these occasions are forever tainted if bad news is associated with them. It saddens me deeply when I hear children say, "They told me on Christmas. They turned the time when I was always happiest into a season that will make me sad for the rest of my life." Unfortunately, I hear variations on this theme all too often, as birthdays, Thanksgiving, Passover, Christmas, and other occasions around which families build joyful traditions are transformed into times of sadness and loss.

The big message. A single fundamental message is the foundation for all of the explanations and discussions that follow: "Whatever changes take place between Mom and Dad, one thing that will not change is our love for you. We will always be your parents and we will continue to take good care of you. Both of us love you very much, and the kind of love we have for you is the kind that will never end." Such a message provides children of all ages with a powerful core of reassurance and stability that allows them to deal more confidently— although still sadly—with the major changes in their lives.

Physical contact helps to reinforce this loving message. Sitting close to your children so you can reach out to hug or touch them helps them to feel your nurturing presence during this intensely emotional time.

Children may not always reveal how important your message of enduring love is to them, or how frequently they need to hear it. But telling them again and again and sustaining the message with actions throughout their lives are great sources of comfort and confidence.

What else to say. Children are better able to cope with life-changing news when you let them know that you have had a difficult time making this major decision, and that you are not undertaking the divorce lightly. While the message needs to be tailored to children's ages, the fundamental theme is that you've had serious problems in your marriage that you have been unable to solve. These problems have nothing to do with the children—they did not cause them and they cannot fix or change them.

If both of you agree that one of the best parts of your marriage is your children, then it is comforting for children to hear you say so. They also need to know that your paramount concern is to take good care of them. They are further reassured when you continue to live this promise by keeping their needs a top priority and not introducing additional changes and new partners into their lives too quickly.

Establishing a stable home and family life with structure, warmth, and limits, and staying connected to children as an authoritative parent go a long way toward helping children to feel "normal," secure, and loved.

Explain what will happen next. Children of all ages benefit from advance notice and preparation for the changes that soon will occur in their family. Telling them about the separation or divorce is the first step in a communication process that continues for many years. Children's uncertainty about what will happen to them and to the two people they love best in the world is exceedingly stressful for them. As they try to absorb the news in that first conversation, children need to know that they will continue to have a home and their parents' ongoing love, attention, and guidance. They also find it reassuring to know some of the specifics about what will happen to them.

It is ideal if you have made some preliminary plans before you tell the children about your plans to divorce. Then you can share the most important facts of their immediate future—where each parent will live, where the children will live, and approximately when they will see each parent. Having this information helps to allay their biggest concern—what will happen to me? Children who are not given information about family changes nor explicitly told that their parents will continue to take care of them often fill in the gaps with their own worst fear—that their parents might leave them, too.

If it is not possible to have a general plan in place at this time, it is helpful to tell your children that you are working on this together and will take into account their needs, schedules, and input as you make plans for their time with each parent.

Tell the children together. Children benefit if you are able to break the news of your pending separation together, if at all possible. I understand how very difficult this can be, particularly when your own emotions are raw.

After an especially emotional meeting in which Jerry and Suzanne worked out the details of how and when to tell their children, Suzanne expressed their shared hopes for the future and their commitment to working together on behalf of their children. "Once we focused on a plan for making sure our children were our priority, telling them—and the divorce itself—became more bearable to contemplate. It's all about them. We want to make sure they know how deeply we both love them, and know that both of us will always be their parents—in every sense of the word."

Making careful, well-considered decisions together about what to tell the children is best accomplished when you can make enough quiet, private time to have thoughtful conversations and agree on the ways and the words that are just right for each of you. As you undertake this planning together, you may find it helpful to think about your own relationship in a new way—as professional partners in the extremely important job you must work at together, now and for the rest of your lives, parenting your children. Making such a transition demands enormous self-control, sound judgment, and sensitivity, but is easier to manage if you can view it as an investment in your children's healthy development, and hence well worth your time and effort. More information about how to develop an effective, business-like, coparenting relationship is included in chapter 5.

Because it is often hard to set aside all the issues that led them to part ways, many parents find it helpful to consult with a mental health professional who specializes in families and divorce. Together, they can find the optimal ways for the parents to talk with their children and prepare them for the changes that lie ahead.

But sometimes it is necessary to tell them alone. Sometimes, of course, it is either not wise or not possible for parents to break the news to their children together. When one parent leaves without notice, talking together with the children is, of course, impossible.

If the degree of volatility or hostility between parents is extremely high, it may be impossible for them to sit down together for this conversation with their children. If there is a history of violence or the safety of children or a parent is in question for any reason, the parent's first priority is always to protect the children. If telling the children together has the potential to become violent, then one parent must tell the children alone. Children need that parent's reassurance that they will be cared for and safe, and the parent needs to take the steps necessary to ensure their safety.

In any situation when parents cannot tell the children together, the parent who takes responsibility for telling the children about the separation explains what will and will not change in their lives. Particularly in these situations, children need to be reassured that this parent is wholeheartedly committed to caring for them and keeping them safe. Chapter 5 provides information on parallel parenting practices that may be adopted to minimize opportunities for conflict.

Avoid the rumor mill. Children need to hear the news of your divorce directly from you. Over the years, I have heard painful stories from children who learned about the possibility of their parents' divorce from a grandparent, aunt, uncle, cousin, or close family friend. Others learned the news from peers who had overheard their parents repeating a rumor. In all cases, these children understandably felt betrayed. Hearing about their parents' divorce from someone else undermined a fundamental sense of trust and honesty at the very time when they most needed the security of a strong and loving relationship with both parents.

The only foolproof way to protect your children from hearing the news secondhand is to make sure that no one hears about your decision before your children do. Telling family, friends, and neighbors is the next tier of communication. In some cases, it is helpful to tell adults who are close to your children very soon after you tell your children, so they can talk with these trusted individuals about their feelings and fears.

Because the decision to divorce is such a major one, however, you may need a trusted confidante who provides a listening ear and support during this difficult time. If you have a friend or family member in whom you can entrust such personal information, insist that they keep it confidential. Other safe alternatives are to have such discussions with a licensed mental health professional who specializes in marriage and family issues. Not only are people considering divorce assured of the privacy of their conversations, but they also benefit from the support of an experienced therapist.

Many individuals want to share their thoughts and feelings with other close family and friends. While having support is unquestionably helpful, my caution is to confide in people who can be completely trusted to keep confidences and are able to be discreet. Even a single overheard remark can cause children unnecessary fear and worry.

Sometimes friends and family, out of a sense of loyalty and love for you, may unwittingly contribute to conflict and animosity—and to your children's distress—by taking sides and criticizing the other parent. To prevent or minimize this additional burden for children, I often recommend that both parents tell their friends and family that, for the sake of their children, they want to handle the divorce in the most respectful way possible, and ask for their full support in this. It is also advisable to explicitly ask them to discuss your family matters with no one else, and particularly to make it clear that you want to be sure that your children hear the news from you before they hear it from anyone else. If these are people who are important to your children, it is important to let them know when you will tell the children and what messages you want the children to hear from them.

Tell your children without "telling on" your former partner. Four out of five divorces are not by mutual choice, so in a great many situations, the spouse who is left feels abandoned, betrayed, painfully sad, deeply hurt, and often very angry. In such cases, this parent may want the children to share their belief that "we are all being left" and to see themselves as injured parties, too. In nonmutual divorces or high-conflict situations, it can be very difficult to avoid making blame, vengeance, rage, or sarcasm part of telling the children. "I don't know why you are so mad at me, this was entirely your mother's idea—I had nothing to do with it," or "I know how sad and angry you are—I'm devastated by his selfishness, too, since your father left us for her."

It is all too easy to slip across the line from "telling the children" to "telling on" their other parent. While a parent may feel justified in telling children about their other parent's faults, this knowledge jeopardizes their relationship with both parents over time. Information about a parent's affair or character flaws is painful and corrosive for children and puts them in the untenable position of having to decide which parent is the good guy, and which is the one to blame, to the detriment of their own healthy development. Very often, one outcome of too much negative information about their parents' divorce is for children to have misgivings about ever trusting someone enough to commit to a long-term relationship of their own. Ultimately, it is children who suffer most when they are directly or indirectly pitted against a parent. Blaming fuels conflict and puts children on a path toward jeopardizing their relationship with a parent, which can create enduring problems.

Children in our support groups or the privacy of therapy often talk about how overwhelmed and troubled they feel when their parents share the details of their adult problems, or describe the other parent's faults or limitations. When children role-play being "experts" on divorce, they inevitably offer this advice to parents: "Tell us about the changes in our family and what will happen to us, but *please* spare us the gory details."

When children hear that their world is about to change in a major way, they urgently need their parents to focus on loving and nurturing them, and not to be pulled into the middle of their hurt and anger. Except in situations of abuse or violence, children benefit when each parent helps them to maintain a good relationship with the other and avoids alienating them from their other parent. In so doing, parents also earn their children's respect for taking the high road. Many parents find this mantra helps them to focus on what is most important, especially in the early days of a breakup when emotions are intense: "My children need me to love them more than I hate my former partner right now."

If you are struggling with the desire to "tell all," you may find it helps to put these feelings into perspective by envisioning how you want your children to think about their family in the years ahead. As a loving parent, you want your children to benefit from the certainty that both of their parents have deeply loved and cared for them, and not for them to feel trapped in the middle of your conflict. By imagining your children in ten years and focusing on what will make them happy and confident, you may be better able to contain your own hurt or anger and speak respectfully and positively about your children's other parent.

Fostering a good relationship with the other parent is not a favor to your former partner, but a lifelong gift to your children. Research has shown that children who maintain strong relationships with both parents after a divorce are much more likely to have a loving relationship and marriage in the future than those who have been estranged from one of their parents.

How much information you give your children about the divorce should be based on their age and level of maturity, of course. But by focusing on the desired outcome for your children, you can probably avoid telling them stories they will wish they had never heard. In these cases, less is always much, much more.

The Best Ways to Handle Some of the Most Difficult Situations

Divorce is almost never easy, but some situations are far more difficult than the "average" breakup. There are proven ways to help children through these particularly difficult adjustments.

When one parent leaves abruptly. When one parent leaves suddenly, without notice, the other is left with the difficult task of delivering the news to the children. Often the reasons for a sudden departure are complex adult issues—alcoholism, drug abuse, incarceration, emotional problems, or an affair.

As hard as it is for a parent who has been left abruptly, it is even harder for children to comprehend and deal with this new reality. When they do not have accurate information that is appropriate for their age, they replace the unknown with their own worst fears and fantasies: "Maybe it was because of me. I wasn't good enough—or lovable enough. He left because he was mad at me for not picking up my stuff and arguing with my sister." Children and teens sometimes connect a parent's sudden departure with their own rebelliousness or an argument they have had. "We had a big fight. I wished she would disappear, and now she is gone."

Children need to be told that a parent left because of adult problems they need to work out—and that it has nothing to do with them or their lovability. If there are issues such as alcoholism or drug abuse for which the parent is getting help, it is important for children to be told that their parent is safe and getting the help they need for their problem.

In the desire to protect children from painful realities, sometimes a remaining parent makes up a reason for the other's absence, such as "Dad is on a very long business trip." Or she simply tells the child nothing except "He left." Although such statements are usually based on the deepest desire to shield children, they leave a big void in children's minds that is almost always filled with negative possibilities. Even if children do not fill it with their own fears, fantasies, or guilt, they often hear rumors that they are powerless to address.

In the absence of information, children often worry that the parent on whom they are now completely dependent is keeping an important secret from them. Such secrecy often breeds a sense of shame, which undermines their relationship with this parent. So although parents need to avoid sharing the "gory details," they can best help their children by giving them age-appropriate, accurate facts about their other parent's absence, combined with reassurances of their own abiding love.

When there has been little overt conflict. Recent research has shown that children react differently to their parents' divorce when they have witnessed a great deal of conflict than when they have seen little or none. Studies reveal that children in high-conflict marriages actually fare better after their parents' divorce. These studies reinforce the long-established finding that divorce can be an effective solution to a marriage marked by animosity and conflict. On the other hand, children in families with low overt conflict have a harder time adjusting to their parents' divorce. For children who have not been aware of problems in the marriage, the news of the divorce comes as an unwelcome shock. They feel caught off guard and blindsided by news that contrasts sharply with the family life they have experienced.

In these situations, children benefit from some advance preparation. I am not suggesting that the solution is to fight in front of children. Rather, if you anticipate separating, you need to let your children know well in advance that you are having problems. If it turns out that you do not divorce, the children will have had a valuable lesson about the benefits of working diligently to resolve problems in relationships. If you do divorce, the news will be less of a shock because of this advance notice.

Here is an example of how to prepare children in a seemingly placid household for the possibility of a divorce:

"Mom and Dad are having some really big problems getting along. None of these problems has anything to do with you—they are between us. We are working hard to try to solve them, but we may not be able to continue to live together."

"We know this is hard stuff for you to hear, and we're sad about it, too. We are not sure yet what will happen, but we will tell you when we have made a definite decision. We are sorry to have to tell you about these problems. You will probably have some questions and feelings about all of this. Always know you can talk to us about your feelings and ask any questions you might have."

Regardless of the explanation that you provide, this message helps children through uncertainties and fears: "Whatever happens between us, we want you to know that we both love you with all our hearts and we will always be your parents and take good care of you."

Such conversations are undeniably difficult, but if the decision to divorce becomes final, you will have cushioned the blow with a compassionate message that helps to prepare your children for the changes that may lie ahead. As in other situations, in a low-conflict separation, you will do well to share the planning and delivery of these messages, avoid placing blame, and reassure your children that they are deeply loved and always will be.

When a parent has done something wrong. Although divorces are almost always the result of complex situations rather than a single cause, some are marked by events that result in additional stress for children. If a parent has been violent or done something illegal, it is important for them to acknowledge their hurtful behavior, take responsibility for their actions, and apologize for the impact it has had on the family. As always, children are best served if they are given the basic facts delivered in a way that is appropriate to their age and ability to understand, but spared complicated adult details.

If parents have been involved in incidents of physical fights or verbal abuse, they need to acknowledge how frightening and confusing these must have been for their children. Children need to learn that it is unacceptable to use violent or hostile expressions to deal with anger. Under no circumstances is it acceptable for one parent to blame the other for "causing" them to lose their temper and become abusive or violent. Children need to hear a sincere apology and a commitment to behave differently in the future. And then, of course, it is imperative for parents to live up to that promise.

What Children Need at Different Ages

Children reflect stress differently at each stage of their development. Excessive crying, regression in behavior, emotional outbursts, and

physical complaints such as headaches and stomachaches are mani-
festations that can occur in various ways throughout children's and
adolescents' years of development.

Because children are able to process information and emotions
differently at different times in their growth, the specific messages
that you deliver and the way you deliver them need to be adjusted for
each child's age. In this section, I will provide ideas, suggestions for
communication, and other tools and activities that you can use to help
your children at each stage of development understand and cope with
the changes brought about by the initial decision to divorce.

Infants and young toddlers. Children younger than two are not able
to grasp the concept of divorce. What is important to them is what
they experience, and babies absorb the emotions that surround them—
happiness and contentment, but also anger, frustration, and depression.
Even very young children can sense a parent's distraction or stress.

Although infants have no words and young toddlers only a few,
they express their feelings with the only "vocabulary" they have—
their behavior. Little ones respond almost immediately to what they
experience. When they undergo daily stress, they also develop patterns of behavior substantially different from those of calmer times.
Regression in developmental accomplishments is a hallmark of stress
in infants and toddlers. For example, they may prefer a bottle after
having been weaned, refuse foods they once enjoyed feeding themselves, revert to pointing instead of trying to name an object, stop
interacting with others, and give up on standing, crawling, or walking in favor of being held. Disruptions in sleep patterns, loss of appe-
tite, becoming easily frustrated, and having more frequent illnesses
can also be signs of stress at this developmental stage.

Infants and young toddlers are not able to manage their own emotions, so they depend on the consistent, day-after-day efforts of a
loving adult to help them do so. Research reveals some of the proven
ways that parents can protect their young children with responsive,
nurturing care that helps them thrive.

They need to have a solid attachment to at least one parent, and preferably both. They thrive when they experience a warm, nurturing environment in which their physical and emotional needs are reliably met, regardless of whether they are in a home with one parent or two. If their parents are attentive, patient, responsive, and available for them, then they feel secure and safe.

What Infants and Toddlers Need

- A secure attachment to one, and ideally both, parents
- A warm, nurturing environment in which their physical and emotional needs are reliably met
- Reminders of parents' love and reliable presence
- Continuity and consistency of care
- Protection from conflict and hostility

Older Toddlers: Eighteen Months to Three Years. Secure attachment to at least one loving adult, and optimally to both parents is central to older toddlers' healthy development. Yet beginning around eighteen to twenty-four months, they also begin to need some independence and autonomy. No wonder this toddler stage is called the "terrible twos," with "no's" and temper tantrums side-by-side with exuberant laughter and affectionate snuggles.

At this stage, children still show stress through behavior more than words, and a change in their behavior patterns often signals a change in the core of their feelings. Since this is a time of significant growth and change in children's behavior, it can be difficult for parents to decipher which behavioral changes are part of children's normal development and which reflect stress.

Changes in eating and sleeping habits, increased irritability or crying, and refusing to be soothed as easily as before can all be signs that toddlers are absorbing difficult emotions that they cannot process any other way.

Backsliding in developmental accomplishments, such as lapses in toilet training, regressing in language, reverting to other behaviors they had outgrown, and becoming more anxious and shy with a caregiver are all classic symptoms that something is wrong in their lives.

Temper tantrums and demanding, defiant behaviors are part of the mix of expected behaviors for toddlers and signs of growing independence. When these become excessive, however, or there is a marked change in the frequency, duration, or magnitude of these outbursts, parents may rightly suspect that they are feeling out of control, frightened, or otherwise upset. Such displays may occur particularly when children must separate from a parent, either going to child care or with the other parent. They may become clingy, crying, and distraught when they part from a parent, even when a parent leaves the room to go to another part of the home. Becoming unusually withdrawn or sad also signals that they are having trouble coping. As at any age, children may have more frequent illnesses when they experience stress because it suppresses their immune systems and leaves them more vulnerable.

Toddlers under the age of three need some very simple explanation of the changes they are experiencing. An explanation, such as "Mommy will live here in this house and Daddy will be at his house, and you will spend time with both of us," is about all they can process. Because very young children cannot grasp concepts of time beyond today or tomorrow, they need to see both parents without lapses of more than a few days in order to feel safe and secure. When both parents have frequent contact and give consistently high quality of care, they foster their children's healthy attachment to them, despite the marital changes. I recognize this may be difficult if you are in the military or your job requires travel, but to the extent that you can control your schedule, you will help your children by fostering the development of these important early attachment bonds.

Hugs, snuggling, smiles, and other physical contact are very important in helping toddlers feel loved and secure. Talking with them in soothing tones about how much they are loved also helps to reassure them. Protecting toddlers from the stress of divorce requires parents to contain conflict and maintain continuity of nurturing care, both physically and emotionally. You can accomplish much of what these very young children need by giving them responsive care at both homes and creating a stress-free environment. Taking care of yourself physically and emotionally helps you maintain a calm atmosphere and give loving attention to your children. I realize that is a tall order for a sleep-deprived parent whose own world has often just been shattered. Chapter 5 offers some proven strategies and suggestions for how to take care of yourself in ways that help your children to thrive.

Toddlers benefit from simple explanations and reassurance from parents about when they will see them again. Concrete reminders, such as a book prepared especially for the child with pictures of them at both homes, can help these very young children understand that both parents will continue to love and care them, and also affirm their special place in the family. While no single tool solves all problems, these personalized books help young children process and understand the changes in their lives at the same time they reinforce the important message of a positive connection and attachment to both parents.

What Older Toddlers Need

❄

- A secure attachment to one, and ideally both parents
- A warm, nurturing environment in which their physical and emotional needs are reliably met
- Frequent reminders of parents' love and reliable presence
- Continuity and consistency of care
- Protection from conflict and hostility
- A simple explanation of family changes

Preschoolers: Ages Three to Five. When five-year-old Joanna came to see me, she spoke so quietly I could hardly hear her. Her kindergarten teacher was concerned about her withdrawn behavior at school, her lack of interest in play, her refusal to eat lunch. She had also begun sucking so hard on her hands and arms that they were red and chafed. Joanna's parents and teacher were disturbed and puzzled about her behavior.

When she entered the playroom she seemed almost literally tied in knots. For a long time, she sucked on her sleeve and then her hand, without moving. Children's behavior has a purpose; it is their way of conveying their inner experience to the world. In this case, Joanna was sending a distress signal. Why was she so deeply troubled, and what could be done to help her? When I encouraged her to explore the playroom, she finally began to move around tentatively, not speaking and unable to engage in play. I gently reminded her that the playroom was a place where she could choose how and with what she wanted to play.

It took several weeks of encouragement before she started to play, finally filling the playhouse with five dolls—the same number of people in her family. Slowly she took them out of the house, one by one, leaving just one little girl doll alone in the house. As she played with this doll she called JoJo, she began to cry. When she was finally calm enough to talk, she choked out, "All the sadness and madness is because of her. Her mommy and daddy are gone. They're getting a divorce and it's all her fault—just like me!"

Joanna, so small and vulnerable, was carrying a huge emotional burden. I commented on how hard and confusing divorce can be for kids and suggested that sometimes it can *seem* like kids can cause divorce, but it's really a problem between the grown-ups—not one that kids can cause, or fix. Joanna was not convinced. Tears streaming down her face, she whispered, "No, no, it's true. It's because I wet the bed. I hear my name over and over when they fight. Now they don't love each other anymore, and they're both going to go away, and I won't have anyplace to live—and it's all because of *me*." Added to her deep sense of guilt were profound distress and fears of abandonment. "What will happen to me?"

Preschoolers are prone to misconceptions about family changes and the reasons for the separation. Their confusion and misconceptions may range from benign puzzlement, such as I heard from one four-year-old, "My parents got divorced because Mommy would get up so early in the morning and clomp around in her wooden sandals," to more disturbing self-blame, like Joanna's.

Their other almost universal reaction is fear of abandonment. Young children often conclude that if the marital bonds could dissolve—if Mommy and Daddy could stop loving each other—what is to guarantee they will keep on loving their children? Their deepest worry, most often unspoken, is "What is going to happen to me? Who will be here to take care of me? What if Mom (or Dad) leaves me, too?"

Children at this age are unable to grasp a concept as complex as divorce. When they hear their parents' angry voices, they absorb those emotions and feel stressed and frightened. Young children who lack both the cognitive ability to understand the meaning of words like "divorce" and "custody" and the verbal skills to express their inner experience often feel like their world is falling apart. Even when parents carefully explain their situation and the changes that will occur, preschool children seldom fully understand them. Their ability to think logically—to understand cause and effect, and what happens next—is significantly limited, even when they act as if they understand completely. Magical thinking that typifies this developmental stage often leads to beliefs about their parents' divorce that seem wildly improbable to adults but can cause preschoolers a great deal of anguish.

Changes in preschoolers' behavior often reveal the stress they feel. Some, like Joanna sucking on her hand, adopt extreme self-soothing behaviors that border oddly on self-punishment. Many revert to imitating earlier developmental behaviors they'd outgrown—begging to be picked up or fed, clinging to parents, playing with baby toys, talking baby talk, and bedwetting and other toileting lapses. They may become demanding, defiant, or uncooperative. Or they may cry easily over "little things" and not want to sleep alone.

The best time to prepare three- to five-year-old children for an impending separation is approximately one to two weeks before a parent moves out. Children will best be able to understand and accept the changes if explanations are very clear, simple, and reassuring. Telling the children for the first time about family changes is just the beginning of communication that continues in the days and months ahead. Close physical contact is especially meaningful to children at this age, so sitting close together, hugging, and touching help to reassure them that they are still loved and that their parents will still take care of them.

It is best to keep explanations simple with young children, and then to follow up the initial conversation frequently. At these times, they benefit by being reassured of your unconditional love for them and reminded about what will and will not change in their lives. These are also times to ask them what they're thinking and feeling about all these changes and pick up on any misconceptions, worries, or fears.

What to Tell Three- to Five-Year-Olds

❊

- Provide a very simple explanation of family changes.
- Make sure children understand they are not at fault and they cannot fix grown-up problems.
- Express unending love for them, coupled with reassuring hugs and snuggling.
- Allay any fears that they, too, will be left.
- Reassure them that both of you always will be their parents and take care of them.
- Assure them that they will continue to spend time with both parents; explain their schedule.
- Explain in simple terms what will and will not change for them.

Sample Script—No script is perfect, nor can it remove the pain that goes along with telling children about divorce. But I hope you will find this sample a helpful guide as you think about how to tell your children in a way that helps to ensure they feel loved and protected, even as they learn about the big changes in their lives.

"Mommy and Daddy have some grown-up problems that make it very hard for us to get along with each other. We have been fighting too much. That's not good for any of us, so we have decided not to live together anymore. We will have two houses. You will spend time with each of us at each home. Mommy will stay in this house and Daddy will live in a new house that you can see sometime soon. Bo will stay with Mom, so you will still be able to play with him here. Dad will have Kitty at his house. You will still be able to take swimming lessons and see your friends. And we can still have your birthday party at the playground if you want to.

"We want you to know that you did not cause any of these grown-up problems; none of this is your fault. We both love you so very much, and we always will. The kind of love we have for you is the kind that will never end, no matter what. Some other things will never change, either: Mom will always be your mom and I will always be your dad. You will always be our special Amy and we will always take good care of you."

Calendars, Books, Movies, and Other Resources—Young children need concrete reminders of when they will see each parent. Having them color two calendars—one for each home—using different colors for their days with Mom and those with Dad, can help to break down the mystery of time away from each parent, which can seem like an eternity to young children. Daily reminders, such as "You'll see Daddy again after two more sleeps" and "Mommy will pick you up after preschool today," further help them to understand. These reminders are also reassuring to them when they are missing the other parent or begin to worry about when they will go to their other home.

Children need a safe, nonthreatening way to put their feelings into words. Talking about other children and their parents' divorces is one way for children to explore their own feelings without having to acknowledge what they are feeling, which can be intimidating and confusing to them. For example, if a child is hesitant to acknowledge any feelings, comments like "Some kids worry about what will happen to them, or they might even think that they caused the problems—but kids don't cause divorce . . . it's a grown-up problem" help them realize their feelings are normal.

Reading an age-appropriate story about divorce with your children snuggled in your arms offers another comfortable way for them to begin understanding all the emotions they may feel. There are a number of books available and more coming out all the time. I often suggest to parents of preschoolers that they use books written especially for children at this age. Books can be used interactively, reading one page at a time and pausing to talk about how the character in the book is feeling. You may want to preread books you plan to read with your children so you can be prepared to deal with the ideas and emotions, as well as to be sure that you are comfortable with the messages in them.

Ages Six to Eight. Most school days, Seth woke up with a stomachache. Always a quiet, serious boy, he now became even more withdrawn. His teachers noticed changes in his behavior. He often seemed distracted and unable to focus on his schoolwork, and when he was unable to grasp concepts the first time, he immediately became upset. His grades began slipping. Whenever an assignment was returned to him with a grade lower than his typical A's and B's, he became teary.

Like many seven-year-olds whose parents are locked in conflict, Seth absorbed the stress of the situation, and it found expression in both physical and emotional disconnects. In one of our group sessions, Seth told us that he wanted to make everything right by getting good grades, "but I worry all the time at school, so my grades are getting worse and worse"—which made him still more worried. Poor Seth was so concerned about both his parents that he had trouble concentrating on anything. He desperately wanted to protect his mother, who was very sad, but he also was troubled that some of the things she said about his father were not true, and he thought that was unfair. He did not know how to talk to her about that, and he certainly could not ask his dad, who seemed so mad at his mom. All of this anxiety and turmoil in his mind essentially paralyzed him.

When their parents divorce, young school-age children are often deeply sad, yearn for the absent parent, and hope fervently for reconciliation. It is common for them to feel guilty and responsible for the big family changes. Even though these children may have strong and growing verbal skills, the signs of their stress are often nonverbal. Because they worry about adding their feelings and fears to the concerns that already upset their parents, they often try to hide their own feelings. The stress they are experiencing may be manifest in a variety of ways—becoming withdrawn and easily upset. Boys are more likely to become uncooperative or uncharacteristically angry and aggressive. Both boys and girls may regress to less mature behaviors. They often worry about one or both parents, and girls especially may make extra efforts to behave well. At the same time, many children have trouble concentrating and their grades may slip. Headaches and stomachaches are among the most common physical symptoms of stress, but increases in allergies and asthma-related symptoms are also indicators. Recent advances in the field of psychoneuroimmunology help to explain the connections between emotional and physical well-being and the impact of stress on the immune system.

By the early school years, children have developed some ability with logic; they are able to understand the connections between events and predict some outcomes. They are generally able to manage their own behavior based on how they expect others to respond. They cannot yet think in abstract terms, however, so even very bright children may misinterpret some of the expressions and experiences surrounding their parents' conflict and divorce.

At this point in their lives, they have a very strong sense of fairness and often become quite upset when someone violates their inflexible rules for right and wrong. They often find it very stressful to discover that one or both parents may have done something "wrong" or "bad" to the other, or to hear someone say that divorce itself is "wrong." As so many children have said, they did not get to vote on this major change in their family. Their lack of a voice and resulting loss of control they feel over their lives strike them as deeply unfair. They are often torn between their loyalties to both parents, and they go to great lengths to try to keep things fair and equal between them.

As is advisable with all age groups, it is best to keep explanations short, clear, reassuring, and loving. Because they can understand more about what divorce means and how it will impact them, children at this age usually feel more emotional than younger children may. Whether they express their feelings openly or not, they often find it hard to process information that causes them anxiety. Many times they forget what they have been told. This is not because they're not paying attention, but because their emotions are on overload and they're simply unable to take in and process any more information. For these reasons, frequent one-on-one follow-ups with each child are very important to their understanding and well-being.

What to Tell Six- to Eight-Year-Olds

❋

- Provide a simple explanation of family changes.
- Express your unending love for them.
- Convey regret for the divorce, because you understand the changes will be hard for them and make them sad.
- If it is true, tell the children you agree that they have been the best part of your marriage.
- Make sure the children understand they are not at fault and cannot fix your problems.
- Reduce their worries about what will happen to them and reassure them that both of you will always be their parents and love and take care of them.
- Explain what will change and what will stay the same, and how the new way of life will impact them.

- Encourage children to express their feelings, now and always. Let them know you realize some of their feelings may be pretty tough.
- Encourage the children's healthy relationship with both parents. Let them know they do not have to choose between the two of you.

Sample Script—As with all scripts in this chapter, this is simply a model that may help you think about how to explain your situation and how to incorporate the most important messages for children at this age.

"We have some sad news to share with you. As we told you, we have been having a lot of problems and have not been getting along together. We are sorry to say that we will be getting a divorce. You know what a divorce is, right? It's when a mom and dad are not married to each other anymore and they live in different homes.

"But one thing we really want you to understand is that just because we are getting a divorce, it does not mean that we will ever stop being your mom and dad. One thing we really agree on is how much we love you, and nothing will ever change that. We want you to love and spend time with both of us. You don't ever have to choose between us.

"We know this is hard news to hear, and you probably feel sad or maybe even mad at us for this, and that's normal. We have some of those feelings, too. Whatever feelings you have, it's good to talk about them, and we both want to listen and talk about ways to help you feel better. We want you to know that you did not do anything to cause the divorce. It's because of problems between us, not because of you, so it is not anything you can fix. This is a sad time in our family right now, but we love you and we will do everything we can to help you. These are big changes for our family, but we will all get through this.

"In a couple of weeks, I will be getting a new apartment and you will spend some time there with me and some time here with Mom. I'd like to show you my new home next week when it's ready. It's near here, so we will still see each other a lot and I will still coach your soccer team. You will go to your same school, and you'll be able to have all your friends come to both of your homes.

"We know this is a lot to hear right now and you may have more questions later. Always know that it is good to ask any questions you have and talk to us about how you are feeling. And just always remember that we love you very, very much, and that will never change."

Calendars, Books, Movies, and Other Resources—Like preschoolers, early school age children also benefit from a calendar with different colors designating "Mom days" and "Dad days." They thrive on routine, and a regular, predictable schedule can help to reduce their stress. You can use books as a way to open up conversations with your children, help reduce their worries and misconceptions, and reassure them of what will remain constant in their lives.

Many schools offer support groups to help children cope with family changes. Once you have told your children about the divorce and one parent has moved, it is usually helpful to inform your child's teacher about the changes and find out whether your child's school has a support group program or other resources available for your child.

Preteens: Ages Nine to Twelve. "My parents are so selfish—all they think about is themselves! Why are they doing this to me? Why can't they just act like grown-ups and learn how to solve their own problems? All my friends are going to think I'm some kind of freak." Eleven-year-old Casey was very outspoken about her parents' divorce. Like other preteens, she was consumed with her peers' opinions and terribly upset by anything that might negatively influence her reputation.

In addition to new social concerns, preteens have developed fairly strong reasoning skills. Keen observers, they are likely to have a sense of their parents' problems. They are capable of real insight, but they do not have a depth of experience that allows them to see the whole picture, nor is it in their best interest to know the details of their parents' marital problems. They understand that, unlike death, divorce is not inevitable. They realize their parents made this decision without consulting them, which often leads to anger, resentment, and other strong emotions.

Compounding the situation are the highly unpredictable feelings that accompany the emerging physical and emotional changes they experience during this period of their lives. So the experience of their parents' divorce may include many elements not evident with younger children.

Gender plays a role, too. Preadolescent boys have a harder time adjusting to family life in which the mother is the primary residential parent. The loss of a responsible male presence complicates their adjustment. Both boys and girls at this age may take on the role of an absent parent, a role reversal in which they become the family caretaker. While taking on some responsibility can add to their maturity and self-confidence, being thrust too fully into adult roles can be unhealthy for them. They feel much more secure when one or both parents are in charge.

As preteens attempt to deal with their own worries and sadness and their concerns about remaining loyal to both parents, they often hide many painful emotions. Apparent indifference may mask other feelings that trouble them deeply. Physical complaints such as frequent headaches or stomachaches, or visits to the school health office with vague complaints also reveal the stress they feel.

There are negative emotional consequences for children who get entangled in loyalty conflicts between their parents, and the negative effects can extend throughout their lives. For this reason, it is important to avoid placing blame or engaging preteens in conversations about who is right, who is wrong, or who is the injured party or victim.

Preteens benefit when a parent takes the high road and refuses to belittle the other, sparing them the dilemma of divided loyalties. Conversely, hearing accusations and blame only adds fuel to their anger and may contribute directly to an increase in behavior problems.

Just as we want our children to accept responsibility for their behavior, it is important for parents to acknowledge responsibility for problems. Preteens do not need—and should not hear—intimate details, but an honest admission and a genuine apology for the pain that a parent may have caused helps them to begin dealing with the reality. This relieves them from trying to decode a mystery, or deal with rumors from outside the family.

Preteens often need help with expressing their inner feelings about the divorce. As with younger children, using comments like "Some kids your age worry about what to tell their friends and what their friends might think . . . those feelings are understandable" helps them to realize their feelings are normal. You can help your children address their worries by talking with them about their options for letting others know. Do they want to tell their close friends, or do they want you to break the news? If they prefer to handle it on their own, it's important to respect that decision. You can help them think through how to share the news in a way that will help to ensure their friends' understanding and support.

Sometimes, preteens prefer to have you tell their friends' parents so that they can tell their children and smooth the way for later conversations on the topic. If your children prefer to have you deliver the news, it will help them to plan with you in advance what you will say and to anticipate how to respond to questions their friends may ask. If your child wishes to, she may invite one or two close friends over to give them the news. With her permission, you can tell them that she wanted to share important information about some changes in your family with them because they are such good friends. Then you can provide a very brief explanation of the changes—that you are divorcing, and that they are always welcome to be with your child at both homes. You can also tell them that their friendship is very important to all of you and a divorce does not change that. It's best to keep such a conversation brief, and take cues from your child as to whether to talk further—or wrap it up and move on to some pleasant activity for them.

Giving children a choice about telling their friends and other such matters gives them a sense of control over some aspects of family changes at a time when they otherwise may feel completely powerless.

On the brink of adolescence, preteens are beginning to make their own break with the family, but they need to push against bedrock, not sand. You can help them greatly by emphasizing in words and demonstrating through behavior that you will continue to be fully responsible parents. Their "job" is to do well in school and continue participating in wholesome, enriching activities. They can best do so when you provide consistent care, supervision, and guidance.

What to Tell Nine- to Twelve-Year-Olds

❋

- Tell your children that your marriage is ending, and briefly why.
- Express regret that you cannot solve your problems, acknowledging that divorce will impact their lives.
- Accept responsibility but refuse to blame each other.
- If true, tell children they have been the best part of your marriage.
- Make sure children understand they are not to blame and cannot fix your marital problems.
- Express unending love for them—repeat often.
- Reassure them that both of you will always be their parents and look after them.
- Encourage them to have a healthy relationship with both parents.
- Explain what will change and what will stay the same.
- Seek their input on the schedule now and later on, as changes occur in your lives and theirs.
- Explain that their input is important, but you will make the decisions about the schedule.
- Reassure them that the schedule will include time with both parents, time for their activities, and time to see their friends.
- Encourage them to express their feelings and let them know you will listen.
- Let them know you'll also respect their wishes when they don't want to talk.

Sample Script— This sample script provides some guidelines for talking to your nine- to twelve-year-olds.

"We need to talk with you about some sad and difficult things that are happening in our family. As you may have noticed, we have not been getting along for a long time now, and we have decided to get a divorce. There are a lot of things that have contributed to our problems, and we are both sorry that it has come to this point. As a married couple, we have not been able to agree on many things.

"But the two things we *do* wholeheartedly agree on are that we both love you very much and always will, and that both of us will always be your parents. The kind of love we have for you is the kind that will never end.

"Even with the changes in our lives, we want you to be able to continue to focus on all the things that are important to you—doing your best in school, enjoying your other activities, and seeing your friends. We'll both help to make sure you can be involved in all of these.

"We also want you to know that the problems we have are between us. You did not cause them, and you cannot solve them. We do not want you to take sides or choose between us. It is important for you to continue to spend a lot of time with both of us, just as you do now.

"We know this is hard for you to hear, and it was hard for us to come to this decision. Like us, you will have a lot of feelings about it. We want you to know that you do not have to keep any secrets. You can talk to your friends, your teachers, and your counselor at school, and we want you to talk to us, too, about any of these changes in our lives and your feelings about them. It's hard, but we'll all get through this. If you would like our help in telling your close friends, we can do that. You can decide what feels more comfortable for you and tell us what you would like us to do.

"Here is what we have been thinking about the schedule and how the changes are going to look for you and for us: You will spend part of every week with Dad and part with Mom, and you'll alternate weekends with each of us. You can have your friends come to both homes, and you'll still be able to do all your same activities. We want you to have input on how the schedule is working for you, and we want to know how you feel. So we'll test it out and make any changes so that it works well for you. We love you so much and care very deeply about you, so we will be checking in with you from time to time to see how you're doing. We understand that you might not feel like talking sometimes, and that's okay. But just know that we're always here, always ready to listen.

"Above all, just remember that we both love you very, very much, and nothing will ever change that."

In the days, weeks, months, and years that follow this first conversation, it will remain very important for you to make time for frequent one-on-one time together, and to have conversations not just about the divorce, but everything your children are interested in. When you can, find ways to laugh together and share experiences that make you both happy. And of course, plenty of physical affection will help to reinforce your words of abiding love and strengthen the bond between you and your child.

Calendars, Books, Movies, and Other Resources—Because many preteens already lead very busy lives, with school activities, sports, music lessons, band practice, and social time with friends, the schedule changes associated with divorce usually add a layer of complexity to their lives. Calendars, whether paper or electronic, help them to stay on top of where they are going and how they will get from place to place. Bags to carry things between their various destinations and checklists of what to take to each place can help to reduce their worries about not being in the right place, or not having the right books or equipment.

There are some books that preteens may want to read on their own, and these can provide openings for conversations about what they are reading and how it relates to them. Sharing novels and watching movies in which divorce has an impact on some of the characters can be an excellent way of allowing children at this age to talk about divorce without putting them on the spot. Making journals and art supplies available and encouraging your children to express their feelings in these ways can also provide them with outlets for their thoughts and feelings. And of course, simply spending time together in shared activities of any kind helps to create a platform for open dialogue.

Licensed mental health professionals in schools and in the community who specialize in helping children and families through divorce are also valuable resources in helping preteens deal with tangled emotions.

Adolescence: Ages Thirteen to Eighteen. Continuing on the path they began to travel in their preteen years, adolescents take still bolder steps toward independence. From their perspective, divorce seriously disrupts their lives. Most have developed physical and intellectual skills, including logic and the ability to make predictions about what may happen in various situations, but they still lack the depth of life experience and brain maturation that provide a deeper and wider context for much of their knowledge.

The behaviors sometimes associated with adolescence—shifting moods, egocentricity, finding fault with adult positions, impulsiveness, being overly dramatic at times—all have their roots in the rapid biological, psychological, and neurological changes they are undergoing. In the brain, the gray matter continues to form and thicken neural connections, and its exuberant growth peaks around puberty. Then pruning begins and continues through adolescence. Thus cognitive abilities undergo considerable shaping during these teen years, as the brain strengthens neural pathways that are used and discards those that are not.

Other changes in the brain also have huge ramifications for adolescents' behavior. Functional MRI studies show how differently teen and adult brains process emotions. When shown pictures of people wearing fearful expressions, adolescents had more activity in the amygdala (the part of the brain involved in discerning fear and other emotions) than in the frontal lobes (the seat of rational thought)—the reverse of adults' response. Younger teens, in particular, often misread a fearful facial expression as sadness or anger, which may explain, in part, why they may have more difficulty dealing with emotional situations. Older teens showed a shift of activity from the amygdala to the frontal lobes. These studies help to explain the physiological reason for teens' emotional responses and the growth in ability to use reason.

At the same time that teens are neurologically prone to emotional responses, their frontal cortex—the brain's CEO that keeps things under control—is still under construction. So while teens' anger circuits easily get red hot, the switch that keeps emotions and impulses in check is being rewired. Just as these major neurological changes are taking place, teens are also buffeted by hormonal surges and psychological tension.

Even though they have the ability to think logically, adolescents' judgment may be compromised by impulsiveness, resulting in risky behaviors. Unfortunately, some of these lapses in judgment can have dire consequences, as evidenced in the high proportion of teens' car accidents, excessive drinking, and experimentation with drugs.

Substance use during adolescence is especially risky because the adolescent's brain is susceptible to addiction. Research suggests that adolescents are more vulnerable than adults to the effects of alcohol on learning and memory, and that it causes more damage to the formative brain than was once thought. Early drinking also increases the risk of alcoholism. One recent study found that 47 percent of those who began drinking before age fourteen experienced lifetime dependence on alcohol, compared with 9 percent who did not drink until age twenty-one. It seems a particularly cruel irony of nature that adolescents' brains are most vulnerable just when they are most likely to experiment with risky behaviors.

Even as they struggle to find their own identity and stretch or break some of the family bonds, adolescents have a strong desire to be loved. A 2007 MTV and Associated Press survey asked thirteen- to twenty-four-year-olds, "What makes you happy?" Their number one response: "Time with family." Although they might not express it openly, teens have a deep need to know how much their parents value them and to feel their unconditional love. Yet another survey found that only 47 percent of American teens think that adults like and respect them.

Most teens feel some stress just because of where they are in their lives, leaving the comfort of the protected past and moving into the uncertainty of a future for which they must be responsible. Some exhibit signs of serious rebellion, while others move away more gently. Teens feel especially stressed when they do not have input into major decisions affecting them and when schedules do not allow for flexibility. As with other age groups, conflict between parents and unstable or weakened relationships with parents are major sources of stress for adolescents.

Divorce creates enormous additional challenges for adolescents as they add all the family changes and heightened emotions to "normal" tensions. Changes in family structure further erode the stable foundation from which teens launch their quest for independence because they make the future seem even more uncertain. Divorcing parents need to be particularly watchful for signs of stress and anxiety in their teenagers.

For most teens, the news of divorce comes as an unwelcome disruption to their lives. For this reason, they need plenty of advance notice about the changes that will impact them. Because of the ongoing changes in adolescents' cognitive and emotional development, preparing them for family changes requires sensitivity, judgment, patience, time, and a realistic expectation that, despite your best efforts, the transition may not go the way you hope—at least initially. Adolescents' immediate concerns include: What will happen to me and our family? What will my friends think? I don't want people to feel sorry for me! Does this mean I have to have two houses and go back and forth with all my stuff? Will I still be able to get my driver's license? What about that trip I wanted to take over the school break? If I spend the weekend at Mom's, will Dad feel like I don't want to be with him? Who will pay for college, or help me when I finish school? And at some point, they almost always want to know—whose idea was this, anyway?

In preparing to talk with your teens, you can anticipate that you will need to address just such questions—and more! Usually, these conversations are more successful if both parents discuss and agree in advance how you will prepare your adolescents and set the stage for how life will unfold in the future. The first conversation is only the beginning. Teens, in particular, need multiple ongoing opportunities to talk about this, along with all the other emotions and experiences related to their breaking away from childhood and entering adulthood. In addition to talking and listening—and sometimes refusing to do either—they also observe your behavior and use it as a yardstick for their own.

At this stage in their development, teens may be especially concerned about the parent they perceive as the injured party. They may feel a strong need to discover who was at fault for the breakup and align with the parent they deem less culpable for the decision to divorce. When an extramarital relationship is a factor in a divorce, a parent who honestly acknowledges it and expresses real regret for the hurt it has caused has a better chance of maintaining a teenager's respect than one who glosses over the facts or defends his or her behavior. Trying to keep big secrets almost always puts further distance between parents and teens.

Although parents who feel hurt and betrayed may find it comforting and even gratifying to have teenage children side with them, their doing so almost always comes at a cost. Teens are most likely to thrive and be resilient if they have a positive relationship with both parents. Exceptions to this are when a parent is abusive or has such chronic mental health or substance abuse problems that it is unsafe to maintain regular contact.

What to Tell Thirteen- to Eighteen-Year-Olds

❄

- Tell them your marriage is ending, and why—briefly and without intimate details.
- Express regret for the divorce; acknowledge the impact of this decision on their lives.
- Accept responsibility but refuse to blame each other.
- If true, tell them they have been the best part of your marriage.

- Make sure they understand they are not to blame and cannot solve your marital problems.
- Express unending love for them—repeat often.
- Reassure them that both of you will always be their parents and share a commitment to them.
- Encourage them to have a healthy relationship with both parents.
- Explain what will change and what will stay the same in their lives.
- Seek their input on the schedule now and later on, as changes occur in your lives and theirs, but let them know you will make the final decisions.
- Explain that they may not get exactly the schedule they want, but it will include good time with both parents, time for their activities, and time to see their friends. Encourage them to express their feelings and show them that you listen.
- Let them know you'll also respect their wishes when they don't want to talk, but you will check back with them because their feelings matter to you.

Sample Script—In addition to the words they hear, adolescents are quick to pick up on the prevailing tone of their parents' conversations and behavior. Even more than the words, the tone influences how they think and feel about the changes ahead. Teens perceive underlying hostility, sarcasm, and blame, and these often lead to danger ahead. But they also can sense parents' genuine sadness and mutual respect, and these reinforce the knowledge that both parents will provide a safety net of support, even in the midst of major life changes. Thus, as you prepare to tell your adolescent children about your divorce and the changes ahead, you can positively influence the transition by being attuned to your own feelings and finding ways to convey genuine respect for your former partner, along with their sadness and regrets.

While there is no one "right" way to tell teens, the example below provides some suggestions. This is a blueprint of what might be ideal for parents to communicate, but given the emotions that are likely to surface, it is unlikely that the conversation will go quite this smoothly.

"We have something very important we need to talk with you about. As you know, we have been finding it very difficult to get along together for quite some time. We have tried hard to solve our problems, but we just have not been able to. And so we have decided that it is best for us to get a divorce. We are sad about this and we know that you will have a lot of feelings about it, too. Above all, we want you to know that even when we are living in different homes, both of us will always love you and be there for you. You should also understand that the problems between us do not have anything to do with you. You did not cause them, and you cannot solve them. In fact, the one thing we both strongly agree on is that we are grateful for our marriage because we got to have you.

"We both want to stay close to you—you do not ever have to choose between the two of us. We have decided to share joint legal custody, and we are working out the schedule so that you will have a lot of time with both of us and you will be able to continue with all your activities and see your friends at both homes. You will get to have some input on this, and although we cannot promise that we will be able to make every aspect of the schedule exactly as you may want it, we do want to hear how it's working for you when we first separate and as time goes on. We will both be in this house for a few more weeks and then Mom is moving to an apartment until she finds a house near your school. We will tell you in advance about changes once we know more.

"Most of all, always know that no matter what, you have two parents who love you very much—nothing will ever change that. This is hard stuff to hear about all at once. You probably have some questions—and a lot of feelings about this. We are sad about it, too, and we deeply regret that this is happening. As hard as this is, our hope is that it will be better for all of us in the long run without all the tension and arguments. We want to hear about what you are thinking and how you are feeling now and in the days and weeks ahead. Just know that no matter what, we love you, and we will get through this."

Calendars, Books, Movies, and Other Resources—Most teens have full lives and schedules, so the need for transitions between households will almost certainly add a layer of complexity for them and for you. If they do not already use a planner or calendar—whether paper or electronic—now they will probably need to do so. Having all elements of their schedule combined in a single tool helps to give them a sense of control over their lives and reduces their worries about where they are to be at any given time. If checklists for each activity or day can be attached to the calendar and in each home near the door, so much the better. Calendars and lists help them to take responsibility for their lives and belongings and feel more in control. Book bags, gym bags, overnight bags, and dedicated shelves to hold their gear as they transition from place to place can all help to bring a sense of clarity and order to their lives.

In addition to helping teens manage the physical aspects of their schedules and their belongings, you can help them make emotional adjustments with a variety of tools. Conversations about novels and movies whose characters experience divorce can help teens feel less isolated and more "normal" and at the same time provide a way to talk about the experiences and emotions they are now having. Licensed mental health professionals can also be an important resource, allowing teens to work through their feelings and grapple with the changes in their lives with someone who has special skills and knowledge in this area.

Planning for All the Days to Follow

By now, you may feel so overwhelmed that you want to close this book and think about something else—anything else! Telling the

children is undeniably one of the hardest parts of the process of ending a marriage, but every family is unique, and I realize that your
conversation may be different from the versions I have presented in
this chapter. What I have provided are idealized sample scripts, and
your conversations may not necessarily follow them or go smoothly
even if they are very carefully planned.

Despite your best preparation, the number of things that can go
awry seems daunting. It may be hard for you and your former partner to manage the intense emotions you are feeling so that you can
talk together with your children. Or even if you manage to talk with
them together, you might get sidetracked and fail to say everything
you meant to. Your spouse might detour from the plan you thought
you had agreed upon. Your children might storm out of the room in
tears after the first few sentences. Your adolescent or preadolescent
might stare into space and refuse to respond. But even if the first
attempt does not go as you had hoped initially, you can try again,
perhaps aiming to accomplish just one piece at a time.

More important, though, is understanding that "the big conversation" is only the first of many, many conversations to follow. It is very
important to follow up the initial conversation—however it goes—
with each child one-on-one, and then to keep the communication
lines open. Going out for a walk or driving in the car can provide
opportunities for you to "just check in about how you're feeling"
without putting children on the spot and forcing a conversation they
may not be ready to have.

So the guidance in this chapter is not just to help you determine
what is important to tell your children the first time, but to help you
focus on the messages you will continue to embed throughout many
more conversations in the days and years ahead. Your children will
need to be reminded over and over again of your unconditional love
for them and your commitment to be there for them as a loving parent. They will need to be reminded that they are not to blame, and
that they cannot fix your broken marriage or mend your hurts. They

will need your help in managing the changes in their schedules and lives, and in making adjustments when things change or don't work out. They will need you to hug them when they are happy and hold them when they are sad. And they will need the sense of comfort and security that comes with structure and new family routines and rituals.

Chapters 4 and 7 provide more information about how healthy routines, structure, and traditions can help make the changed situation feel normal and secure. Backing up your words with consistent behaviors is one of the most important—and sometimes most challenging—aspects of the period following a separation, and you will find more information about how to accomplish that in these chapters and others.

Of course it is not possible—or wise—to hide all of your feelings from your children. Such a pretense would put an unnatural barrier between you and them. But you will help them greatly by focusing more on their feelings than your own, acknowledging the difficult emotions they express in words or behavior. "This is hard stuff we're going through. We are all having a lot of feelings right now." In addressing your children's needs, you will provide them with the foundation they need for the long term. As for your own intense feelings, you certainly do need to express them and even spill the horrid details, but these are best handled with trusted friends, confidantes, or a therapist—*not* your children.

At the same time that you focus on making life after divorce the best it can possibly be for your children, I hope you will give yourself permission to be human. Most of us zig and zag our way through painful times, growing with each turn in the road. Healing and adjusting to major life change takes time as well as effort. Research suggests that the average time for individuals to feel whole again after a divorce is one and a half to two years.

As I work with parents who diligently and lovingly prepare their children for all the changes in their lives, I am always reminded that the root of the word "courage" is the Latin *cor*—heart. As you prepare yourself and your children for the changes ahead, I hope you will take heart in the possibilities of your love and support and remember that even an uneven, zigzag pattern of progress may still be a pathway to resilient, healthy adjustment in the long run.

FOUR

Parenting Plans:
Positive Approaches
to Difficult Decisions

I t's Tuesday, but do I go to Dad's house today after soccer practice, or to Mom's? What do I need for tomorrow, and where is it? Are the books for my report at Dad's or Mom's? Where's my gym bag?"

These were only a few of the questions Ted asked himself regularly after his parents divorced. They separated when he was ten, and from then until he finished high school, he went back and forth between their homes every other day, including weekends. He felt constantly confused and anxious, since he did not go to the same home on the same day each week. As he packed his belongings each morning, he was never sure whether he had all of his schoolwork or sports equipment in the right place. As a result of his complex schedule, this deeply conscientious boy spent most of his childhood worrying.

To compound matters, Ted's parents frequently changed his schedule to accommodate various needs of their own—work and otherwise— often at a moment's notice. The slightest mention of a problem—missing homework or activities—could unleash a torrent of hostility between his parents, and this conflict put more knots in Ted's stomach. His frustrating situation and lack of control over it contributed to depression and anxiety that proved hard to shake, even in adulthood.

Now in his forties, "Ted" is a successful business executive, accomplished in many ways. But he still feels anxious every time he packs for a trip, even a happily anticipated vacation. His suitcase has come to symbolize the worry and angst he felt daily throughout his childhood.

"Ted"'s emotional burden was largely preventable, as we now know from a sizeable body of research. Had his parents contained their conflict, reduced the frequency of his transitions during those critical years, created a schedule incorporating some input from him, taken greater control over their erratic work and social schedules, and developed a cooperative parenting relationship—no small feats in the midst of their own life changes and emotional turmoil—they could have spared him much of his enduring anxiety. At the outset, had they understood that they might need to modify their son's schedule and known what to watch for, they could have made changes and prevented some of his anxiety then and even now.

This chapter will give you some critical information that "Ted"'s parents did not have. It begins with a brief overview of the legal options that form the context for most parenting plans. Its primary focus, however, is on the factors that have proven to influence the success of custodial arrangements. The schedule is one of the most critical factors, and I will explain how to make scheduling decisions and parenting plans that are best suited to children at various developmental stages.

The ideas and recommendations I include throughout this chapter are based on a substantial body of research; I also draw from my own extensive experience working with children and their parents.

Some Options in the Legal Matters

Divorcing parents often wind up in a maze of intimidating legalities, and in choosing among them, they may easily be more influenced by strong emotions than logic, and lose their focus on the outcomes they want for their children and themselves. Traditional litigation is usually an adversarial legal process that by its very nature escalates conflict between parents. Although about 90 percent of divorce cases ultimately are settled outside of court, legal negotiations are influenced by the amount of collaboration, or lack of it, in the legal proceedings. Negotiations between attorneys can be reasonably cooperative or intensely aggressive.

For individuals who feel that their safety or their children's is at risk because they have been abused or threatened or feel deeply intimidated by a former partner's aggressiveness, it is essential to seek the vigorous representation of an attorney. Only a relatively small number of situations fall into this category. Unfortunately, however, the aggressive tactics required in these situations are used all too frequently in situations that do not require them.

Many times, intensely aggressive tactics have the undesirable effect of further fueling conflict between divorcing parents who still need to share parenting responsibilities. Hurt, fearful, angry parents often choose an aggressive path for emotional reasons. Feeling vulnerable because of the losses they've suffered, they respond to instincts to hurt back, and they choose the most potent weapon they can find—an aggressive attorney. Unfortunately, the aggressive, acrimonious legal path often intensifies the pain and anger for both individuals, who leave the courtroom with a mind-set opposite to what they will need in order to share in parenting their children for many years ahead.

In choosing an attorney and the process you will pursue, it is important to remember that you are your lawyer's customer. You can choose one whose approach suits your goals and your children's needs, and then insist that the path he or she pursues remains true to those goals. You are seeking professional advice and services, but your attorney should be willing and able to help you pursue both the end and the means in a way that keeps your children's needs a top priority. He or she should be willing to negotiate, not always litigate.

One of my patients' experiences illustrates the point. After making considerable progress, Anna came to her session one day and announced she was ending therapy. "My lawyer says when I come to see you, I'm not as full of anger and ready to get even. He said I need to stay angry in order to win," she said. From the standpoint of aggressive litigation, anger is a good weapon. But from the perspective of negotiating a reasonable agreement and establishing a healthy platform for sharing in the parenting of children, staying angry undermines the desired outcome. Once Anna and I talked through her real objectives—protecting her children and finding a way to coparent effectively with her soon-to-be-ex-husband, she determined to pursue one of two options. Her first course of action was to reassert her goals with her attorney and insist that he pursue the course of action she wanted. If that did not work, she was prepared to find someone else to represent her. Fortunately, her lawyer listened to her wishes, changed his approach, and ultimately helped her negotiate a win-win parenting agreement in which her children thrived. Although aggressive representation is still considered the legal standard, initiatives are being considered in many law schools to structure the training of lawyers specializing in family law to include a more holistic view of the family and children's developmental needs.

Fortunately, in addition to traditional litigation, other alternatives are now available to resolve marital disputes. Mediation and collaborative law are increasingly sought out as effective alternatives to adversarial legal proceedings, which can intensify parent conflict and negatively impact children.

Mediation is a form of alternative dispute resolution (ADR) that involves both parents coming together with a neutral third party. A major goal of mediation is to reduce conflict by helping separating parents arrive at mutually agreed-upon decisions about their children. Mediators are usually mental health professionals or lawyers with special training to help divorcing couples negotiate agreements, but they do not have the power to make a final decision if the parties fail to reach agreement.

One of the benefits of mediation is that the process involves both parents as decision makers about the most important aspects of their children's lives. Mediation has been shown to result in a host of positive results for families for many years after a divorce. The Virginia Mediation Study followed people who were randomly assigned to traditional litigation in court or mediation. The results were remarkable, with positive outcomes for family relationships twelve years later. Parents who mediated their own agreements were significantly happier with the process and the results, and both parents were more involved in their children's lives than those who litigated. Children whose parents mediated their divorces had more contact with the parent they did not live with than children whose parents went through litigation. Twelve years later:

- 28 percent of children whose parents mediated saw their non-residential parent once a week, compared with 9 percent of parents who litigated.
- 36 percent of litigating nonresidential parents had not seen their children in the past year, compared with 16 percent of mediating parents.
- 59 percent of parents who mediated had weekly phone contact with their children, versus 14 percent of parents who litigated. These differences in telephone contact were particularly notable since many of the children had left home or moved away.

Especially noteworthy is the fact that increased contact did not result in increased conflict between parents, perhaps because former partners had learned to resolve issues together through the mediation process.

These benefits were the result of just five hours of mediation with specially trained facilitators. So not only were the outcomes better for children and parents, but the process yielded huge cost savings for both parents and the taxpayer-funded court system.

This study found that one of the most important components of the practice of mediation was its emphasis on teaching about emotions. For example, when parents were becoming hostile and arguing, mediators would point out how they themselves felt just being in the same room with them, and wondered out loud how their children must feel being in the middle of those conflicts far more often. This corresponds to what I have found with so many separating parents in my practice. When we take time to sort out other feelings behind the anger, we commonly find sadness and grief. This awareness does not make those painful emotions disappear, but it does help parents to acknowledge their emotions, get help to work through them, and learn how to manage them so they can negotiate an effective parenting plan.

As with any professional who is to work with your family, it is important to choose a mediator carefully. I encourage parents to choose a mediator who is accredited in your state and has special training and experience in divorce and family mediation. In some states, an individual can be designated a mediator with only twenty hours of training but no other background in family relations, psychology, or law, so in these states, it is particularly important to inquire about a mediator's background. It is always advisable to meet with the person first to see if you and your former partner feel comfortable and confident with the mediator's style, knowledge, experience, and skills. For your welfare and your children's, it is imperative that any agreement reached through mediation be reviewed by your lawyer before you sign it.

Collaborative law, also known as collaborative practice, is an increasingly popular way for divorcing parents to work as a team with trained professionals to help resolve disputes respectfully without going to court. In this model, both parents have the support and protection of their own lawyers while working as a collaborative team to arrive at legal agreements. It differs from mediation in that it involves a team of people rather than a single mediator.

Collaborative practice is different from traditional litigation in four major ways:

- In this client-centered approach, parties negotiate mutually agreed-upon settlements without ever using the court to decide any of the issues.
- There is an understanding that the legal professionals will withdraw if either parent goes to court.

- The process is characterized by openness in communication and information sharing.
- The collaborative team uses communication skills, problem solving, and shared solutions that consider the interests and priorities of both clients and their children.

Lawyers in the collaborative process embrace a new way of working with clients by focusing on the family going through a divorce in a holistic way. The lawyer's role is multifaceted, providing information and education, facilitating negotiations between clients, as well as advocating for their client's needs and interests. The collaborative process emphasizes effective communication, conflict resolution, and positive ways of negotiating agreements.

Some models of collaborative practice include a *financial specialist*, a neutral expert who helps to clarify financial issues, available options, and consequences. This addition to the team helps clients make sound financial decisions for themselves and their children. A *coach*, or family relations specialist, is often part of the collaborative team as well. The coach is typically a licensed mental health professional who facilitates communication between team members, helps to manage difficult emotions that could block effective resolution, and model effective communication and positive coparenting behaviors. The team also usually involves a *child specialist*, a licensed and specially trained mental health professional who provides a voice for children in the process. The child specialist also gives parents information and guidance about how they can best support their children, reduce conflict, and provide the most effective parenting to foster children's adjustment. This person assists the team in developing effective parenting plans, tailored specifically to the needs of the children and their family.

In my own experience as a child specialist and coach in the collaborative process, most parents deeply appreciate having a voice in decision making about their children. While a long-term study of collaborative practice is just beginning, preliminary evidence suggests that the vast majority of separating partners complete the process.

Anecdotal information suggests that parents who engaged in the collaborative process are more likely to continue with a cooperative approach to parenting over time.

Parenting coordination is a relatively new area of conflict resolution that addresses disputes between parents that occur "post judgment," after the divorce is final. This child-focused approach is often recommended for parents who are in high conflict and cannot agree on basic child-rearing matters such as the schedule or extracurricular activities. The goals of parenting coordination are to reduce conflict and resolve disputes in a timely manner without resorting to litigation, to educate parents about children's needs, and to help parents implement their parenting plan or court orders. The approach combines knowledge of both mental health and legal issues with awareness and insight about parenting and child rearing. If parents are still unable to come to an agreement after a mediated approach, resolution may come in the form of arbitration, in which the parenting coordinator will make a decision for them.

Parenting coordinators are most often licensed mental health professional or lawyers specializing in family law, divorce, and child custody, with additional training in mediation and conflict resolution. More information about parenting coordination and other services for families in transition is available through the Association of Family and Conciliation Courts (AFCC), an organization dedicated to improving the lives of children and families through the resolution of family conflict.

Parenting coordinators do not take sides or advocate for either parent in a dispute but remain objective in efforts to help parents come to an agreement.

Among the objectives and functions of parenting coordination are:

- To resolve disputes about children.
- To help parents comply with the parenting plan.
- To make decisions together or accept the decisions of the parenting coordinator.

- To refocus attention and energy on their children's needs, emotions, and best interests.
- To improve communication and parenting skills.
- To strengthen and stabilize families.

Whether you choose traditional litigation, mediation, collaborative practice, or parenting coordination, you are likely to have the most positive outcome if you choose professionals who will work *with you* to help you develop the best separation agreement and parenting plans and to find ways to adhere to those plans and focus on your children's best interests.

The Power of Language in Parenting Relationships

For parents who feel overwhelmed by their own feelings of grief, loss, and anger, having civil discussions with an estranged partner is anything but simple. Even the terms used to describe how parents make decisions about their children can either encourage cooperation or inflame conflict. The word "custody" implies a sense of ownership of children, and "visitation" suggests a marginal role for one parent. Such terms may intensify anger and feelings of loss, and thus undermine a spirit of cooperation and shared responsibility for children's support and well-being. In a study that asked what words people associated with various legal terms, the phrase "joint legal custody" was related to being fair, good, and equal, whereas "sole legal custody" was most often associated with being selfish, unfair, bad, and useless. Parents who had primary custody were viewed as more powerful, dominant "winners," as compared with noncustodial parents. These terms and their connotations can further intensify feelings of loss and despair for a parent who is already feeling marginalized and may add to disengagement between nonresidential parents and children.

As we've seen, children benefit most from having two capable, responsive parents involved in their lives in supportive and meaningful ways, not just "visiting." Increasingly, legal and mental health professionals are calling for new terms to replace "custody" and "visitation," and promote a message of shared responsibility and commitment to children. Fortunately, many states are taking decisive steps to move away from such terminology and its implications.

Like many professionals, I prefer the term "parenting plans" to describe the legal agreements and guidelines parents negotiate, often with the help of a mediator, lawyer, and mental health professional. These describe how they will share responsibilities to meet their children's needs. At the heart of most parenting plans is a thoughtfully developed specific schedule that enables both parents to spend meaningful time with their children. These plans become part of the legal divorce agreement and can provide helpful guidelines for navigating unfamiliar territory after a divorce. Equally important, when well executed, parenting plans help to provide children with the sense of security they need.

Ultimately, though, how any custody arrangement or parenting plan works for children depends heavily on how parents carry it out. As you read this chapter, you'll find descriptions of qualities that relate to better outcomes for children in different living arrangements. The best parenting plans are those that two responsible parents create together after taking time to consider their children's developmental needs and then working hard to ensure that those needs are met.

The Court's Role in High-Conflict Custody Situations

The parenting plan options presented in this chapter have proven effective for many separating parents. Unfortunately, however, some couples remain at an impasse or entrenched in conflict, despite efforts to reach agreement. If your legal negotiations have ground to a halt and your custody case is headed to court for a judgment, here is what you can likely expect.

A "forensic evaluation," or psychological evaluation, may be ordered. This process is conducted by a mental health professional with specialized training in custody evaluations. The American Psycholog-ical Association, the Association of Family and Conciliation Courts, and the American Academy of Child and Adolescent Psychiatry all have clearly established ethical guidelines for custody evaluators. The process includes an evaluation of you, your former partner, and your child, with the goal of making a recommendation to the court as to what kind of parenting plan is in your child's best interests.

The court may also appoint a lawyer or specially trained advocate to represent your children's interests. Terms for this individual vary from state to state, but the terms "guardian *ad litem,*" "law guardian," and "attorney for the child" are among those used. The advocate's role is to serve "the child's best interests," which many profession-als consider a vague standard without clear definition. Many in this role consider it their responsibility to assist the court in weighing and assessing the conflicting information that is brought to court by both sides, and to focus on the child's developmental needs.

Ironically, after all the conflicting information is gathered, allega-tions against both parents are heard in court, and a variety of experts offer differing testimony, the advocate's recommendation often boils down to focusing on the child's need to have a positive relationship with both parents. So, if it is possible to work out your parenting plan and custody arrangements outside of court, you will be able to bypass this often arduous, expensive, and stressful process.

Understanding the Legal Definitions of Custody

Despite concerns about its emotional overtones, the term "custody" is still used in most courts of law. "Legal custody" of children means having the right and the obligation to make decisions about their upbringing.

Many divorcing parents find the differences among the types of legal custody confusing or even intimidating. The information that follows is based on current law in many states at the time of publication. Because laws vary from state to state and change over time, I encourage you to consult an attorney in your state to address any legal aspects of planning for your children's needs after divorce.

The terms commonly used to describe parents' options in caring for their children are "sole legal custody," "joint legal custody," and "joint physical custody."

Sole legal custody gives one parent the right to make all the major decisions about a child's home, health, education, religious training, and all other matters, without consulting the other parent. Because such an arrangement seriously limits one parent's involvement in the children's lives, this agreement is used far less frequently than joint legal custody.

Even when one parent is awarded sole decision-making rights, the court may determine that the other parent is legally entitled to spend time with the child and share in parenting. This usually involves legally establishing "visitation" rights, in which a parent is allowed a fixed amount of time with the child.

Joint legal custody requires both parents to share in making decisions on key issues, usually including the child's health, education, and religion. Studies have shown that parents who use mediation are more likely to opt for joint legal custody than those who choose a more adversarial legal process. Joint legal custody does not mandate any particular living arrangement and does not necessarily provide for children to spend equal time with both parents. It is possible for parents to share joint legal custody and joint physical custody (see below), or they may share legal custody while one has sole or primary physical custody.

Joint legal custody has become standard practice in many parts of the country, used in 50 to 90 percent of post-divorce decrees in states where statutes allow it. This represents a dramatic increase since the early 1990s, when only 20 percent of parents opted for this arrangement. The increase is probably due to the growing understanding among parents, judges, and legal and mental health professionals of how important it is for children to have both parents actively engaged in their lives.

In addition to allowing better adjustment for children, joint legal custody is related to more positive relationships between parents as well. Because this win/win approach to decision making inherently acknowledges the rights of both parents, it fosters an emotional climate that in turn produces more positive parenting behaviors. Studies show that parents who share legal custody spend more time with their children, pay child support more regularly, and remain more involved with their children over the long term than parents who do not have joint legal custody.

Joint physical custody provides for children to reside with each parent part of the time. In most states, joint physical custody laws do not require that children's time be shared equally with both parents. Definitions and legal requirements vary from state to state, but in general, children average two overnights a week, or between 33 and 50 percent of their time, with one parent and spend the rest of their time with the other. Legal scholars point out that this shared-time allocation helps ensure that neither parent will be assigned to "primary custodial" or "visiting" status. Joint physical custody is still relatively rare; some estimates show only 5 to 10 percent of children in the United States regularly living in both parents' homes. Even in states such as California and Arizona, which enacted joint physical custody statutes in the early 1980s, about 12 to 27 percent of parents opted for joint physical custody, and children still spent the majority of time with their mothers.

In some states, child support payments may be tied to levels of physical custody, so it is important to consult a lawyer to understand the guidelines in your state. Unfortunately, these provisions sometimes become bargaining tools in negotiations. Many judges find it distressing when parents in a custody dispute count the exact number of hours with their children for financial reasons, rather than focusing on their children's developmental needs.

Research shows that some form of joint custody generally results in children having more connected relationships with both parents and a higher standard of living. A meta-analysis of thirty-three studies assessed children in joint legal custody, joint physical custody, and sole maternal custody. Compared with children in the sole custody of their mothers, those in some form of joint custody were more successful on multiple measures of emotions, behaviors, self-esteem, and adjustment to family circumstances. These studies incorporated information from a wide range of sources, including mothers, fathers, teachers, clinicians, and the children themselves.

Shared residence does not guarantee such benefits to children when parents are embroiled in conflict, however. Children in shared custody with battling parents have more emotional and behavior problems, including depression, physical symptoms, withdrawn behavior, and lack of open communication with their parents. Frequent contact that exposes children to ongoing conflict or high levels of anger and hostility between parents puts children in the middle of a toxic situation. Research shows that children whose parents shared custody but were engaged in very high conflict fared worse than children in sole custody.

Although each family situation is different and custody decisions should be made carefully, sole custody should be considered in highly volatile or abusive situations. Children do not benefit from frequent contact, if any at all, with a parent who is abusive, violent, has untreated mental illness, or one whose inadequate parenting or substance abuse risks a child's safety. In such circumstances, it is essential to have a safety-based parenting plan that protects children and parents from harm. Some excellent models of parenting plans under these circumstances are now available. For example, the Oregon Family Law Courts, courts in Arizona and Alaska, the Association of Family and Conciliation Courts (AFCC), and others have developed models of research-based parenting plans. Parallel parenting (see chapter 5) with a clearly specified agreement is a safer alternative when there is a history of high conflict. Supervised visitation to ensure a child's safety may be warranted in some situations. Above all, when domestic violence is present, courts should be sensitive to the need to provide sanctions and guidelines that protect children and abused parents from further harm.

Despite the potential benefits of joint physical custody or shared parenting, these agreements do not always work well, even when no abuse, violence, or unmanaged psychological problems or addictions exist. In deciding whether to negotiate joint physical custody, it is important to understand what makes these arrangements work well, and what undermines their success for children.

What Factors Influence the Success of Joint Custody?

The joint custody situations that serve children best are built on a high level of communication and cooperation between parents. In "shared residence," as I prefer to think about it, parents manage their own emotions, negotiate schedules, solve day-to-day problems, and are flexible with schedules and transitions between homes. Parents who are most satisfied with joint custody that incorporates shared residence tend to be those who willingly choose it, reflecting a belief in the added value of both parents' active involvement in their children's lives and a willingness to work together. Another factor that positively influences shared residence is simply the proximity of the two homes. It is far easier for children to go back and forth when the travel time between them is short.

Research provides additional information about characteristics of parents who succeed at shared residence agreements. The results are not surprising. When both parents are well-adjusted, cooperative, and amicable, and they agree on joint custody, it is most likely to succeed. The parents who make shared residence agreements work well are:

- *Flexible*—They are willing to adjust the schedule to accommodate a child's activities or the other parent's work.
- *Empathetic*—They are able to understand and appreciate both the child's and the other parent's point of view.
- *Judicious*—They exercise good judgment, maintain boundaries within their relationships, and avoid pulling children into declaring loyalties or taking sides.

- *Businesslike*—They are able to shift from their previous marital relationship to new roles as professional partners in parenting.
- *Fair-minded*—They do not remain mired in anger and blame the other parent for the family's problems.
- *Respectful*—They communicate effectively, maintaining an attitude of mutual respect.
- *Child-oriented*—Most of all, they keep their children's best interests front and center and make decisions accordingly.

For a variety of reasons—not the least of which are their own hurt and anger—many parents are unable to adopt these attitudes and live by them consistently. By honestly assessing your own ability to practice these behaviors as well as analyzing the status of your relationship with your former spouse, you will be in a better position to reflect on exactly what it will take to make joint physical custody work. Consulting with a specially trained mental health professional, mediator, or lawyer may help you to choose a legal and practical framework that allows you to adopt the type of residential arrangement and parenting plan that will be best for your children.

Parenting Plans: A Framework for a New Way of Life

There is no single "best" parenting plan for children; there are as many variations as there are families. Other than the studies of sole custody compared with joint physical custody, there is no research that provides answers to what specific schedules work best for children. It takes creativity and often exploration of many different possibilities to arrive at each family's own "best" plan, but the payoff is worth the effort. Studies have shown that over the long term, the most comfortable, confident, and happy children are those whose parents have worked together to create a plan that protects them from conflict, promotes healthy parent-child relationships, and provides quality parenting.

Parenting plans incorporate all those factors that influence children's lives day-to-day, month-to-month, year-to-year. Generally, they include:

- *Responsibilities*—What will each parent be responsible for in the new situation? How will you ensure that all of the parenting responsibilities for your children are addressed?
- *Decisions*—How will you make decisions that affect your children, in both the short and the long term? How will you make changes to your parenting plans as future phases of children's lives unfold?
- *Communication*—What do you expect of each other in regard to communication? What information must be shared? How frequently will you communicate? What means will you use— e-mail, telephone, texting, in-person conversations?
- *Schedule*—When will each of you see each child? How will you divide their time for holidays and vacations?
- *Finances*—How will you manage the costs of providing for your children? What will the plans for child support entail? How will you arrive at a reasonable budget? What can each of you afford, and what impact will the finances have on your children's activities and schooling, now and in the future?
- *Education*—Will the children continue in the same schools, or will moves require changes to different schools?
- *Religion*—How will matters of faith be handled? Will the practices that the family had established be maintained? If not, how will differing beliefs and perspectives be addressed?
- *Health*—How will decisions be made about doctor visits, medications, or braces for the children's teeth?
- *Conflict*—Knowing that disagreements are almost inevitable, how will you deal with your differences? How will you contain conflict so that it has the least possible impact on your children?

Children, of course, see parenting plans through the filter of their own needs and feelings. These plans provide the structure for their lives and solve many of their concerns. In the best circumstances, communication about plans and changes is open and abundant and gives children a voice. These are some of the major topics and questions that effective parenting plans answer for children:

- *Fears*—What will happen to me?
- *Homes*—Will we have to move? Where will Mom and Dad live? Where will I live? Will I have a room of my own? Will I be separated from my siblings? What will happen to all my stuff?
- *Schedule*—When will I spend time with each parent? Will I still be able to see my friends? How will they know where to find me? Will I still be able to play soccer, sing in the chorus, get my driver's license?
- *Money*—Will there be enough to buy the things I need or want and let me take lessons? Will they be able to pay for my college education?
- *Rules*—What is expected of me? Are there going to be changes in what I am allowed to do or not do? Will curfew and bedtimes be the same at both homes? Can I take my stuff back and forth between Mom's and Dad's houses?
- *Communication*—Will Mom and Dad talk with each other about me, my grades, what I can do with my friends, how late I can stay out? What will happen if I want to do something and they don't agree? Can I call Dad if I'm with Mom? Can I text Mom if I'm with Dad? And will Mom or Dad be upset if I choose to do that?

Creating Child-Focused, Developmentally Tailored Parenting Plans

While parenting plans must address all of the practical matters—work schedules, finances, school or child care, cultural considerations, and more—they are most effective when they also take into consideration the unique personalities and needs of each child, the quality of parenting each parent can provide, and the degree of conflict between them.

Parenting Plans: First Steps

1. Create a schedule based on your children's developmental needs and quality parenting time.
2. Establish a process to review periodically and adjust plans as needed.
3. Manage your emotions.

As you begin to develop your parenting plans, I encourage you to focus first on three things: developing a schedule based on your children's developmental needs and healthy relationships with both parents, establishing a process to review and change the plan as needed, and managing your emotions. Once these are in place, you can work on developing ways to make decisions and resolve disagreements together, nurture your children's adjustment to changes, and support their positive relationships with both parents.

1. Establish a Schedule. As I indicated in chapter 3, well before all the legal aspects of the divorce are finalized, it is important to have some temporary plans ready to go into effect at the time of separation. During this time of enormous change, children of all ages—including teens—are subject to many fears and worries. Having a schedule helps to reassure them because it communicates that their parents are still in charge, still taking care of them.

In shared residence agreements, it helps to think about schedules in broad terms of months and years. When too much emphasis is placed on counting hours and days, parents tend to focus on their own entitlement to their children's time, and as a result, they often wind up feeling frustrated, angry, and deprived. The more important outcome of such thinking, however, is that it shifts attention away from what is best for the children—how their time can be shared to ensure they feel truly connected to and loved by each parent and avoid unnecessary disruptions that leave them feeling anxious, confused, or harried.

Although schedules may seem like straightforward calendar exercises, a number of important psychological considerations influence their success.

> *Children's inner needs.* While parents' obligations are necessary considerations in any schedule, building one that meets children's inner needs is essential for it to succeed. Children's ages, stages of development, temperament, emotional needs, and degree of adjustment to their new situation are all fundamental considerations. The amount of time children spend with each parent, the number of transitions, the changes to their own routines, and all of the other aspects of the plan have the potential to make them feel secure and comfortable, or to make them feel anxious, fearful, or sad. In general, children thrive when the schedule allows for both parents' involvement in their school and recreational activities. For those parents who are able to manage it, bird-nesting—in which the children remain in one home and the parents move in and out—can provide stability for children. As you develop your plan, you may find it helpful to review the information in chapter 1 on interpreting the signals they may be sending and in chapter 3 on behaviors that reveal stress at various developmental stages.
>
> For children with significant medical, learning, or emotional problems, additional considerations impact parenting plans. Children with these special needs usually fare best with more consistency in their lives, so for them, a relatively simple schedule with routines they can count on and the fewest possible transitions may be comforting.
>
> To maintain as much consistency and time with parents as possible, some parents opt to have an agreement that children will be in the care of the other parent when the parent they are scheduled to be with has to be away for work or travel. Sometimes

called "right of first refusal," this agreement can be put into a parenting plan to increase children's time with a parent and reduce the need for child care during large blocks of time when a parent is unavailable. This agreement must be clearly spelled out with specific times and circumstances, to prevent conflict. For this reason, many parents find it helpful to apply it to overnights or extended time away, rather than just for a few hours or an evening out.

Age-specific guidelines for scheduling based on children's developmental needs and capabilities are provided later in this chapter.

Quality of parenting. The quality of parenting each parent is able to provide is a major factor in children's healthy long-term adjustment. This means that each parent needs to build time into the schedule to attend to their own needs so that they can be better able to provide warm, patient, and authoritative parenting for their children. And if a parent becomes physically ill, depressed, or extremely stressed, the schedule may need to be altered temporarily to allow for recovery, so that the children are cared for by the parent who is better able to provide attentive care. Chapter 7 provides more information on proven strategies for quality parenting, and chapter 5 incorporates guidance on ways parents can take care of themselves.

One-on-one time. Part of quality parenting is individual time between each parent and each child. When I help parents develop their parenting plans, I often recommend building in some time for each child to spend alone with each parent. How frequently this happens depends on the ages of the children, sibling relationships, and other family circumstances. Of course, it is important that each parent support each child's time with the other, without pressuring them or causing them to feel guilty. Children often tell me how much they value this quality time with busy parents. Carving out special time together strengthens relationships and builds a foundation of trust and affection for a lifetime.

Consistency and simplicity. Simple, consistent schedules reduce stress for children and adolescents who are already dealing with the emotional and logistical aftermath of their parents' divorce, whereas inconsistent, complicated schedules add to it. For example, it's helpful for children to have their time with each parent on the same days every week. So your child knows, "Tuesday I'm at Mom's, and Thursdays I go to Dad's after soccer practice."

2. Plan for Change. Establishing a plan for change enables you to address evolving needs that occur naturally as your children grow and develop. It also allows you to adjust the plan as your own lives evolve and to accommodate changing family circumstances. By setting both an expectation and a process for change, you can avoid making this another cause of dispute.

It is unreasonable to expect you and your former partner to quickly make all the important decisions about your children's future while your emotions are in turmoil. Slowing down the process before signing a legal agreement gives you time to deal with your own intense emotions, see how your children respond to the initial parenting plan, establish new ground rules for your relationship, and find ways of working together for the benefit of your children despite your changed relationship.

Stressful situations that may feel overwhelming to children often can be solved with relatively minor adjustments to the schedule—sometimes simply by reducing the number of transitions between households or creating additional one-on-one time with each parent.

As I discussed in chapter 1, children often keep feelings of distress to themselves, worrying that they may hurt their parents' feelings or cause more conflict in an already tense situation. You can alleviate much of this anxiety by observing your children, communicating with them about how the arrangements are working, and fine-tuning your parenting plans. If your children resist when you or your former spouse comes to pick them up, withdraw from communication, or show symptoms of stress or depression such as restlessness, anger, excessive crying, a drop in grades, or loss of interest in activities or friends they previously enjoyed, these may be signals that the schedule is adding to their stress. Check in with your children to ask about how the schedule is working for them, and what you can do as parents to ease the stress of transitions.

The story of fourteen-year-old Emma illustrates how caring parents can respond to signs of stress in their children. When they divorced, Jan and Bob had agreed to share time equally with their daughter. After six months, she came to see me because she felt "stressed out." It was initially hard for her to pinpoint the reasons in words, but she sometimes used art to express herself. One drawing showed a child bent under a large, heavy backpack. When I asked her to tell me about it, she said, "That's how I feel, trying to take all my books and other stuff back and forth."

That turned out to be only one of Emma's burdens. As we talked, it became clear that she was also missing her mom, who traveled frequently and often worked late. She wished she could see her mother more and wanted to spend more time at her house; that would make it easier for her to see her friends, too. She also wanted to go back and forth between homes less frequently. But Emma deeply loved her dad and was very concerned about hurting his feelings. "I wish you would talk to them for me," she said. "I just don't think I can do it right now."

When we met, both Jan and Bob recognized that their daughter was just "not herself." She seemed tired, tense, and withdrawn, and her grades had dropped. Jan acknowledged that her career had overshadowed

Emma's needs, and she expressed regret that they had so little time together. Bob felt the pain of having initiated the divorce, as he realized its impact on the daughter he loved deeply. Although the meeting was very emotional, together we worked out a modified schedule with fewer transitions. Emma would go to her mom's house every day after school and Jan changed her schedule to work late only one night a week. Bob agreed to spend that evening with Emma at her mother's house and have dinner with her at his home on another weeknight. Although he still saw her often, Bob found it painful not to have Emma stay at his home as often as he wished. Yet the changes in the schedule made a huge difference for his daughter at this critical point in her life, and she understood that his flexibility was an expression of his love for her. Jan and Bob displayed courage, responsibility, maturity, and love in putting their daughter's needs ahead of their own emotions.

Building in a process to review the parenting plan over the long term has important benefits for children. Even if the plan is working well, it is helpful for parents to schedule periodic reviews, determine whether the plan best meets their children's needs, and make changes if necessary. I often meet with parents two or three times a year, at the beginning and end of the school year, and before major holidays, to plan changes in schedules, assess needs for additional support, or anticipate major events that may impact the restructured family. At a time when they are still adjusting to big changes in their own lives, parents understandably focus more on their children's immediate needs than on pending changes. It can be helpful to see the bigger picture and to realize that over time, as your own lives change and your children grow, there are possibilities for more peaceful and happy times ahead—and you can help to create such a future for your children and yourselves.

3. Manage Emotions. Creating parenting plans that thoughtfully address children's needs requires both partners to approach negotiations in a respectful, professional way. Managing emotions is essential to this approach so that children are protected from the stress of their parents' conflict.

In the midst of divorce, parents are often buffeted by strong emotions.

Broken trust, rejection, and fears of "losing" even more of the pieces of their lives can fuel wrath, resentment, and retaliation. Like sponges, most children soak up the emotions around them. Angry exchanges about legal agreements, residence schedules, or financial issues cause stress for all children; for young ones, they can produce real fear. Even the most thoughtfully developed plans can be sabotaged by hurt, loss, resentment, jealousy, and anger. Studies show that 40 to 50 percent of parents interfere with shared parenting schedules at one time or another.

Although it can be painful to examine your own emotions, doing so enables you to assess whether you will find it difficult to work out your differences. If you anticipate trouble ahead, you can take measures to protect your children. If conflict seems inevitable, it is advisable for you to include in your legal agreement a plan for how future disagreements will be resolved. If both of you have worked with a mental health professional or mediator whom you trust to help you resolve disputes objectively, it may be beneficial to name that individual in your legal agreement. Doing so can help to ensure that you have a familiar resource in place for resolving differences promptly, with a focus on your children's needs. Although having help is certainly preferable to having none, starting over with a new professional or team of professionals may prolong the time before a resolution can be reached, and thus can increase the risk of allowing problems to escalate.

My own experience supports the value of having sustained help before, during, and after a divorce. I am listed in many divorce agreements as a clinical psychologist and child specialist who will be available to help families through an impasse about child-rearing matters. Because we have a history of working together, we are often able to resolve problems relatively quickly to everyone's benefit, particularly the children's.

The case of Marvin and Alice and their four children is fairly typical of the situations in which I've been involved. When I first met them, Marvin and Alice were locked in bitter conflict. Both were engaged in high-powered careers and focused on their individual success. Marvin had always depended on Alice to manage the children and household as well as the demands of her job. Without consulting her, he had recently accepted a promotion that required him to travel a great deal, putting still more responsibility for the family on her shoulders. This happened just as her career was at a critical juncture and she needed greater flexibility. Her response was immediate, angry, and shrill. He reacted by having a very public affair. The children—aged twelve to eighteen—all began to show significant signs of stress.

For more than six months before their divorce, I worked with Marvin and Alice to contain their anger and bitterness, establish practices to reduce conflict, and focus on their children's needs. I also worked with all of the children, helping them to identify and cope with their own emotions, understand what they could and could not control, and manage their own lives in ways that were healthy and productive. We made some substantial progress in those difficult early months after their separation, and we all agreed that they would continue to need professional help after the divorce. In fact, we worked closely together on developing and adjusting parenting plans as well as continuing to work on managing the parents' conflict and the children's feelings and needs as their lives changed.

There are also strategies parents can use on their own to reduce conflict. One is to develop and stick to a specific, fairly rigid schedule that minimizes their contact with each other. Another is to adopt a child-focused, businesslike relationship, with mutual commitment to ground rules for their own behavior while in their children's presence. Mediation, parenting coordination, therapy, and collaborative law have also proven helpful to many parents in containing and reducing conflict.

Parents in high-conflict situations may find it helpful to use a journal in which both record key information about their children. Communicating in writing allows for both parents to be informed and can help to reduce conflict and create smooth transitions as the children go back and forth between households. A journal provides important information that ensures children get the food, rest, soothing, favorite toys, and medicine they need. For infants and very young children, food intake, naps, diaper changes and bowel habits, fussiness, fevers, medications, and new developments—crawling, walking, new words and skills—are all recorded and shared. As children grow older, their activities, concerns about behaviors and relationships, and happy news, too, can be shared in this way.

Sustained anger and rage hinder good judgment, rational thinking, and problem solving—all of which are necessary for negotiating plans and parenting in ways that will positively impact children's lives. So even though it may be tempting to see your former partner as an enemy, it is better for your children if you can find ways to communicate with civility. Your children will benefit enormously if you are able to manage your emotions in ways that help you work toward a reasonable plan for parenting for resilience—yours and theirs. Chapter 5 provides more in-depth information on how to take control of conflict and explains parallel parenting strategies for those parents who find it difficult to maintain emotional control in each other's presence.

A Special Note About Fathers and Parenting Plans

When I began working with children in divorce support groups during the early 1980s, "missing dad" was a recurring theme. Many were distressed about sporadic contact or long time spans between visits, which typically occurred only on alternate weekends. These children felt that their fathers were "visitors" in their lives, rather than true parents. When fathers move on after a divorce, form new relationships, remarry, and raise new families, some drift away from the children they had with a previous partner.

Recent studies show that nearly half of children and teens wanted more frequent contact with their fathers and a third wanted longer contacts. Fewer than 10 percent of youths wanted less time with their fathers. And more than half of surveyed college students whose parents divorced a decade earlier wanted more time with their dads. Despite this evidence, children who have regular weekly contact with a nonresidential parent are still in the minority. That may be chang-ing, however. An analysis of data from 1976 through 2002 found sig-nificant increases in contact between fathers and their children during those decades. Increased contact between fathers and children also means increased contact between former partners, highlighting the need for them to contain conflict during these contact points for the sake of their children's well-being.

In chapter 2, I described a number of studies that collectively reveal how important it is for children to have their fathers actively engaged in their lives and providing quality parenting. With the overwhelm-ing evidence of how much children yearn for and benefit from both parents' active involvement, I strongly encourage fathers—who are statistically the most likely to disappear from their children's lives—to take an active role in developing parenting plans and then remain fully engaged as loving, communicative, and authoritative parents. There are many factors that influence stronger relationships. Among them, research has shown that reduced conflict between parents and having authoritative parenting by fathers help to sustain young chil-dren's relationships with them.

Given the rewards of close father-child relationships, parenting plans that build in meaningful time with both parents enable most children to adjust in the short term and thrive over the long term.

Tailoring Parenting Plans for Children's Developmental Ages

Research in child development provides a large and growing knowledge base of what children need, understand, and can do at each stage of their development. Parenting plans built with an understanding of children's current and evolving developmental stages are most likely to help chil-dren thrive. Having this knowledge does not guarantee that transitions will be without problems, but it can help you plan for adjustments as your children grow. The information in chapter 3 on the behaviors that signal distress at each developmental stage may help you detect trouble spots—even hidden ones—and make changes as needed.

Infants and Young Toddlers: Birth to Eighteen Months. Babies' primary need is to have a secure attachment relationship, or bond, with at least one, and preferably both parents. While not all researchers agree, there is considerable evidence to suggest that most infants bond with both of their parents at approximately six to seven months of age. In order to maintain these attachments, infants and toddlers need regular and frequent interaction with both parents through a variety of caregiving activities such as bathing, feeding, playing, soothing, diapering, and tucking in at bedtime.

More controversial is the question of whether babies need a single, primary attachment relationship, and whether regular separations from the primary caregiver are harmful to them. There is also some conflicting evidence about whether separation from their primary caregiver while spending time with the other parent results in babies' distress and subsequent difficulties. But recent research based on attachment theory suggests that infants and toddlers can bond with more than one parent or caregiver, and they benefit from frequent contact with two responsive parents. Much depends on the quality of caretaking, emotional sensitivity, and responsiveness of parenting in both homes.

From my own experience working with families, I am convinced that it is not only possible but important to support a baby's attachment to the primary parent in the first year of life, while at the same time encouraging the baby's attachment to the other parent. There are multiple benefits when infants and toddlers develop secure attachments to two responsible parents. An important goal of parenting plans with young children is to have frequent enough contact with each parent to keep the infants secure, trusting, and attached to each parent. Avoiding long separations from either parent reduces babies' separation anxiety. For young children, a "long time" is three or four days. For these frequent transitions to flow smoothly, parents must be prepared to communicate about essentials such as feeding schedules, bedtime routines, food preferences, illnesses, soothing techniques, and any information about their babies' needs, and then to provide as much consistency as possible in their patterns of care.

Babies' schedules also need to accommodate their sleep, feeding, and awake time. If breast-feeding has been established, the feeding schedule must be factored in—along with the understanding that this schedule will change over time. Some nursing mothers offer their former partners the opportunity to give a bottle between breast-feedings. When it is feasible, this can be a benefit to all concerned. Mothers get time to themselves, and the bottle-feeding helps to foster the attachment between fathers and babies. Some mothers I have worked with felt comfortable having the fathers come into their homes to give them more time and involvement in their children's care, but this is not always possible or even desirable, especially in high-conflict situations.

SAMPLE SCHEDULES FOR INFANTS AND YOUNG TODDLERS (YOUNGER THAN EIGHTEEN MONTHS OLD)

Assumes two responsible parents. Times shown are with the parent who does not provide the infant's primary residence.

NOTE: These are just examples, not intended to apply to every family situation.

For a Child Who Has an Established Relationship with Both Parents	For a Child Who Is Not Yet Attached to Non-residential Parent
• Two blocks of four to five hours during the week • One weekend day (e.g., 10:00 a.m. to 5:00 p.m.), or overnight (Saturday noon to Sunday noon) if infant is attached to both parents • If both parents are comfortable with arrangement, the nonresidential parent may initially come to the other parent's home to feed and care for infant for designated blocks of time (7:30 to 8:30 p.m.) • Occasional overnights during the week if the infant adjusts well	• Two times a week for two-hour blocks of time • Allow several weeks or months for child to feel secure • Extend to full day (e.g., Saturday 10:00 a.m. to 5:00 p.m.) when child's behavior reflects attachment (smiling, cooing, or otherwise demonstrating feelings of ease and safety in the parent's company) • Gradually add an overnight, once child is securely attached and adjusting well

At the time of the separation, if babies are attached to only one parent or are accustomed to having only one parent give them care, they may benefit from a schedule that gradually increases their time with the less involved parent. This allows infants and young toddlers to strengthen bonds with that parent over time. In these situations, starting with one to three supervised contacts during the week in the home of the primary caregiver or a responsible third party, such as a grandparent or family friend, may help to foster the attachment to that parent. Each visit can be two to three hours long. If the baby responds well, the length and frequency of the visits can be increased, and depending on the situation and quality of parenting, eventually include overnights.

Even early in life, children absorb the emotional climate around them, and it has a profound influence on their sleep, digestion, and growth—and certainly their disposition. One challenge for divorcing parents is to ensure that the emotional climate throughout their own time with their babies and during transitions between households remains calm. This is understandably difficult for a parent who is not only managing strong emotions and adjusting to the challenges of parenting an infant, but is also experiencing sleep deprivation! But by making a commitment to sustain a nurturing, emotionally responsive environment in which their babies' needs are met consistently and helping them to bond with both parents, they promote their children's long-term emotional well-being.

Toddlers: Eighteen Months to Three Years. Toddlers benefit from schedules that provide frequent contact with two responsive parents who foster healthy routines and emotional security. When both parents provide continuity of nurturing care that consistently meets their children's needs, they foster strong attachments with their children and give them a secure, stable foundation.

Toddlers fare best when their parents maintain consistent schedules and routines. When a toddler is attached to both parents, and parents can communicate about their child's needs and reactions and are willing to be flexible, they can test having their child spend one or two overnights per week in the home of the nonresidential parent.

If parents' work schedules can accommodate daytime visits, they may opt for blocks of five or six hours at a time, three days a week. When toddlers are in day care, I often recommend creative scheduling to increase the time they spend with their parents and reduce their time in day care.

SAMPLE SCHEDULES FOR TODDLERS (EIGHTEEN MONTHS TO THREE YEARS OLD)

Assumes two responsible parents. Times shown are with the parent who does not provide the toddler's primary residence.

NOTE: These are just examples, not intended to apply to every family situation.

FOR A TODDLER WHOSE PARENTS COOPERATE	FOR A TODDLER WHO IS NOT ATTACHED TO ONE PARENT
• Frequent contact, every other day or so, with separations not longer than three to four days • Alternate weekends, overnights on Friday or Saturday so that each parent has child one weekend night (e.g., Friday 5:00 p.m. to Saturday at 5:00 p.m.) • May also have weekday overnight; pick up after day care, and return at 9:00 the following morning • Schedule should allow time for each parent to engage in normal child-rearing routines, including feeding, bathing, playing, putting to bed	• Two weekly contacts of two to three hours in a supportive setting (e.g., pick up from day care or preschool and return to other parent at 7:00 p.m.) • Extend to full day when child shows comfort and attachment to parent, which may take weeks to occur (e.g., Saturday noon to 5:00 p.m.) • Primary caretaker to provide information on toddler's care, routines, ways to soothe, favorite activities, etc. • Gradually add overnights if child is adjusting well.

Preschoolers: Three- to Five-Year-Olds. At this age, children need frequent contact with both parents. It is difficult for them to be separated from the people they know and love for more than four or five days at a time. These little ones are often bewildered and confused about the flurry of changes surrounding them, and they struggle to make sense of it.

Having one or more overnights a week with the nonresidential parent has been shown to provide significant benefits for children aged four to six. Parents reported fewer attention and social problems compared with children who had no overnight time with one parent. Maintaining a consistent schedule was key to these positive outcomes. Children fare best not only when their schedules are consistent, but also when their routines at both homes are consistent. Bedtime rituals and schedules, nap times, meals, and beloved stuffed animals or favorite blankets are all elements that make them feel comfortable and secure.

Children at this age also find it very reassuring to know when they will see each of their parents. You can help them to feel secure by communicating very clearly and often about when they will see each of you, and which parent they can expect to see at any given time. For instance, when you drop off the children at preschool or day care, you can remind them which parent will pick them up that day. One very useful tool for preschoolers is a calendar clearly marked with color-coded lettering or stickers so they can understand which days and times they will be with Mommy and which with Daddy.

Since children at this age are quite perceptive, they not only pay attention to information about their schedules, but they also absorb attitudes and feelings. Although it can be difficult to talk with or about a former partner in positive tones, you do your children a great favor when you consistently communicate to them that both of you will always love and care for them. Ease their transition to the other parent's home with positive comments and a smile. This can make a big difference in helping your little one to feel secure.

SAMPLE SCHEDULES FOR YOUNG CHILDREN (THREE TO FIVE YEARS OLD)

Assumes two responsible parents.

NOTE: These are just examples, not intended to apply to every family situation.

Options for Shared Residence	Options for Time with Non-residential Parent
• Three or four weekday contacts: pick up at child care or preschool • Two or three overnights each week • Overnights on alternating weekends (e.g., Saturday through Sunday afternoon) • One-on-one time for each child with each parent	• Every other weekend (e.g., 5:00 p.m. Friday to 2:00 p.m. Sunday) • One weekday after school or day care to 7:00 p.m. • Every Saturday from noon to Sunday at 2:00 p.m.

Early-School-Age Children: Six- to Eight-Year-Olds. Developmentally, children around the ages of six through eight are better able to manage their emotions and separations from their parents than they were at earlier stages. Yet these youngsters still usually need to see both parents frequently. They often long for a parent who moves away after a divorce, and distances or travel costs make it difficult for them to see that parent at least once a week. This is an age when children develop a keen sense of fairness, feel deep connections, and have a strong sense of loyalty to both parents. As a result, they often place importance on spending equal time with each of them. Because they also feel protective of their parents, they often hide their feelings and try not to upset them. So as you create and adjust schedules, you can reduce your children's stress by encouraging them to talk openly about their needs and desires to spend time with each parent, and to reassure them that expressing their wishes is a good thing to do and will not hurt your feelings.

SAMPLE SCHEDULES FOR EARLY-SCHOOL-AGE CHILDREN (SIX TO EIGHT YEARS OLD)

Assumes two responsible parents.

NOTE: These are just examples, not intended to apply to every family situation.

OPTIONS FOR SHARED RESIDENCE	OPTIONS FOR TIME WITH NON-RESIDENTIAL PARENT
• Parents share time somewhat equally (e.g., Monday and Tuesday with one parent; Wednesday and Thursday with the other parent and alternate weekends from Friday through Sunday, or Wednesday after school until 4:00 p.m. Saturday with one parent; from 4:00 p.m. Saturday until Wednesday morning with other parent) • Include one-on-one time with each child in developing these schedules	• Every other weekend (e.g., Friday after school until Monday a.m.) • Every Wednesday after school until 7:00 p.m. • Builds in one-on-one time

Eight-year-old David was having trouble in school and had begun to visit the school nurse quite regularly with complaints of stomachaches. He had enjoyed a close relationship with both of his parents before their divorce, six months earlier. Now he only saw his dad every other weekend and one evening each week. As I soon discovered, recently his father had been traveling a lot, so their time together had been further reduced.

In my office, David seemed solemn and listless; he couldn't decide what to play with. As we talked, he mentioned that his stomach hurt a lot and that he "kind of" wanted to see his dad, whom he hadn't seen for two weeks. David's eyes flooded with tears when I commented, "That's kind of long to not see your dad. Maybe you're missing him."

"Yeah, I really miss him," he whispered through tears. David's sadness and overwhelming sense of loss were at the root of his stomachaches. Like many children his age, he had tried not to burden his parents with his own feelings. When David and I explained to his parents how he felt, they made a special effort for him to have more time with his dad, particularly one-on-one time. I encouraged them to keep revisiting the schedule to adjust and modify it for the benefit of David and their other children as the changes in all their lives continued to evolve.

Children at this age take note of all that goes on in their presence between their parents, and suffer—though often in silence—when they witness conflict. Parents who are unable to control their emotions in each other's presence may help their children by reducing the frequency of their in-person interactions. Sometimes, by picking up and delivering children at school or child care instead of at their other home, parents can arrange transitions with almost no contact at all.

Preteens: Nine to Twelve. With the growth in their cognitive development, preteens are able to spend longer periods apart from one parent. They understand how the schedule works and are usually very comfortable and adept at using the phone, e-mailing, and text messaging to stay in touch with both parents.

They also have an ever-increasing sense of right and wrong, and they often have strong feelings of anger and resentment at the changes being foisted upon them. At this age, many children are very industrious and motivated to achieve in many different ways. So parenting plans for this age need to take into account the importance of their school and other involvements. In a time of a great deal of upheaval, school is often a source of stability, and it is important that children not lose opportunities to be involved in healthy school activities because of the divorce.

Whenever it is possible, parents can help their preteens greatly by staying very involved in their lives. By staying close to the school and teachers and showing strong and consistent interest in school-work and all their extracurricular activities, parents give preteens a sense of security in a situation fraught with change and uncertainty.

This is also a time in their lives when peers may take center stage. Preteens are concerned about others' opinions, and they often worry that having divorced parents will negatively impact their friends' views of them.

These are all matters that influence the schedule. It is important to establish significant blocks of time with each parent. It is also important for both parents to build enough time into their own schedules to stay actively involved in school and outside activities. In so doing, they can best provide encouragement and support for those activities in which their children are involved and motivated to achieve.

SAMPLE SCHEDULE FOR PRETEENS
(NINE TO TWELVE YEARS OLD)
Assumes two responsible parents.

NOTE: These are just examples, not intended to apply to every family situation.

Options for Shared Residence	Options for Time with Non-residential Parent
• Monday through Wednesday with one parent; Wednesday after school to Friday with other parent • Alternate weekends (e.g., from 5:00 p.m. Friday to 5:00 p.m. Sunday) Or • Alternate weeks with each parent, with transitions on weekends and one evening with other parent during "off" week • Build in one-on-one time with each parent	• Primary residence with one parent. • With the other: • Every other weekend (e.g., pick up Friday after school, drop off at school Monday morning) • Every Wednesday after school to 7:30 p.m. • Build in one-on-one time with each child and parent

Joyce and Tom juggled busy careers and the care of their two children, ages nine and eleven. Joyce was a surgeon with responsibilities to be on call four times each month. Initially angry about the divorce that she never wanted, she resisted Tom's repeated efforts to have the children with him for her on-call nights. She insisted that she would hire someone to be at home with the children if she were called to the hospital to deal with an emergency. Her emotions about the divorce extended to not wanting to coparent with him in a way that would allow for flexibility with the schedule.

As we worked through her feelings of loss, hurt, and anger, she gradually began to separate her own emotions from her children's needs—and their own strong preference—to have a parent, rather than a paid nanny, care for them. They adopted the concept of "right of first refusal" for her on-call nights, and for Tom's travel schedule. They worked out their schedules in advance as much as possible to accommodate a clear understanding of changes, and prevent conflict over last-minute changes and miscommunication. Their children were relieved to have a parent with them when the other was away, with little or no disruption to their schedule of school and extracurricular activities.

Adolescents: Ages Thirteen to Eighteen. Teens are very concerned with the logistics of their lives and benefit from having input into their schedules. They want to know what will and will not change, which parent is moving where, when will they see each parent, when will they get to see their friends, whether they will have a say in the schedule, and whether there will be enough money for their present activities and future plans such as college. They fare best when the activities that are important to them are not disrupted, and they are reassured when their parents make it clear through the schedule, communication, and their own commitment that their teenagers will have reasonable continuity in their lives and parents who are still in charge. Like preteens, teens benefit from their parents' continuing support for achievement in school and the activities they cherish.

In a large study of adolescents, fewer had shared residential arrangements than lived solely with one parent. Yet teens who spent time in both parents' homes had better grades, were less depressed, and described their "worst problems" in less disturbing terms than their peers in sole custody. They also had closer and more positive relationships with their parents. Regardless of the living arrangements, however, teens fared best when they had fewer life changes, stable living arrangements and household structure, parenting that included reasonable limits, attention to their daily lives, monitoring of their activities, and a close relationship with at least one parent.

Parenting plans for adolescents also need to take into account their needs for autonomy and increasing independence, while still providing clear rules and monitoring between households. Teens can become quite adept at manipulating to get what they want, and this can become tempting and easy for them when parents are already divided. They may tell one parent that they are at the other parent's home, only to use this ruse to mask risky behaviors and activities.

Since parenting adolescents is challenging even in the best of circumstances, divorced parents need to work especially hard to communicate about their teens. By agreeing on consistent rules, curfews, homework, and the use of the car, they will provide the structure teens need through the years of turbulent emotions, helping them grow toward adulthood with minimal harm. At the same time, teens benefit if their parents can maintain a relationship that allows for some flexibility and teens' input—especially regarding their social lives. As one study revealed, high school and college students whose parents were flexible about schedules were less angry and reported being closer to their parents than those whose parents were resistant or rigid about schedule changes.

Parents are often distressed when their teens balk at transitions between households. Many outbursts occur not because they don't want to be with that parent, but because they resent the disruption to their lives. Many prefer to have a schedule that allows them to have primarily one home base so that their friends know where to find them, or they want more time with the same-sex parent. As one wise father of two teens told me, "I have to step back and see this from my daughters' eyes. They want time with me, but they don't want to have to sacrifice their own already demanding schedules. I'd always seen overnights as important because they meant that I was as much a part of their lives as their mother is. But now I realize that overnights are really not all that significant; after all, they're asleep most of the time! So it ends up being better to have the quality time I do have with them—both individually and together."

SAMPLE SCHEDULES FOR TEENS (THIRTEEN TO EIGHTEEN YEARS OLD)

Assumes two responsible parents.

NOTE: These are just examples, not intended to apply to every family situation.

OPTIONS FOR SHARED RESIDENCE	OPTIONS FOR TIME WITH NON-RESIDENTIAL PARENT
• Split weeks, usually Sunday evening through Wednesday morning with one parent; after school Wednesday through Friday with the other parent • Alternate weekends Or • Alternate weeks between parents, with flexible time in between for contact with the other parent • Incorporate one-on-one time with each teen and each parent during scheduled evenings or days	• Primary residence with one parent • With the other: • Every other weekend (e.g., Friday after school through Monday morning) • Weekday contact each week, on a day that fits teen's schedule (to be decided jointly, with teen's input) • Additional time for teen and parent may occur at school and extracurricular functions, or during drive time

The schedule is an important tool, but regardless of how it is structured, research repeatedly reveals that it is the quality of parenting, the parents' commitment to their children's developmental needs, and their ability to contain conflict and work together that contribute most to children's adjustment to living arrangements.

Making Plans Successful: Minimizing Children's Stress

All of the sample plans in the previous section are based on known child development factors. But these are only examples, and children benefit greatly when their parents continue to watch and listen particularly for signs of stress. Often, relatively small changes to the schedule go a long way toward solving issues that may seem inconsequential to an adult but can keep children tied in knots.

In talking with several thousand children over the years, I have been able to extrapolate some of the major factors that can increase or reduce the stress of their changed lives.

These are some of the factors that reduce stress:

> *Minimal distance between households.* This has multiple benefits for children—less travel time, more quality time with each parent, minimal disruption to school and other important activities, proximity to friends, and the comfort of a familiar neighborhood. Shorter distances also make it much easier when children forget something at the other parent's home.
>
> Conversely, it can be very hard on children when divorce requires them to undertake long trips. Taking plane trips on their own may make them fearful, and long trips—even by car—take them away from familiar routines and activities they enjoy. As many children have told me, "I didn't choose the divorce, but I'm the one doing all the traveling and dealing with all the changes." When children must travel significant distances, it is especially important for parents to coordinate plans. They may ease the stress by accompanying their child on trips, at least initially, providing plenty of advance preparation, and communicating all the details of travel and the children's concerns with one another. Siblings traveling together can provide meaningful support to one another as well.

Knowing the schedule. Children are far more comfortable when they know what to expect. Although their understanding is influenced by their developmental age, all children can sense change, and they feel more secure when they are prepared for it. For infants, this can be a calm and loving routine. Surprisingly early, they can absorb what it means to be "going to Daddy's house." For young children, having a color-coded calendar and counting the number of "sleeps" before the next time they go back to Mommy's house help them to feel secure. Older children and teens who have an understanding of time and the future often find it reassuring to know what will happen over longer periods of time, and to be able to have input on changes related to their school and activity schedules.

Positive preparation. Parents can also make a huge difference in how their children feel about going to the other parent's home by preparing them in a positive way. I greatly admire parents who not only help their children understand what will happen during their time with the other parent, but also encourage their children's enthusiasm for what the other parent has planned. Helping them look forward to a favorite dinner or activity makes the transitions easier for children.

Terri and Steve were remarkably successful in helping to smooth transitions between homes for their three-year-old daughter. Their own emotions were still raw, but through our meetings, they worked hard to contain their hurt and pain in order to provide Jenny their best parenting. At first, when Steve came to pick her up, she would often balk and cry. Once we realized that Jenny was upset because she did not know the plans and was always surprised, they solved the problem by telling her what to expect.

In order to give very specific information to Jenny, Steve e-mailed or texted Terri in advance of each visit, letting her know exactly when he would arrive to pick Jenny up and what he had planned for her. Each time, before Steve arrived, Terri would tell Jenny that Daddy was on his way. As she helped her gather her favorite stuffed animals to take to Steve's house, Terri talked enthusiastically about how much fun Jenny would have with him, mentioning her favorite grilled cheese lunch and the trip to the park, or whatever Steve had planned for that visit. The transitions became smoother with time and this consistent positive communication, and Jenny began to look forward to her time with her father. It was not easy for Terri and Steve, but by staying focused on their daughter's best interests, they managed to help her adjust.

Having special things at both homes. At all ages, children need to feel that they really belong in both homes. Having clothing, school supplies, and personal treasures in both households—particularly having their own bedroom in both places—helps greatly to create that sense of belonging. For young children, stuffed animals, blankets, pictures of themselves with each parent and a beloved pet, or night-lights can often be important. School-age children often want books, games, equipment for their favorite activities, and pictures. Preteens and teens usually have favorite posters, artwork, and music that are important to them.

One diligent mother went out of her way to duplicate her child's favorite things at both her home and her former partner's. While replicating belongings to such a degree is not usually necessary, parents can help by ensuring that children have things that are comforting and important to them in each home.

Letting children take belongings back and forth. With busy lives and tight schedules, most parents understandably try to keep the transitions as quick and simple as possible. When their children want to haul a lot of their belongings back and forth, this can add time to their schedules and clutter to their homes. Some of these are items that children need for school or activities. Some are things they think they might need. And others are often just belongings they feel attached to. Whatever the reason, children usually benefit if parents allow them to bring whatever they believe they need or especially want.

Allowing children access to each parent through phone calls, e-mail, and texting. Letting children communicate with their other parent reinforces the message that both parents belong in their lives, regardless of whose "time" it is. That said, parents may need to set boundaries on when and how long these conversations can go on and guard against allowing children to use them in ways that are manipulative or disruptive. Free access to each parent is especially important for adolescents.

Containing conflict during transitions. As research has consistently revealed, witnessing their parents' conflict is inevitably stressful for children. Because the pickup and drop-off times are occasions when separated or divorced parents see each other most frequently, these are times when emotions can overflow. Hostility—whether expressed in words or icy silence—adds to children's stress with each exposure. Understanding this, conscientious parents can maintain a respectful, businesslike approach during transition times by greeting one another respectfully, staying focused on the children, and not discussing issues that may invite conflict. When parents are unable to manage their emotions, creating schedules that eliminate or greatly minimize contact is often a good solution.

Creating opportunities for healing. It is important for children to overhear parents sharing positive information about them. Children often say that this does not happen very often. A statement like "Michael did a great job getting all his homework done this weekend" is welcome and encouraging praise. Such comments also help children realize that, despite the divorce, both parents continue to love, cherish, and take pride in them, and to share in parenting them.

Continuous open communication with children. While communication is always important in maintaining strong relationships, it is particularly critical during times of change. Sometimes a third party is needed to help children sort out their feelings and learn how to broach difficult topics. This may occur when children who feel protective of their parents are worried about burdening them with any more problems. Or they may feel overwhelmed by feelings and unable to express them. Trusted adults, including friends, teachers, or family members, may be able to assume a helpful role.

Of course, licensed mental health professionals who specialize in children and family issues can usually offer a valuable perspective and set of skills. Although it can be hard sometimes for loving parents to accept that their children need such intervention, I always hope they will see it as a strength to seek help when it is needed, and to recognize that all of us have times when a little help can be beneficial.

Special Considerations for Vacations and Holidays

Vacations and holidays are wonderful opportunities to strengthen relationships and make special memories with children. Yet these times can also be fraught with tension, conflicts, and miscommunication.

I encourage you to begin communicating with your former partner about vacation and holiday plans several months in advance and agree on a schedule for them. Doing so helps to prevent last-minute conflict, tension, and disappointment. Once plans are made and children have been informed of them, following through on these promises is one of the most important things you can do to avoid big disappointments.

Vacations. Children benefit if their vacations include some quality time with each of their parents. Even though vacations may be happy times, going to unfamiliar places and changing routines can be unsettling for children and produce a certain amount of stress. They often benefit if you can arrange their schedules to allow for some much needed "downtime" in between their trips. Such times provide the comfort and security of routines between vacations that involve a lot of change to the patterns of their lives.

Sometimes the best vacations for children do not involve any travel at all. During the summer, children and the parent who has had less contact during the school year can spend more meaningful blocks of time together. For preschoolers, parents may choose to stay at home with children for a week or two—a short vacation from day care. For school-age children, parents may establish a different schedule during the summer than during the school year, allowing greater flexibility and the chance to do special things with each parent.

Holidays. For most of us, emotions often are intensified around the holidays we celebrate. The first round of holidays after a separation almost always presents especially difficult emotional challenges. The occasions that families have celebrated together become painful reminders of what no longer exists, often causing a deep sense of loss. Holidays may hold either fond memories of good times together or painful memories of past hurts and disappointments. Mixed in with these are often hopes and wishes for the happiness these occasions could bring.

Unfortunately, holidays are a time when I hear the most poignant comments from children of all ages. For example, four-year-old Maria wondered whether Santa would come to her house at all "since nobody loves each other anymore and lots of bad things have happened."

Although holidays in changing families inevitably contain a certain amount of sadness, they need not result in enduring feelings of loss. There is much that you can do to take control over making these times better for your children and yourself.

Holidays like Mother's Day, Father's Day, and parents' and children's own birthdays are important to children. Just as you want to share your own special days with your children, they place great importance on celebrating these times with the appropriate parent. You can do your children a great service by helping them make a card or pick out a present for their other parent. This practice gives children a wonderful gift—the right to openly express their love and respect for both parents.

In the first cycle of holidays after a separation or divorce, it can be helpful to establish new traditions and create new formats for celebrating. It is wise to anticipate, however, that these will likely need some adjustments, and you will feel better about making them if you have not overloaded the new activities with too many hopes, expectations, and plans for permanence. By staying attuned to your children's feelings and remaining flexible, you can add changes to make future holidays happier, less stressful times for your children.

If you anticipate and understand your own emotional response to each holiday, you can put some forethought and extra effort into taking care of yourself and reaching out for support to get through these times. By taking more control over your feelings about holidays, you will be better able to give your children genuinely positive attention and to spare them some worry.

When both you and your children's other parent want to celebrate the holidays with your children, negotiating a schedule can be especially emotional and challenging. Particularly at these times, everyone benefits when you take care to communicate in a professional, respectful, and tactful way about each other's wishes and your children's needs and desires. Here are some tips that can help make these negotiations a little easier:

> *Be open to compromise.* Of course all parents would love to have their children with them on all the holidays. But for children, what is most important is to have quality time and a meaningful celebration with each parent, regardless of the day on which that happens. Even more important than the celebrations themselves is the spirit of goodwill and cooperation that children observe and experience between their parents during the holidays and every day.

Clarify the specifics of the schedule for each holiday in your agreement. For example, does Thanksgiving mean the day or the entire weekend? Does Chanukah mean the first night or all eight nights? Does Christmas Eve mean overnight? By agreeing to and communicating specific time frames well in advance, and then sticking to them, you can avoid putting your children in the midst of tension and conflict at a time when they are particularly excited and happy.

Be flexible about adjusting the regular weekly schedule to meet holiday schedule needs. This is important not just during the holidays, but immediately before and after. If one parent has the children for an extended period of time, then providing a similar amount of time for the children to spend with their other parent is good for them and helps to reduce friction with the other parent.

Think creatively about scheduling and develop plans to suit your family's unique needs. Many families have found creative ways to have two Christmas, Passover, or Thanksgiving celebrations, with different morning and evening, or night-before and day-of celebrations, or even declaring control over the calendar and having celebrations on unofficial days. Some families rotate holidays, so one year, children spend a holiday with Dad, and the next year, the same holiday with Mom. Others plan for larger time blocks, still ensuring some special holiday time with each parent. For example, children can spend the first half of the December school vacation with Dad until noon on Christmas Day, and Christmas afternoon through the second half of the school vacation with Mom.

Share the special time, if possible. Many parents find it painful to think about missing children's birthday parties or their opening of gifts on Christmas morning. If both parents agree and can remain reasonably cordial and focused on their children, they may enjoy sharing these times with their children. In some cases, it is wise to limit the amount of time that parents spend together on these occasions. Here again, agreeing in advance to a specified amount of time and living by the agreed-upon schedule help to prevent stress.

Children's birthdays deserve parents' most thoughtful attention, especially in the early stages of a divorce. Most children want to celebrate their birthdays with both parents. When approached thoughtfully, these occasions remind children how deeply both of their parents love them. Preschool and school-age children often want both parents to be present at their celebration. Teens may want plenty of celebrating with friends, but they are often comforted to know that their parents can set aside their differences long enough to join in celebrating their birthdays.

Preserve special traditions with the extended family, if possible. If there are special times that children enjoy with extended family, it is desirable to maintain those if possible. Children benefit not only from the continuity of traditions, but even more from the sense that they belong to a loving circle of people who care about them. Again, this may require flexibility in scheduling and the graciousness of other family members.

Manage emotions and contain conflict. As you have discovered, this is a recurring theme in this book. Particularly during the holidays and all the special events in a child's life, managing emotions is the most important gift parents can give their children. In this way, they allow their children's feelings and memories of holidays to be positive and not marred with bitter associations for years to come.

Focus on what really matters. You do your children a great service when you and your former partner coordinate your gifts and ensure that they receive the most yearned-for gifts, within reason but avoiding excess. Modest, thoughtful, loving gift-giving helps children to feel happy and secure. By contrast, competing for children's gratitude by overloading them with gifts may make them anxious or contribute to undesirable values and behaviors, including entitlement and manipulation.

You can also reassure your children by helping them make cards or gifts for their other parent. While this may be difficult for you, such gestures help children learn that when we love and care about people, we honor the relationship and remember them in some special way. These experiences help teach children the value of acknowledging and nurturing their relationships with the people they love. They also help them to feel secure in the love of both parents and remove some of the stress associated with living two separate lives.

Maintain healthy routines. Particularly during holidays, children's schedules and diets are often subject to dramatic swings. They stay healthier, happier, and more secure when their schedules and habits are not wildly out of control. Regular bedtimes with time for books and snuggling, a core of healthy foods to offset sugary treats, and continuity of family rules and routines all help to make the holidays happier and more peaceful.

Vacations and holidays can still be very special times after a divorce. These times provide natural opportunities for parents to express through words, gifts, and actions the joy that their children's presence brings to their lives. And that, above all, is what every loving parent wants to accomplish, every day.

Throughout this chapter, I have introduced several important themes that are explored in greater depth in future chapters: managing conflict and taking care of yourself (chapter 5) and effective parenting (chapter 7). As you work your way through these topics, the one thing I hope you realize above all else is that children can thrive when they have an effective parenting structure. Through research, we now know a great deal about what that means and how you can apply it. Despite all the worries you may have as a result of your divorce, your children can thrive when they have the security of quality parenting, protection from conflict, and the nurturing love of parents and other adults who care deeply about them.

. . . .

FIVE

Taking Control of Conflict and Taking Care of Yourself

It is natural for discord to occur in any intimate relationship, and it is inevitable during divorce. As couples grieve the loss of a dream they once had for their marriage, not only sadness, but anger, fear, betrayal, guilt, and other strong emotions often erupt or hover just beneath the surface. Such turbulent emotions make it especially difficult to resolve differences calmly. As a result, conflict often occurs, involving anger, antagonism, and sometimes even physical aggression. If parents handle their disagreements well, they may arrive at effective solutions and cause few, if any, negative consequences for children. When children are exposed to constant antagonism and unresolved conflict, however, they are vulnerable to unfortunate social, emotional, and even physical consequences.

Ten-year-old Tony speaks for many children who are exposed to their parents' ongoing conflict. "Don't use us as weapons and bullets or say bad things about each other. We need to love both of our parents." His words reflect how unresolved conflict seriously undermines the all-important relationships children need to have with both parents.

The outcome of any difficult situation often depends not on whether painful emotions and powerful urges exist, but on how we deal with them. What American journalist Dorothy Thompson said about global issues also can be applied to individual behavior: "Peace is not the absence of conflict but the presence of creative alternatives for responding to conflict. . . ."

Achieving peace is seldom accomplished quickly or easily in the process of a divorce, but this chapter provides proven approaches you can use to manage anger and conflict, as well as ways to take care of yourself. These matters are related. Research has shown repeatedly that staying physically and emotionally healthy has a strong influence on the ability to control anger and other strong emotions and transform highly charged conflicts into productive problem solving. When divorcing parents take such an approach, they benefit not only themselves, but they also provide their children with a positive example of healthy ways to deal with disputes.

As always, I want to stress that safety is the top priority. If contact between parents becomes violent or abusive toward each other or their children, the first course of action must be to ensure the safety and well-being of their children and themselves. In such situations, maintaining any contact may not be advisable and a safety plan should be in place.

The Perils of Unresolved Conflict

Conflict is usually highest during the period immediately following a separation. For about 80 percent of those who end their marriages, anger and conflict gradually decrease within two or three years after divorce. But for another 8 to 20 percent, the level of conflict remains high, marked by blame, physical and verbal hostility, high levels of tension, and minimal resolution of problems.

Ongoing conflict is a destructive force in parents' lives. It erodes your ability to provide attentive and effective parenting for your children. As a result, the warm, loving, and attentive parent-child relationship that most conscientious parents crave deteriorates. Conflict

also destroys your ability just to enjoy your children in a relaxed and happy way—to simply take pleasure in good times together. Moreover, unresolved, protracted conflict robs you of your own sense of inner peace, preventing you from healing and moving on with your life.

As you read in earlier chapters, children also suffer the consequences of their parents' conflict. First, as described earlier, it is a major cause of stress, which puts them at risk both emotionally and physically. Second, parents in conflict model behaviors that few would want their children to adopt. Children learn what they live. If they observe their parents treating each other with rudeness, sarcasm, or verbal or physical abuse, they learn that these are acceptable behaviors and become more likely to engage in them. Third, when they hear a parent criticized, they may become concerned about being "defective" themselves, since well before they can understand genetics, they realize that they are "made of" their parents' traits. Finally, conflict also deprives them of truly effective parenting—the kind of emotionally intelligent parenting described in chapter 7. They lose out on having their parents' loving attention and a consistent structure to guide their behavior.

High levels of continuous conflict nearly always result in difficulties for children, and these problems may last a lifetime. As a large body of research reveals, children's lives and their relationships with their parents are changed—for better or for worse—by how parents handle conflict following their divorce.

Research has shown which aspects of conflict have the most negative impact on children's adjustment. Among the factors linked to the greatest difficulties for children are:

- Witnessing or overhearing their parents' aggressive or violent conflict, whether verbal or physical.
- Feeling guilt and responsibility for parents' problems because of child-related conflict.
- Hearing one parent denigrate the other with sarcasm or criticism of their character or their mistakes.
- Being caught in loyalty conflicts that require them directly or indirectly to side with one parent and against the other.
- Being used to carry hostile messages or convey a parent's anger.
- Being forbidden to mention one parent in the presence of the other, either expressly or tacitly.

There are no winners when parents continue to engage in conflict, even if they temporarily enjoy a sense of having "control" over the other parent. Fortunately, most parents are able to learn how to manage their anger and address their differences in ways that allow them and their children to survive and thrive.

From Conflict to Cooperation: The Story of Lisa and Mark

Like so many recently separated parents, Lisa and Mark had frequent volatile arguments that left them frustrated, angry, and too depleted to provide attentive parenting for their three children. Over the last several years of their marriage, they had fallen into a destructive often-repeated pattern of behavior—quick anger, followed by quarreling and blame, and then icy silence. Their separation did not change that pattern.

The parenting schedule was a chronic source of irritation, but almost any of their children's problems turned into fresh ammunition for their battles and exchanges of blame. When an outbreak of illness caused five-year-old Crystal's kindergarten to close for three days, they fought about who would stay home from work to take care of her. When seven-year-old Timmy left his homework at Mark's house after an overnight with him, they battled over whether Mark should take it to his school or whether he should "learn his lesson the hard way." When ten-year-old Marcie couldn't stop crying after her best friend moved away, even that was a source of conflict: Should Marcie be allowed to visit her, and if so, who would drive the hundred miles each way?

Many long-term underlying factors contributed to the high levels of hurt and anger that both Mark and Lisa experienced. They were continuing to play out the cycle of anger, quarreling, blame, and the silent treatment that had characterized their marriage and ultimately resulted in their separation. Now their anger and conflict were what kept them connected to each other. On their own, they were unable to end these hurtful behaviors and focus on being effective parents.

They sought help when all three of their children were showing signs of stress. Both Mark and Lisa were especially worried about five-year-old Crystal, who now had recurring nightmares from which she awoke sobbing and trembling. Each time, she was inconsolable and unable to get back to sleep for hours. When she woke up in the morning after one of these nightmares, she was exhausted and unwilling to go to kindergarten.

Play therapy sessions helped to get at the source of Crystal's nightmares and uncover the enormous emotional burden she felt. Ultimately, these sessions also provided a therapeutic avenue to help her adjust. We began with a wishing well game. As we tossed iridescent stones, she called out her wishes: that "Mommy and Daddy would not get divorced," that "Mommy and Daddy would be nice to each other and not fight," that "Mommy and Daddy would please get along enough to talk to each other." As Crystal threw her last colored stone into the wishing well, she said quietly, "I wish all divorces would disappear. They're really sad and scary for kids because the kids might need their parents sometimes, but the parents won't know because they don't talk to each other."

Later in the session, Crystal chose some puppets and began to act out a story. She was silent but intent as at first she made the girl puppet play alone. Then she made two bears sneak up behind her and grab her. When I commented on how scared the girl must be, Crystal replied, "Yeah, just like in my dreams." She described how in her recurring nightmare, she was being chased by huge, angry bears. She screamed for her parents to help her, but because they were not speaking, they could not help each other find her. Without her parents to rescue her, Crystal was terrified that she would be lost to the bears forever. Her dream was a manifestation of deep fears that in the midst of their own strife her parents had abandoned her. She felt frighteningly alone—through Crystal's eyes, her safety, security, and her very life were all at risk.

She urgently needed reassurance in both words and behaviors that the two people she loved and depended on would work together to keep her safe. When I described to her parents the fears that Crystal had revealed through play therapy, Mark and Lisa were clearly upset—horrified that their beloved little girl felt terrified and unprotected. Only now did they begin to understand the relationship between their angry battles and their children's well-being.

Mark and Lisa are not alone. Studies show that parents often underestimate the impact of their behavior on their young children. This may be especially true for divorcing parents who are already struggling with painful emotions and guilt about their children.

With their new knowledge, Mark and Lisa acknowledged the sadness and guilt they felt about their focus on "fighting for their own rights" instead of focusing on parenting their children. It took courage for them to confront and examine their own behavior, accept responsibility for its consequences, and do the hard work of changing long-held habits of anger and conflict. Because both loved their children deeply, they were determined to become more attentive, affectionate, and effective parents.

What they needed was to redefine their relationship with boundaries, as coparents rather than spouses or lovers, and stick to guidelines on how they communicated with each other. Together, we developed ground rules for keeping their relationship more professional and less emotional. This required them first to focus completely on the children and their needs, and then to communicate respectfully with each other about those matters. They agreed that all changes to the schedule would be made well in advance unless an urgent matter, such as illness or unexpected travel for work, intervened. We established a consistent schedule that provided both of them with one-on-one time with each child. The schedule also included time for Lisa and Mark individually to engage in activities that helped them replenish the physical energy and emotional resources they needed to provide compassionate, quality parenting to their children.

Changing their long-standing habit of conflict and establishing new patterns of behavior and a new parenting partnership was far from an overnight fix. But both Mark and Lisa worked hard to make these changes because they understood the importance for their children.

Understanding and Managing Anger

Anger is a normal, healthy response to injustice and a natural reaction to emotional or physical injury or loss. It is sometimes the other face of sadness, fear, or other painful emotions, and it often erupts when we are afraid of losing something—or someone—we value deeply. Understanding its sources and relationship to other emotions can be helpful in learning how to manage it.

In separation and divorce, anger is often perpetuated for a variety of reasons. It can be a substitute for painful emotions like sadness and loneliness. Anger may also be a way to deflect blame and avoid looking at one's own culpability for problems in the relationship. It can also confer a sense of power in situations when individuals feel powerless. Sometimes anger just provides an easier way to let go of a partner than to maintain good feelings or even sadness. For couples ending a relationship, angry, conflict-filled interactions sometimes provide a way of staying connected to each other; their strong feelings signify their emotional attachment to a former partner.

It is tempting to hope that the finality of a divorce, coupled with time and distance, will cause festering anger and resentment to dissipate. But for many whose marriages end, that optimism is unjustified. A long-term study of divorce found that even decades later, many divorced partners were still deeply mired in anger, pain, and resentment. Half of the women and one third of the men were still intensely angry at their former spouses ten or more years later. Sadly, anger had become "an ongoing . . . dominant presence in their children's lives as well."

Despite its normal and even healthy origins and its understandable roles in ending a marriage, anger that is unmanaged can be a very dangerous and even destructive force. Outbursts of temper are usually frightening not only to those at whom they are directed, but also to others around them. They are particularly frightening to children, who are terrified by a parent's rage, even when it is not directed at them. In the most frightening of all situations, uncontrolled anger leads to violence. Anger, no matter how intense or even warranted, never justifies violence.

Anger can be channeled in productive ways to create positive changes. But the ability to redirect anger requires an understanding of what to do—and not do—about it.

One popular misconception is that it is healthy to "let off steam" by venting anger intensely and frequently. Although the adrenaline rush of expressing strong emotions can leave an individual feeling temporarily powerful, when the underlying problems remain unresolved, anger does not diminish; it escalates. Carol Tavris addresses the myths surrounding anger in *Anger: The Misunderstood Emotion*. She warns of the dangers of emotional venting as the only ways of dealing with anger and resentment. Not only does unleashed expression of anger lead to more anger, but intense venting can result in imposing destructive rage on others.

Just as habitual venting of intense anger can be dangerous, ignoring or suppressing anger is not healthy either. The key is to find the balance of expressing anger in healthy ways, but not stay mired in it.

What are the alternatives to remaining stuck in anger when you have been hurt, betrayed, and injured by someone you once loved? Several methods of managing anger have proven helpful to many individuals whose marriages came to an end.

Identify the source of your anger. A healthy first step is to reflect about your anger when you are not feeling angry. Examine its sources in yourself, and seek to understand what emotions and problems are at its source. Try to define those clearly in your own mind. Does it come from hurt, humiliation, a loss of your own sense of self-worth? Is it triggered by certain memories, situations, words? It can be difficult to be objective and to examine very painful emotions on your own. In such cases, a licensed mental health professional may be able to help you to understand your emotions more clearly.

Address the causes. Once you have identified the underlying issues, the next step is to find ways to address them. Try to understand your own motivation. Are you focusing on your former partner's behavior or faults as a way of not having to focus on more painful issues such as your role in the problem? No matter what the reason, painful emotions and feelings of loss take a long time to heal, and this process cannot be rushed. Grief over the loss of anyone or anything that has been important to us often hits us in waves. After a period of relative calm, a memory may arise and suddenly trigger a wave of grief that soon turns to anger. During such times it helps to take a step back, take some deep breaths, perhaps shed a few tears, talk to a trusted friend or therapist, or write out your feelings. By separating your anger from its source and addressing the problems in which it originates, you may be able to curb the anger before it gets a foothold. Looking at your own role in why your marriage ended is important for your own emotional health and future relationships.

Consider the consequences. As I emphasize to the children I work with, emotions are temporary and always change—for better or worse—depending on how we handle them. Although emotions pass, however, the consequences of behavior endure. So I always encourage parents in emotionally charged situations to step back and reflect before making decisions or taking action. "I need some time to think about this" is among the most valuable phrases that divorcing parents and others going through major life changes can add to their vocabulary.

Talk about your feelings. Being able to talk openly about your angry feelings is important, but it is also important to do so without denigrating your former partner when your children are within earshot. Family and friends may be willing to listen and provide support and caring. In talking with them, it is particularly important to elicit their help and cooperation if they feel angry on your behalf, as many sympathetic loved ones do. Explain that you are trying to contain your anger and reduce conflict for the sake of the children, and specifically ask them to help you cool down in situations when your children are present. Ask them, too, to help you deal with the triggers that ignite these feelings. For instance, you may ask them to remove certain topics from conversation when your children are present: your ex's faults, how you've been wronged, how your ex mistreated friends and family, for example. If some of the people you are close to are not able or willing to abide by your wishes, then it is important to confide only in those who will, and avoid situations that undermine your determination to manage your anger.

Consider getting professional help. Mental health professionals also can be an excellent resource, and I am convinced that most people would benefit from seeing a skilled therapist during the process of divorce. Therapists not only allow you to express your feelings but may offer an objective perspective and advice on how to manage specific triggers. They can also help you work through the deeper personal issues that almost always emerge with the pain of a divorce, and help you develop strategies to set your life on a course toward healing and the vision of a happier future.

Ramp up your exercise. Physical exercise is an excellent way to release anger and reduce stress. Many find that activities like kickboxing, racquetball, or other aggressive sports allow them to vent their anger and frustration. Others find they can release a lot of powerful feelings through walking, running, dancing, swimming, yoga, or engaging in other physical activities that use up some energy and have pleasant associations. My personal favorite way to reduce stress is to team up with a friend to combine the benefits of good exercise with the joy of shared conversation and friendship.

Laugh out loud. Another favorite way to defuse anger and stress is with humor. As Bill Cosby, who suffered significant losses in his own family, said, "Through humor, you can soften some of the worst blows that life delivers. And once you find laughter, no matter how painful your situation might be, you can survive it." In one study that measured the effects of purposeful aerobic laughter in the workplace, participants reported a significant increase in several different aspects of self-efficacy, including self-regulation, optimism, positive emotions, and social identification, indicating that even "manufactured" laughter confers significant benefits.

By twisting the lens slightly to look at your situation from another perspective, you may be able to find humor in it. But even if that is not possible, finding ways to enjoy a good belly laugh at times can help to melt anger. Laughing with our children is a wonderful way to bond with them—as long as the joke does not demean them or their other parent. This is the time to find the movies, cartoons, books, and friends that make you laugh.

Listen for what's behind your ex's anger. While it is challenging to manage your own feelings of anger, it can be particularly difficult to do so when an ex is behaving with animosity. Former partners know how to push each other's buttons. After all, they installed some of them! They are usually aware of each other's vulnerabilities, and are sometimes tempted to hurt back with caustic remarks. Although it can be difficult not to get caught up in a negative exchange, the best way to avoid conflict is not to take the bait.

Instead, in such situations, it often helps to take a mental step back and listen to what is behind your former partner's strong emotion. Even if you do not agree with the reasons for it, you can employ an active listening technique to bring the focus back to your roles as coparents and the specific parenting issues you need to address.

The first step is to let him know that you've heard what he's saying by paraphrasing what he has just said—but removing the anger. A sincere apology and expression of empathy also help to defuse anger. For example, "I know you're hurt and angry at me for things that happened in our marriage. We both made mistakes. I'm sorry for the hurt I have caused you; that was not my intent."

The next is to bring the focus clearly back to the parenting issue. "But I hope we can put past hurts behind us for the sake of our children, and focus instead on how we can work together and create a schedule that makes it possible for Jenny to have good quality time with each of us and not get caught in the middle of our conflicts." Such listening and reflecting feelings without judging them can help to de-escalate an emotional conversation.

If you don't succeed in getting your ex to calm down or you feel yourself ready to erupt in anger, take a time-out and agree to continue the conversation later. If it is safe to meet in person, establish meetings in public locations that are not conducive to public displays of anger, such as the library, the mall, or a coffee shop. Above all, exercise every ounce of will and take every precaution so that your children are never in your presence or able to overhear you vent your rage at their other parent.

Parallel and Cooperative Approaches to Parenting: A Range of Options

There are effective options you can employ as you face a future of parenting with your former spouse after your marriage ends. Parallel and cooperative parenting represent two different approaches to sharing the responsibilities of raising children. But it is certainly possible—and often desirable—for you to use techniques from both, and to continue to make changes to your parenting strategies over time, as you adjust to the continuing changes in your relationship.

The chart below describes the behaviors associated with parallel and cooperative parenting. Many parents I work with find it helpful to understand these options as they begin to develop their plans for the next phase of their children's lives and their own.

PARALLEL PARENTING	COOPERATIVE PARENTING
Parents communicate infrequently or in emergencies.	Parents communicate regularly and frequently.
Parents use e-mail, texting, a third party, or a parenting notebook to communicate.	Parents can communicate in person or over the phone.
Major decisions are reached through a third party or via a legal agreement.	Major decisions about the children are jointly discussed and agreed upon.
Households are separate. Each parent makes decisions about the children for the time they are in that home.	Parents work together as needed to resolve issues related to the children and to plan activities.
Parents work separately for the best interests of the children.	Parents work together for the best interests of the children.

(continued)

Parallel Parenting	Cooperative Parenting
Children's transitions from one household to the other may be at a neutral site with limited but respectful communication between parents.	Smooth transitions can occur from one home to the other, with in-person communication between parents.
Written parenting plans or court decrees are followed exactly. Parents need an external authority to resolve disputes when they cannot agree.	Schedule changes are made between parents, with flexibility and openness to requests and negotiation.
Each parent is responsible for his/her own relationship with the child.	Parents can discuss various parenting issues that involve both of them and their children.

Parallel parenting. The concept of parallel parenting was derived from "parallel play," a term used to describe the independent but simultaneous play of preschoolers. Parallel parenting implies independent parenting at each home, with little communication or emotional involvement between parents. It minimizes the amount of direct interaction between parents, and gives each parent total responsibility for the children while they are in that parent's care. These very clear boundaries often help to reduce or prevent conflict.

Tips for Successful Parallel Parenting

1. Work to disengage emotionally from your former partner and past hurts. Separate your feelings about your former partner from your child's needs and feelings. Stay focused on what you can control—doing the best you can for your child.
2. Contain your emotions when communicating with your former partner; maintain an attitude of respect. This includes greeting each other, especially when children are present.

3. Behave in a professional manner; use the courteous practices typically associated with more formal business interactions. Do not discuss personal issues; stay focused on the children.

4. Approach child-related concerns with a respectful, problem-solving approach. State the problem, propose solutions, avoid blame, and work toward creating effective solutions over time.

5. Use written communication if speaking in person is difficult. One particularly useful approach for parents of very young children is a shared notebook, in which both parents can make note of all the important things that need to be communicated—from fevers and fussiness to schedules for meals, naps, and activities.

6. E-mail, texting, notes, and letters can help to keep communication child focused and professional. Make a practice of keeping them respectful, clear, and brief. If emotions are running high, save the draft and try to reread it from the other parent's perspective before sending it.

7. When face-to-face communication and/or negotiation are necessary to resolve a dispute, consider using a neutral third party to assist in resolving differences.

8. Follow up in writing on all agreements and discussions regarding the children, with a summary of any decisions that were made.

9. Respect the other parent's time with the children. Do not plan activities for children during your former partner's time with them. If an important event is to occur, make a request in writing well in advance. Maintain an attitude of noninterference with your children's other parent, unless it is an issue of safety.

10. Pay child support on time. Studies show a strong link between regular support payments and major benefits for children, including higher academic success and fewer behavior problems.

11. Do not use your child as a messenger, spy, or delivery person. Mail the check or use direct deposit. Use a phone call, text message, or e-mail to share information.

12. If communication is becoming heated and emotional, defuse it by requesting time for both people to cool off, consider some alternative solutions, and agree to come back to the issue at a later time.

Cooperative parenting. A positive parenting relationship involves a high degree of cooperation between parents, maintaining an attitude of respect toward each other and effective ways of managing conflict. Parents are engaged in a much greater degree of direct communication, shared decision making, and flexibility regarding schedules than parallel parenting allows.

Tips for Successful Cooperative Parenting

1. Continue to work toward a positive relationship with your former partner and minimize conflict. Above all, do not allow conflict between you to spill over during your time with the children.
2. Treat your interactions with your former partner as you would with a respected colleague. Build a relationship that thrives based on collaboration, courtesy, and mutual respect.
3. Plan for brief phone communication at a regular time each week or so, preferably when children are not at home or calls can be made from work, so that children cannot overhear. Make an agenda ahead of time, and stick to it. Keep the calls short (ten to fifteen minutes) and focused on your children's needs, information sharing, schedule changes, or plans for future activities. Avoid personal issues and past history, and be mindful of personal boundaries.
4. If more involved discussion of your children is needed, and you believe that both of you can contain your emotions and be professional and productive, meet in person. Make an appointment to meet at a neutral place at a relatively stress-free time when the children are not around. Agree to an agenda in advance and stick to it.
5. Be specific in communications with the other parent about plans, schedules, and requests. To prevent miscommunication, follow up in writing your understanding of what you discussed and any agreed-upon plans.
6. Do not expect appreciation, praise, or emotional support from the other parent. Such expectations may be unrealistic and can reopen old wounds

that set you up to feel disappointed, hurt, rejected, abandoned—and angry.

7.   In situations where your former partner's motives could be interpreted in more than one way, give him or her the benefit of the doubt.

8.   Pay child support on time. Studies show a strong link between regular support payments and major benefits for children, including higher academic achievement and better emotional adjustment.

9.   Do not use your child as a messenger, spy, or delivery person. Mail the check to your former partner or use direct deposit. Telephone, text message, or e-mail to share information, instead of asking your child to tell the other parent.

10.   Try to understand that the pain of being apart from children goes both ways. Your former partner will miss them when they are with you, just as you do when they're at their other home.

11.   Keep adult emotions in check so that children's feelings and needs can be heard.

12.   Nurture your children's healthy relationship with their other parent. When problems arise between them, help your children discuss them respectfully and help them find ways to ease their distress and learn to problem-solve.

Children benefit from having a healthy relationship with both parents, whenever it is safe and possible for them to do so. Higher levels of cooperation between parents are related to children having more time with their fathers and better relationships with them. On the other hand, more hostility between parents is related to less contact between children and fathers and worse relationships.

When cooperative parenting is safe, possible, and successfully executed, it usually provides greater benefits for children. Studies have shown, however, that children can be well-adjusted regardless of whether their parents adopt cooperative or parallel parenting, or some blend of the two, as long as conflict is kept to a minimum, there is responsible parenting at both homes, and legal agreements clearly specify custody, schedules, and decision-making arrangements.

Family relationships are like mobiles—when there is a change or imbalance on one side, the entire system is affected in some way. The relationship between parents affects not only each of them directly, but also the ways in which they relate to their children and their ability to parent effectively.

Children are likely to be affected by the quality of the relationship between their parents in a variety of ways. If they experience relative cooperation and minimal conflict, their own relationship with each parent is likely to be more relaxed, secure, and positive. They have the security that comes with believing it is not only acceptable but important to have positive relationships with both Mom and Dad. Thus, a cooperative relationship between parents provides a bridge of support on which children can freely move back and forth between their parents and homes.

Yet it can be painfully difficult, if not improbable, for some parents to get to this point, for a variety of reasons. For some, the amount of conflict or potential for violence makes it an unrealistic goal. For others, emotions play a major part. Since the decision to divorce is seldom mutual, the process of adjusting to all of the changes that ensue are generally far more difficult for the partner being left than the one who chooses to end the marriage. The person who did not want the divorce may find it too painful to be in frequent communication or cooperative with a former partner, at least initially. Conflict may intensify as the legal process unfolds, making cooperative parenting seem unrealistic and unattainable—at least at that early stage of the divorce.

There is no manual about how to relate to a former spouse during this time, and how to renegotiate the relationship from former lovers to partners in the important business of parenting. For this reason, many parent education programs nationwide offer information on a continuum of options from cooperative to parallel parenting. Parents engaged in high levels of ongoing conflict generally benefit from using parallel parenting strategies. In situations involving domestic violence or intense conflict, cooperative parenting is not an option. Parallel parenting affords these individuals some measure of safety by minimizing the contact between them.

Even in less contentious situations, many parents find it very difficult to cooperate in the early stages of a separation and divorce when their feelings are still raw and anger erupts easily. During this period, they may find it helpful to maintain emotional disengagement and adopt the clear boundaries of parallel parenting. Because it eliminates the expectation of flexibility and negotiation, parallel parenting reduces opportunities for ongoing conflict, yet still allows both parents to remain an active part of their children's lives.

Some parents are able to move from parallel to cooperative parenting over time as their emotions become less intense and they develop the skills to manage their anger. Some may parent cooperatively on many issues, but still use parallel parenting on certain "hot button" issues. Others may adopt strategies from each approach at various times, as their lives continue to change. Eventually, many parents are able to shift to fully cooperative parenting. Between 25 and 50 percent of parents ultimately adopt a cooperative parenting relationship, with flexible schedules, ongoing communication between parents, and supportive exchanges between homes. Not all parents make that shift, however, and parallel parenting remains a viable long-term approach. By understanding and using these options, parents can maintain their focus on doing what is best for their children.

Managing and Resolving Conflict: Big Challenge for Parents, Big Payoff for Children

Because parents' conflict has been shown to produce a profound negative effect on children, nearly every parent education program nationwide includes a component on managing conflict. One of these is A.C.T. for the Children (Assisting Children through Transition), a program that colleagues and I developed in New York State. This program is based on important research on risk and protective factors and provides information on the many ways that parents can reduce the stress of divorce on their children and support their healthy adjustment. Parents learn a variety of skills for keeping their children out of the middle of their conflict, including communicating effectively with a former partner, behaving in a respectful, professional way, containing conflict, and managing anger. Early research on this program showed that parents were able to learn the core concepts of conflict management and the importance of keeping their children out of the middle.

A follow-up study conducted one year after parents participated in the program found they were still using the skills they had learned, and that ongoing conflict was significantly reduced. Parents were more aware of how easily children could get caught up in their conflicts. They now used a problem-solving approach to resolve and contain conflict, avoided criticizing their former partner in front of their children, and agreed to stick to their legal agreements, or request changes in a businesslike way.

The parents' lasting behavioral changes resulted in significantly reducing stress for themselves and—most important—for their children. Specifically, when parents reduced their conflict with each other, the result was that their children's anger, acting-out behavior, sadness, and depression were all reduced, and children's positive adjustment to the post-divorce family increased significantly.

Parents' efforts paid off in other ways, too. Protecting their children from conflict and avoiding sending messages via their children were related to improvements in their children's school adjustment and higher academic performance and fewer bouts of anger and stress-related physical symptoms such as headaches and stomachaches. Parents' use of effective communication ("I messages") and adopting a businesslike approach to their interactions with each other related to better school adjustment for their children and improved communication between them and their children. The concepts in this chapter are the same ones these parents learned, and from which they and their children benefited.

Setting the stage for change. After they separate, parents often continue the same patterns of behavior that contributed to the end of their marriage. Not surprisingly, this perpetuates problems not only for them, but often especially for their children.

Changing personal behavior, whether long-held habits or more recent patterns—particularly those that involve strong emotions—is seldom easy. From the outset, it is helpful to recognize that although you can learn to control your own behavior, it is impossible for one person to control another's. Although you may make the effort to manage your anger and reduce conflict, sometimes this may wind up in a one-sided effort. The other parent's unwillingness or inability to rein in emotions often means that many of the parallel parenting techniques may work best, at least in the beginning.

In addition, changing patterns of feeling and behavior require consistent effort over a long period of time. Staying focused on the goal of a positive outcome for your children may help you through difficult times when change seems to occur at a frustratingly slow pace, or not at all.

Restructuring the Relationship

The goal of every organization—whether profit or nonprofit, a global corporate giant or a charitable food bank—is success in achieving a fundamental shared mission and goal. In the "business" of parenting, that mission is raising children to be healthy, well-adjusted, and ultimately capable of managing their own lives. The processes that lead to this success are those of loving, authoritative parenting in an environment that is as nurturing as possible.

Professional Attitudes and Behaviors

❋

- Treat others with courtesy and respect.
- Greet individuals by name.
- Fulfill commitments.
- Trust others to do their jobs.
- Make appointments in advance.
- Be on time.
- In communication, stay on the agreed-upon topic and treat others' input with courtesy.
- Respond promptly to all communications.

This business partnership analogy may help you think about how you and your former spouse can adopt some of these attitudes and behaviors in your new roles as partners in parenting. Professional relationships revolve around respect and courtesy, generally demand a considerable amount of trust, and operate with a certain level of formality. Since business partners are dedicated to the same fundamental goals, they need to find areas of agreement, trust one another to behave with integrity and fulfill promises, communicate professionally, respond promptly, and find ways to work through or around their differences in order to achieve success. Business associates operate with a level of distance and formality; they do not make assumptions about one another's time, schedules, beliefs, or other personal relationships.

Neither do they pry into one another's private lives. It is particularly important for divorcing couples to set clear boundaries and make questions or comments about dates, private relationships, and other specified personal matters off limits.

All of these expectations and behaviors are idealized, of course. Not every organizational culture embeds these behaviors. But they form a professional standard that is widely recognized as the foundation for organizational success. Here are some practices you can adopt to achieve a businesslike parenting relationship with your former partner:

Make meetings businesslike. Parents who feel safe being together and are able to undertake cooperative parenting sometimes need to meet to discuss their children. It is a respectful business practice to request a meeting in advance, indicating the reason for the meeting. It is best to schedule appointments for relatively low-stress times when the children are not present. Particularly because of the tensions surrounding divorce, it is *not* advisable to show up unannounced at a former partner's home.

If you must speak by phone, be sure to keep conversations brief, to the point, and completely businesslike in tone. Treat them as closed-door, confidential meetings away from the children, and without distractions. If meetings are set after the children's bedtime, it is particularly important to be sure they are asleep and are unable to hear if they should wake up.

Creating a specific agenda and sticking to it helps to keep the focus on the children and helps to prevent parents from straying into topics that are likely to cause conflict. As with most professional meetings, both have the opportunity to add items to the agenda. Particularly in tenuous relationships, it can be helpful to put the agenda on paper, allot a time frame to each topic, and then monitor the time throughout the meeting to ensure that each item on the agenda is addressed. These practices can be as useful for telephone meetings as they are for face-to-face meetings.

Be attuned to emotions—yours and your parenting partner's. In their classic text *Getting to Yes: Negotiating Agreement Without Giving In*, the authors discuss four principles of negotiation and the problems that can interfere with negotiating agreements. One of the most pervasive is emotion. Unlike most professional situations, divorcing or divorced parents almost always experience intense emotions, particularly in each other's presence. It is helpful to anticipate and understand these, so that suddenly being in a former spouse's presence does not create an emotional landslide that blocks clear thinking and communication about the topics on the agenda.

In addition to anticipating in a general way how it will feel to be in a former partner's presence, it can be extremely helpful to prepare what to say in advance, and then to consider how those words and the expression of them will impact the other person. Most conflicts involve a difference in perception. If we want to work toward an agreement, it is crucial to put ourselves in the other person's position and try to understand their point of view and their feelings.

It can be particularly helpful to keep in mind that your former partner is likely to be feeling much like you are at the thought of time away from the children. Although he or she may act angry and resentful, the underlying emotions may be fear and uncertainty. Fear and anger are common reactions to having interests threatened. Rather than dismissing a partner's emotions as unreasonable, it helps to acknowledge them without reacting to angry outbursts. The goal is not to blame, but to communicate in a way that will create peaceful solutions and agreements built on mutual respect. This kind of decision making will help children in the long run.

If communication between you and your former spouse is likely to trigger deep hurt or intense conflict, it may be wise to consider working with a trained mediator, collaborative law team, or mental health professional to approach the negotiation in a way that will lead to mutual problem solving.

In this self-aware process, parents sometimes discover that an issue they thought was about the children turns out to be more about their own feelings and old wounds. Particularly in these cases, the practice of advance planning and reflection pays off, often by abandoning a topic that turns into something other than the children.

If you anticipate feeling strong emotions when meeting with your former spouse, you can also prepare yourself psychologically in advance. Keeping a "script" in mind can be very helpful. For example, I often recommend that parents tell themselves, "I can do this. I will stay calm and focused on my children's needs and their future. I will stay respectful and manage my own emotions. I will work to solve problems collaboratively. I can do this." This kind of positive self-talk, combined with a few deep breaths, can help you to remain calm and productive, especially in those early, difficult meetings.

Listen and respond thoughtfully. Talking is half of the communication equation; listening is the other, equally important half. Some of the "active listening" techniques that psychologists have long used can be very helpful when communicating about emotional issues, particularly about matters on which parents may not fully agree. The first step is to listen carefully and remain focused on the other person's feelings and message, rather than rushing to respond. This is often accomplished by restating in a neutral way what the other person has said. Doing so helps the listener to remain calm and can buy a little time to reflect on the perspective. It is sometimes helpful to ask for clarification or more information in a calm and respectful manner.

Since "why" questions sometimes make people feel defensive and accused, it is best to avoid these. Instead, a request for clarification with a phrase like, "Help me understand . . ." implies a genuine attempt to understand. It often yields insight into another person's behavior, thus increasing understanding and empathy. Demonstrating that the speaker has been heard and understood helps to defuse potential conflict and usually makes him or her more willing to do likewise. This practice becomes the basis for productive conversation and problem solving.

Communicate with facts and courtesy. The anger and hurt that generally accompany divorce often result in a desire to enumerate perceived injustices and place blame. How easy it is to say, "You're always late! Why can't you ever get the kids here on time?" While the emotions behind these statements are understandable and often justified, attacks and blame almost certainly guarantee that the accused will become defensive and feel compelled to return the volley with firepower of their own. Such exchanges not only fail to solve problems but they also tend to escalate a negative atmosphere and cause an already difficult relationship to deteriorate still further.

It is far more effective to describe a situation with facts and courtesy. One technique for doing so is the use of "I" messages. These statements directly express the speaker's viewpoint as such, and may even explain strong emotions, but do not attack the listener. When "I" statements stay factual, they open the door to further conversation and understanding and make it easier for the other person to respond in a similar manner, with facts and courtesy. Conversely, "you" messages are typical of the kinds of angry, accusatory statements that fuel conflict, defensiveness, and counterattacks. In the following examples, it is helpful to imagine how Bill and Janet's seven-year-old daughter Jaime must feel overhearing her parents' words.

EXAMPLES OF "I" MESSAGES	EXAMPLES OF "YOU" MESSAGES
Janet: It's 7:45, Bill, and she was due back at 7:00. I get so worried when Jaime is late. I'd appreciate a call to let me know.	Janet: You're late again. You're always late. You never have the consideration to show up on time or at least call. What kind of example do you think you're setting for my daughter?
Bill: I'm sorry, Janet. Jaime's soccer match ran late and she was hungry, so we stopped to get a bite to eat. I did try to call you but the line was busy.	Bill: If you'd stay off the phone for a change, you'd have gotten my call. I tried to call you to let you know we were running late, but as usual, you were yammering away.
Janet: Jaime, your dad and I have some things we need to talk about in private. I'm sure you want to say good night and give your dad a big hug before you go in. I'll be along in a minute. (Jaime hugs Dad and goes in the house.)	Jaime's parents continue, as if unaware of their child's presence. Jaime watches and listens as the parents continue . . . and Jaime's stomach begins to hurt.

(continued)

Examples of "I" Messages	Examples of "You" Messages
Janet (after Jaime leaves): I didn't get the check last week, Bill. I count on it for our daughter's food, clothes, and school supplies.	Janet: You're late with the check again. You were supposed to send it last week. How am I supposed to buy Jaime's food, clothes, and school supplies when you don't send the money? She's your daughter, too, you know. The judge said you have to pay child support every month.
Bill: I know, I'm sorry. Things have been rough for me at work. I'll put a check in the mail tomorrow morning. And then I'll put it on my calendar to mail three days before the end of every month—or we could start direct deposit. That way you'll get it on time, and it'll keep Jaime from worrying about the check. I think it will be better for her to keep her out of the middle.	Bill: That's all you ever think about, isn't it . . . the money! If you didn't spend so much putting fine clothes on your own back and showing off to your friends, you wouldn't be worried about when the check arrives. I give you an enormous amount of money. You just need to manage it better and spend it on Jaime—not yourself!
Janet: I agree and appreciate your putting it on your calendar. I'll send you a copy of her soccer game schedule.	Janet: You're such a cheapskate—can't even make sure your own daughter has what she needs.

The language that Janet and Bill use in these exchanges has a strong and direct impact on the eventual outcome, affecting all parties. In the first scenario, Jaime's mom lashes out with angry statements that begin with "you *never*" and "you *always*." She refers to Jaime as *her* daughter, instead of "*our* daughter," which further angers and alienates Jaime's dad. The language is inflammatory and, not surprisingly, begets more anger in response.

One trap that angry individuals sometimes fall into is to disguise insults as "I" statements. "I think you are so narcissistic—always thinking of yourself." Although the structure of the statement appears to offer a personal perspective ("I think . . ."), it instead attacks the listener.

Such statements generally make the listener feel defensive and prone to return the attack—perhaps with a similarly disguised insult: "I see that you're at it again, bad-mouthing me when you should be looking at yourself." And on and on, it could easily escalate.

In addition to effective "I" statements, "we" messages can also be very positive and productive. Using statements that incorporate phrases like "can we . . ." and "let's," one parent can engage the other in shared problem solving. "How can we compromise on this?" "Let's figure out a plan that works for both of us as well as for our children."

E-mail and text messaging offer easy, convenient, and timely ways to communicate about schedules and activities, request meetings, and alert the other parent to unforeseen and unavoidable changes. Electronic communications offer two great benefits that no other form of communication provide: the "send" and "delete" keys. One potential pitfall in emotionally charged situations is communicating on impulse, when we are angry or hurt. E-mail and text messaging give us the ideal means to review a message before it goes out, to make sure that it is clear and reasonably courteous and respectful. Deleting it or putting it in the "draft" file for review in a calmer moment are practices that can greatly reduce conflict. Divorcing parents will help themselves and their children by adhering to the standard rules of e-mail and texting etiquette:

- Make it clear.
- Use the conventions of courtesy and respect: a greeting using the person's name, a closing with thanks for consideration of the matter.
- Keep it short. Longer messages are more easily either misconstrued or ignored.
- Avoid "shouting" with all capital letters.
- Before sending, read it from the recipient's perspective, or ask a trusted friend to do so.
- Consider how you would feel if you were to receive this message.
- When in doubt, rewrite.

Collaborate to solve problems. Just as you may find it helpful to apply professional practices to redefining your relationship, you may also see benefits from using a formal problem-solving model like those used in many organizations.

The process of problem solving relies on both parties coming to the discussion with a win-win attitude, seeking a solution that satisfies both parents and, above all, protects the best interests of the children. This requires that both parents come with ideas but without a predetermined decision in mind. When both listen thoughtfully and remain open to compromise, the result is almost always a better solution than either would have proposed alone. It can help greatly if each individual acknowledges and expresses appreciation for the other's efforts to listen or willingness to compromise. Such expressions help to build a strong parenting partnership even as the marital partnership is dissolved.

If at any time during the problem-solving process emotions get out of hand and the focus on solving the problem cannot be regained, it is best to agree to postpone the conversation to another time. Before the next meeting, both individuals can reflect on what caused the discussion to go off track, to identify and figure out ways to manage reactions when hot-button issues or behaviors arise, and develop a strategy to succeed next time.

Problem-Solving Process

❀

- Define the problem.
- Make a list of agreed-upon criteria for any solution—the "musts."
- Make a separate list of "wishes" or "wants," but recognize these as lower priorities than the "musts."
- Brainstorm possible solutions openly and creatively, without comment or criticism.

- Discuss the merits and drawbacks of each of these in relation to the agreed-upon criteria. Consider "wants" but do not let these overshadow "musts." Think creatively, combining or modifying options.
- Agree on a solution.
- Flesh out details of how it will work.
- Put it on paper, with a copy for both of you.
- Test out the solution for a reasonable—and defined—period of time.
- Review and make any changes needed.

Here's how one couple used a formal problem-solving process to deal with a critical issue regarding their children. Brendan was a high-profile local union leader—a hotheaded character whose strong pronouncements frequently made headlines. When he began turning up at events with an attractive young woman who was not his wife, a scandal ensued. Photos of them together hit the news media, and the gossip in their relatively small community was frenzied and seemingly unending.

His wife, Marcie, who had stood by him through many of his political battles, felt humiliated, hurt, and furious. She abruptly filed for divorce, moving herself and Erin, the couple's fourteen-year-old daughter, to a community eighty miles away where her sister lived, and no one else knew or cared about the scandal.

Despite his affair, Brendan loved his daughter deeply and wanted desperately to remain involved in her life. Marcie refused all his requests to visit or have Erin go to stay with him. For her part, Erin was struggling with the abrupt move away from her school and friends and the loss of her zany, fun-loving father who had kept her laughing and made her feel loved. She seemed listless and withdrawn, showing no interest in making friends at her new school or playing in the school band, which had been her great passion back at her old school.

Marcie talked and talked with her, explaining why it was better to be here, and trying to light a spark. She got no response. Finally, she took Erin to a therapist, who quickly got to the root of Erin's changed behavior. She helped Erin learn how to talk with her mother about her feelings of loss and how deeply she missed her father, and also helped her recognize what she needed to do to take more control over her life and make herself happier.

Then the therapist told Marcie that she wanted to sit down with her and Brendan together and help them identify and solve the problems at the heart of Erin's unhappiness. Even though this was a very painful prospect, Marcie and Brendan agreed because they were so deeply concerned about Erin.

At their meeting, the therapist outlined the steps of a formal problem-solving process and then coached them through it. The first step was to define the problem, and even though it was tempting to lay blame, the therapist insisted that they simply agree on what the problem was. That was straightforward: Erin was not thriving without having her father in her life. So the "must" they agreed on was that any solution would involve him in her life on a regular and frequent basis. A high "wish" was for this contact to be in person as much as possible, not just over the phone or by e-mail.

Their brainstorming yielded many ideas:

- Erin could go back and forth every week, spending a week with each parent.
- She would spend two weekends a month with her father.
- Brendan and Marcie would meet halfway in the middle of every week so that Erin could have dinner with her father.
- Erin would alternate vacation times with each parent.
- She would spend her entire summer vacation with her father.
- If Erin could be persuaded to join her new school's band, Brendan would come to all of her weekend band events when he wasn't working.
- They would talk on the phone every night.

They generated about twenty ideas in all. As Brendan put the first thoughts forward, Marcie was ready to pounce. How could he possibly think of their daughter alternating weeks with each of them; she was in school, for goodness' sake! How could she think of letting Erin stay at her father's house with "that woman" around! Why should she do any driving; this was all his fault! But with each outburst, the therapist stopped her and reminded her of the brainstorming rule: no judgments. Just get the ideas flowing.

Finally, with a long list of ideas, they began to develop a schedule that would form the beginnings of their parenting plan. Brendan would see Erin every other weekend. On those when her band was playing, he would go to see her perform and then take her back to his house for the rest of the weekend. He would drive her halfway back to Marcie's home on Sunday, meeting up with her mother at a library. As they talked about the complexity of the schedule, Brendan suggested using videoconferencing so that he could see Erin during the week. With computers in both of their homes, that proved easy and gave them both the additional sense of closeness from seeing each other's expressions. Brendan and Marcie wrote down their plan and agreed to discuss it with Erin and test it out for three months. At that point, they'd ask her how it was working for her, as well as evaluate it from their perspectives and see whether there was anything they could do to make it better.

Well before those three months were up, it was evident that Erin was much happier. She had joined the band and made some new friends. At their three-month checkpoint, they talked about what was working and what wasn't. Erin said she was not always happy about disrupting her life on weekends to be with her father, but she missed him so much that she decided she'd stick with the plan. The videoconferencing worked well, and they agreed that if something big did come up that Erin wanted to do at her new home on a Dad weekend, he would be flexible, and they could substitute a long visual visit over the computer.

In the future, as all of their lives underwent changes—especially Erin's—they were able to use the problem-solving process without their therapist's help. In the end, Brendan discovered that the painful experience of almost losing his daughter and working through those issues had made him a more sensitive father. He had learned to stay focused on shared interests and avoid the temptation to hold on to a position at all costs. In time, Brendan made a point of apologizing to both Erin and Marcie for the pain his affair had caused.

Taking Care of Yourself

Coping with the waves of emotion and the sense of instability that accompany your divorce, renegotiating your relationship as a partner in parenting, and providing quality parenting for your children all place extraordinary emotional and mental demands on parents. Fortunately, many resources—financial, emotional, physical, and spiritual—can help you acquire the strength you need to deal with all of these challenges. And when you have greater physical and mental well-being, you are better able to manage strong emotions and reduce conflict.

Getting on top of the turbulence in your life provides a critical benefit for your children, too. From their perspective, having healthy, well-adjusted parents brings a sense of security to their lives. As flight attendants always advise, put on your oxygen mask before dealing with small children or others who need your help. Unless you do so, it may be impossible to provide the critical help that others need.

Financial. For nearly every divorcing couple, there are serious financial implications associated with dividing assets, establishing two homes, and paying for the divorce itself. Additionally, there may be costs associated with arranging for child care or transporting children between parents.

As with other aspects of divorce, the natural impulse may be to use money as a punishment for offenses or a salve for wounds. Neither is a productive mind-set when it comes to protecting children's best interests and minimizing conflict.

Some attorneys, mediators, and collaborative law professionals are skilled in helping couples to develop a sound financial plan. In other circumstances, it may be helpful to engage an experienced professional financial planner. In many communities, some financial services are available at low cost or even free of charge through nonprofit organizations or government agencies. Otherwise, professionals in private practice and within financial services firms can offer needed services. Since this field is largely unregulated, it is advisable to seek out a certified financial planner (CFP) who has gone through an extensive training and accreditation process or a certified public accountant (CPA) who has a strong foundation in budgeting, taxes, and other financial matters. Some banks and credit unions have such individuals on their staff, but it is always advisable to ask about the credentials and experience of financial advisors before entrusting this important part of your future to them. In addition, as in dealing with your attorney, it is important to ensure that your financial advisor understands and advances your goal to minimize conflict and find mutually acceptable solutions.

Emotional and Social. Extended family members are the "first responders" for many individuals. Parents, siblings, grandparents, aunts, uncles, cousins—all may be people who know us best and whose love is constant and comes without judgment. For others, it is dear friends who fulfill this role.

Sometimes, however, these same people may know us either too well or not well enough, criticize or judge us, or have such blinding loyalties to us that they are unable to offer objective help. People also vary widely in their ability and willingness to be discreet and keep confidences. In choosing to share your most wrenching feelings, it is important to decide who can best provide the help you need and who is likely to undermine the process.

Many grandparents and extended family members can provide crucial support for children, too. Every child needs to feel precious to someone. Grandparents often fill that need, as long as they can contain their own anger and hostility toward the child's other parent. They need to understand and live by your goal of protecting your children from conflict.

Your children's schools are also important resources. In addition to being your children's "second home," they may also offer information and resources for parents who are undergoing divorce. In many cases, these offer the benefit of dealing with issues related to children whose developmental levels are similar to your own children's.

Support groups and preventive intervention programs can also be an excellent resource to deal with emotional issues and learn new skills. Particularly when these groups are led by mental health professionals, they can provide a way for divorcing parents to feel less isolated, and to learn how others have dealt with similar feelings and problems. They are often associated with universities, mental health clinics, churches, and sometimes schools and community centers. Parent education programs are often sponsored by community agencies and the courts and provide valuable information on ways to reduce the stress of a breakup on parents and children. Research shows the multiple benefits of support groups for both children and adults, especially those that are evidence based and provide support along with skills.

Therapy is a valuable resource for all of us during times of change. If you have never considered therapy, you may now want to consider it as a way of taking care of yourself and dealing with the powerful feelings and inevitable changes that are hallmarks of divorce. It is important to choose a therapist with particular care. In addition to licensing and professional credentials, you may find it helpful to work with a therapist who has experience with divorce-related issues and who is willing to help you achieve your goals of feeling better and taking good care of yourself so you can be the best parent possible to your children.

Here is just one example of how therapy can make a difference. Chris came to therapy in shock and disbelief that her marriage of twenty years was coming to an end. Her husband, Warren, had just told her that he didn't love her—and hadn't for some time. Chris was terrified at the prospect of managing completely on her own and devastated at the idea of her world collapsing. Moreover, since Warren had made all the major family decisions about finances, household maintenance, and even travel, she was also overwhelmed at the prospect of coping with these matters on her own.

"I just don't know how I'll ever get through this," she said at our first meeting. "How can I go on? My entire adult life has been completely centered on Warren and the kids." Frightened and depressed, she had decided to seek help as she anticipated her first round of holidays on her own. She didn't know where to begin on her own, and every attempt just left her spinning around her misery and fears.

"All those happy memories, those wonderful times together—now I find myself doubting if they were ever real. Maybe I was just living some kind of happy fantasy." Her first goals were to feel firm ground beneath her feet again, and to find ways to deal with the deep hurt and losses she felt.

Through months of therapy, I guided Chris in the process of examining herself, her life, and her marriage—and her role in its deterioration. It was hard work, but to her surprise, our work together also led to memories and discoveries that produced laughter and, most important, self-awareness and self-appreciation. Through this process, Chris discovered strengths and resilience she had never realized she possessed. Her first big self-discovery was that she had quite a lot of courage—enough to confront her painful emotions head-on. As she looked at herself and her marriage in a new way, she also found that she was smart, analytical, and insightful, and that she had an unusual capacity to be objective and fair-minded, even though she'd been hurt so deeply. As she began to understand and respect her own talents and skills, her confidence grew, and she became willing— sometimes even eager—to take on matters like finances that she had previously found daunting.

While we worked through a process to develop her understanding, we also worked on developing some strategies to deal with some of the practical matters that had at first stymied her. At the top of the list was how to manage her conversations with Warren about their two teenage daughters. They were both loving parents, and they knew that particularly at this critical period of adolescence, they needed to maintain quality parenting and communicate about their girls' schedules, feelings, schoolwork, activities, friends, and plans for college. Warren joined us for several meetings, and together we developed a plan for frequent businesslike communication and some techniques for keeping their focus on the children.

Since facing the holidays without Warren produced so much sadness and anxiety, we dealt with that soon, too. We explored a number of options, and once she had several that felt okay to her, she decided to have a family meeting with her daughters. Warren was planning to visit his parents for the holidays and suggested that the girls spend Christmas with their mother this year. Chris gratefully accepted his offer. But rather than face a traditional holiday without Warren, she proposed to the girls that they make a complete break with the past and do something entirely different. She offered several options, and they came up with some ideas, too. Ultimately, they decided the three of them would help out on a volunteer housing project in the South. They would know no one else, and on Christmas, they'd help prepare and serve food to needy people at a soup kitchen. It all felt a little strange to anticipate such a completely different holiday, but as they got more details, they felt eager to help out on a worthwhile project, soak up some warmth and sunshine, and learn a lot.

At the beginning of our time together, I guided the therapy with Chris almost exclusively. But over time, she began to apply some of the therapeutic processes on her own. I remember one day when she arrived at my office jubilant: she had just signed up for a course. She had been thinking about what she would need to do to get herself ready to enter the job market for the first time at age fifty-three. She had decided on this course as a way to refresh what she'd learned in college so long ago.

There was no magic wand to wave over Chris's troubles and no way to erase the past. But therapy did give her a structured approach and an experienced guide to help untangle the knot of emotions and facts and find solutions one at a time. Therapy was not the only source Chris drew on. She was also strengthened by her deep faith and a solid group of friends who gave her comfort and support. With effort, courage, and tenacity, she found healing and growth and discovered her resilience, one step at a time.

There are a great many resources now available to people like Chris and other families in transition. On my website, I provide links to some authoritative, research-based sources that you may find helpful.

Physical. The importance of physical health and well-being is well documented, but it is easy to let healthy practices slip away when we are overwhelmed with emotional and logistical issues related to divorce—along with the daily demands of life! Exercise is a proven way to reduce feelings of depression and has multiple benefits for overall mental and physical well-being. Since exercise releases the endorphins that in turn elevate mood, it is particularly important to build daily physical exercise into your routine and make it a priority. Ideally it should be an activity that you enjoy for its own sake. Some may find yoga in a room alone to be calming, while for others, a vigorous game of basketball or a walk with friends may give them the release they need. You may need to engage in physical activity as a strictly "grown-up" activity, or you may share such activities with your children—or both. In either case, keeping your body healthy and fit benefits both you and your children. It helps to improve your feelings about yourself at the same time that you set a healthy example for your children.

Nutrition, too, is an important part of staying healthy. While it is often tempting to indulge in junk food when you're feeling low, use moderation as a guide for your wellness. Likewise, be careful about using alcohol or drugs to self-medicate, soothe anxiety, or numb painful feelings. It can become a pattern that seriously undermines physical and emotional health. As with exercise, doing right by your own body nutritionally also sets an example for your children. There are now multiple free resources, including websites and cookbooks available at the local library, showing easy ways to create enjoyable meals that are also quite healthy. If time constraints make shopping and cooking feel like a burden, there are now many healthy alternatives to pizza and fast food—grocery delis that offer prepared meals, and even frozen meals that provide balanced nutrition and good taste. Children often enjoy the process of teaming up with a parent to plan and prepare a meal or bake a special treat. There are double benefits when you and your children share a pleasant time cooking and then enjoy the satisfying and healthy food you have made together.

Spiritual. A recent study of spirituality and mental health complements those that have been conducted on spirituality and physical recovery from surgery or major illness. These studies have revealed that an individual's spiritual well-being has a positive impact on their physical healing. The new study shows that women, in particular, are affected by their religious habits. Those who had once engaged in religious practice and then stopped were more than three times more likely to suffer generalized anxiety and alcohol dependence or abuse than women who reported always having been religiously active. One possible explanation is that women are more integrated into the social networks of their religious communities. When they stop attending services, they lose access to these networks and their potential benefits. Other studies have shown that spiritual elements alone—specifically prayer and meditation—have a positive impact on physical and emotional healing for both men and women.

I encourage my patients who have a belief structure to explore all the spiritual resources they find meaningful. If they are actively engaged in religious or spiritual practice, I encourage them to continue with it, especially during this time of transition. For those who have once had a spiritual orientation but not actively pursued it in recent years, I encourage them to re-explore opportunities that they may find meaningful. Spiritual practice can provide a source of inner strength, hope, and peace. A spiritual community can also provide a powerful network of compassion and caring, friendship, and support.

Forgiveness Is a Choice

We don't hear enough about the role of forgiveness in healing, especially when it comes to divorce. Yet forgiveness is associated with better physical and mental health, and even better parenting after divorce. In his book *Forgiveness Is a Choice*, Dr. Robert Enright demonstrates how forgiveness benefits those who have been deeply hurt and entrenched in a vortex of anger, depression, and resentment. The research-based program he describes found that forgiveness was related to reduced anxiety and depression, and increased self-esteem and feelings of hope for the future. Studies of divorced men and women found that those who forgave their former partners had a greater sense of well-being and less anxiety and depression than those who chose not to forgive.

Another study of parents of children aged ten to thirteen shows that the benefits of forgiveness can extend to parenting as well. Notably, the more the mother forgave her former partner, the less likely she was to use harsh discipline with her children. The mothers who forgave their former partners the least seemed to redirect their anger onto their children through negative behaviors and harsh discipline.

In considering the possibilities of forgiveness, it is important to understand that it does *not* mean forgetting or condoning the hurtful behavior, justifying or denying the pain, or even reconciliation. The process of forgiveness actually begins with acknowledging the anger, hurt, and resentment and how those emotions may be affecting your health and well-being. The recognition that hanging on to resentment and anger is most harmful to oneself is what usually motivates a decision to forgive. Buddha's wisdom on the subject remains ageless: "Holding on to anger is like grasping a hot coal with the intent of throwing it at someone else; you are the one who gets burned."

The process of forgiveness requires courage to face the hard, painful work necessary to break out of the emotional prison of resentment and anger. But once accomplished, forgiveness leads to the joy of moving on in life with a renewed sense of freedom and purpose.

As Jan, one of my clients, said after a painful divorce, "It's been hard to let go of the hurt and righteous indignation that I wore like a medal of honor. But it weighed me down, and took away a lot of the joy in life. Being able to forgive is not about my ex; it's about me, and taking control of my life again. What he did was wrong, but I'm actually stronger now. Letting go of the pain and resentment has freed me in ways I could never have imagined. Continuing to be resentful about the past kept me in the past. Letting go will help me move forward." Her words reveal forgiveness as strength, rather than weakness, with capacity for compassion and healing.

A Postscript on Lisa and Mark

I wish I could tell you that if you follow all the guidelines in this chapter, your negotiations with your former partner will be smooth and painless and your coparenting relationship will be a model for textbooks. But that would be misleading. Negotiating agreements with a former partner in the midst of the sadness, anger, anxiety, and guilt is one of the hardest parts of the process of divorce, and one that takes tremendous self-control and emotional intelligence. There is no more revealing evidence than the story of Mark and Lisa.

This couple opted to use collaborative law to work out their divorce agreement because they both recognized that there were risks associated with going to court, and clear benefits to working together to plan for their children's future. But the process was not always easy. Negotiating together meant seeing each other and having their emotions stirred up. Like many spouses who did not want the divorce, Mark's feelings of loss were evident in his tendency to object to the proposals and resist finalizing aspects of the agreement. Lisa felt guilty about ending the marriage, but like many partners who have long since disengaged emotionally from the marriage, she was eager to get the agreement finalized and move on. As Mark's resistance increased, tempers flared. During a particularly contentious meeting, Lisa threw up her hands and said, "Maybe we'll just have to see each other in court to get this done—and then we won't have to ever talk to each other again."

I pointed out that the intense grief and painful emotions they each had were the hardest part of negotiating and acknowledging the end of their marriage. Their marriage was over, but with three young children, they would be parenting for many years to come. Even as they approached settlement, their ability to cooperate and work together left them ambivalent, wondering at times if they were doing the right thing.

In individual meetings with me, both Mark and Lisa acknowledged how much easier it seemed to just stay furious at the other. Yet they both recognized that wrapping themselves in anger was a short-term solution to protect themselves from uncomfortable emotions. Although it was tempting to say "see you in court," they both knew that the short-term satisfaction of becoming adversarial was fraught with long-term risk. To their credit, Mark and Lisa did not give up on their commitment to collaborative negotiations on behalf of their children.

Now they are living with the daily realities of their collaborative agreement. Adhering to it and sharing parenting responsibilities remains challenging and emotionally draining at times, but since they were both involved in compromise and ultimately agreed to a plan, they are invested in making it work. As the transitions in their lives unfold, they continue to work through their feelings and negotiate some modifications to their original parenting plan. But they are adjusting, and very importantly, their children are getting the best parenting their parents can give them, not caught in the middle of ongoing conflict.

For Mark and Lisa, the long-term rewards will no doubt be realized in three healthy children who have benefitted from both parents being deeply invested in their lives. Their example, even with all of its struggles, remains an encouraging one, full of hope and healing.

SIX

Building Children's Resilience Skills

Frederick Douglass once said, "It is easier to build strong children than to repair broken men." While that is almost always true, building strong children requires loving, authoritative attention, as well as dedication to teaching and nurturing skills that are the foundation for their emotional well-being.

Chapter 2 provided an overview of research on the primary factors that influence children's resilience or contribute to risks of lifelong struggles related to the stress of their parents' divorce. While those risks associated with divorce are sobering, what I hope you will find truly heartening—and empowering—is that we now have a great deal of solid, research-based knowledge about what parents and others can do to fortify children's social and emotional health.

That knowledge is the focus of this chapter; it provides specific guidance about what you can do to influence your children's emotional intelligence—and resilience. Some external resources contribute to strengthening children, and I will address those briefly. The primary influences on the development of children's resilience, however, are support from caring adults in their lives and the important emotional skills they learn to use. Those will be my primary focus here.

External Resources That Contribute to Children's Resilience

When children experience the physical and emotional life changes after their parents part ways, they need people they trust to help them through the tough times. You can help them develop an important life skill by encouraging them to ask for help and support when they need it. You can teach and promote this concept in a number of ways—by modeling your own willingness to seek help, and by encouraging your children to turn to trusted adults when they need help, encouragement, sound advice, or just a listening ear.

First responders in these situations are often grandparents and other family members, trusted family friends, and teachers. They can be sources of kindness, stability, and wisdom. Promoting your children's relationships with these people can help them to feel loved, comforted, and less alone in times that are difficult for them. Then, when they need to ask for help or support, they already have comfortable relationships with people they love and trust.

Sometimes, however, children's difficulties require special skills and knowledge to address them effectively. At these times, it is important for you to identify appropriate professional resources to help your children. Licensed mental health professionals who specialize in child and family issues can often help children put their problems in context, correct misperceptions, and develop skills—including some described in this chapter—that enable them to cope with the major changes in their lives and become more resilient.

In addition to individual therapists, school- or community-based support group programs such as the Children of Divorce Intervention Program (CODIP) and others nationwide have proven extremely valuable in helping children develop skills and self-confidence. Led by trained mental health professionals and frequently offered free of charge, these can make a great deal of difference for children in a relatively short amount of time. The skills they learn in such settings have been shown to have an immediate and lasting impact on children's well-being, and children are often greatly relieved to discover that others are experiencing similar family changes. In this setting, they sometimes feel much more comfortable expressing emotions they may try to hide from their already distressed parents.

The other important avenues for developing children's resilience are school and healthy activities. Because school is such a big part of children's lives, it is the one place that may feel the most normal to them when their families are undergoing big changes. School can be an important anchor for children during these times, but only if they remain actively engaged in it.

One of the most important things you can do is simply to establish and maintain the expectation that school is your children's most important job, and that they are to give it their best attention and conscientious effort. This is not to suggest that you pressure your children to excel, but rather to ensure that they see education and school activities as a high priority. Important daily routines include seeing that they complete homework on time and helping them understand concepts that are causing them difficulty, or finding others who can. If it is possible for you to work with your former partner in supporting your children's school involvement—attending parent-teacher conferences and school activities—you demonstrate unified interest that underscores the importance of school and reassures them that both of you remain committed to their well-being.

It is often helpful, during and after your divorce, to establish ongoing communication with your children's teachers and others who may be in a position to support them, such as the school nurse, counselor, coach, or a former teacher who remains close to them. With information about the changes children are experiencing at home, teachers are better able to watch for alterations in behavior that may signal a problem.

In addition to emphasizing the importance of school, you can also promote your children's resilience by encouraging their participation in other activities that foster the growth of friendship and skills and provide a framework for support. Some may be after-school pursuits—sports teams, band or chorus, scouts, or classes that develop special talents, involve children with peers who share a common interest, or give them access to adult leaders who can serve as mentors and positive role models. Developing their own special strengths and a network of friends helps to promote children's confidence and establishes a ready source of comfortable companionship and support.

Positive activities are building blocks toward healthy child development and resilience. Without a positive focus and engaging activities, children may decide it's easier to get involved in unhealthy or destructive outlets. As one young teen whose parents were not monitoring her activities said to me, "Some kids do sports. I do drugs." No conscientious parents would want to allow the absence of healthy activities to send their children searching for the other kind.

You may also seek out activities that children and one parent can do together. Some camps and other group experiences are designed especially to bring changing families together in a social and supportive environment. Other organizations may sponsor weekly or monthly activities with a similar mission. Such activities have been shown to offer a number of benefits for children during or after their parents' divorce. They can foster a positive self-concept and an enhanced perception of themselves and their families. Such experiences also help to reduce their sense of isolation and feelings of being "weird and different," particularly when they feel comfortable expressing their feelings.

How to Help Your Children Develop Core Emotional Skills That Foster Resilience

Most of the information in the remainder of this chapter is based on my work over more than twenty-five years in developing, implementing, and studying the results of preventive interventions for children. The Children of Divorce Intervention Program (CODIP)—or Changing Families Groups, as it is called in some schools—is designed to reduce the stress of divorce on children through group support and training in skills known to relate to children's healthy adjustment. Started in just four schools, this award-winning program has since spread to more than five hundred schools, serving thousands of children in the United States, Canada, Germany, Australia, New Zealand, the Netherlands, Cyprus, and South Africa. Research on CODIP has proven conclusively that children's adjustment problems can be reduced or prevented and resilience can be fostered by providing support and effective skills to enhance children's capacity to cope with family changes.

In CODIP, we taught children strategies to develop these skills that are the foundation of emotional intelligence and contribute to resilience. Since its inception in 1982, the program has served more than twenty thousand children, and my colleagues and I have undertaken numerous controlled studies to assess its impact. The evidence clearly shows that the skills and concepts taught in the program make a significant difference in children's healthy adjustment to family changes, in all the important parts of their lives—home, school, family, and peer relations—in their feelings about themselves and their families, and even in their hopes for their own future.

Like many children's programs, CODIP uses a group support model to address children's needs. In my practice, I have taught many parents to use the same concepts and strategies with their children during and after divorce.

Here are some techniques and strategies that you can use to strengthen your children's ability to cope with the challenges they face. These same skills will help them deal effectively with other issues throughout their lives.

> ## Skills That Promote Resilience and Emotional Intelligence
>
> ❈
>
> - Self-awareness (the ability to identify and express one's own emotions in healthy ways)
> - Empathy (awareness of and sensitivity toward others' feelings)
> - Self-regulation (the ability to anticipate the consequences of choices, manage strong emotions, and control impulses)
> - Ability to solve interpersonal problems
> - Optimism (the ability and habit of mind to see positive possibilities)
> - Self-motivation
> - Zeal and persistence
> - Hope for the future

Develop children's awareness of their own emotions. As you read in chapter 1, developing the ability to identify and label emotions is essential to understanding and managing them, and you can help your children learn to do this from a very early age, putting words to emotions even before they can talk. As your children's vocabularies, skills, and the ability to play games develop, you can use drawing, stories, imaginative play with puppets, dolls or animal figures, therapeutic storytelling, and other types of games to help your children learn about a range of emotions and healthy ways of expressing them. Here are some ways you can make learning about feelings fun and engaging for your children.

Feelings Grab Bag—Many children enjoy a Feelings Grab Bag game that gives them practice identifying a range of emotions and developing empathy through an awareness and sensitivity to another person's nonverbal signals. They learn that they are not alone in having these feelings—everyone has them—and that people may respond differently to the same things. They learn that some emotions are comfortable and some are not, and that all of their feelings are acceptable. Moreover, the game provides parents with the chance to help children learn that feelings can change and there are ways to soothe themselves when they are struggling with difficult emotions. Here's how it works:

- Write one-word names for feelings on individual cards or pieces of paper (for young children, you can use pictures). Include words your children are able to understand for all kinds of feelings—comfortable and uncomfortable—including those that have arisen in your family since your separation or divorce: angry, furious, hurt, disappointed, painful, sad, frustrated, frightened, worried, ashamed, embarrassed, guilty, missing, lonely, timid, uncomfortable, jealous, stressed, sorry, interested, shy, good, happy, hopeful, surprised, proud, excited, confused, loving, safe, comfortable, silly, peaceful, giddy, relaxed, joyful, loved, relieved, satisfied, confident, secure, lovable, and others that may be especially relevant for your child. Be sure to include concepts like "silly" so you and your child can act that out and laugh together and "mixed feelings" to help them learn that it is normal and acceptable to feel two ways about the same thing. For example, during transitions between homes, they may feel both sad and happy—sad to leave one parent but happy to see the other. Put all these feelings into a bowl or bag and mix them up.
- Each child and parent takes a turn drawing a feeling card from the bowl, making sure everyone has a turn.
- The person who draws the card silently acts out the feeling so that the "audience"—which may be just you and one or more of your children—watches for nonverbal cues to guess what feeling is being expressed. With young children, the adult should take the first turn, showing them how to act out a feeling dramatically.
- Then each person talks about a time when they felt that way or describes a situation in which someone else might have that feeling. Begin with examples that are relatively neutral, such

as "I'm excited about our camping trip coming up" or "I felt frustrated when I locked my keys in my car." As the game goes on, you can deal with more difficult situations but also bring balance to the process of dealing with heavy emotions through funny, dramatic demonstrations of feelings. Allow children the option to talk about their own experience of an emotion, or choose the safety of attributing it to someone else. For example, if a child draws the "anger" card but doesn't wish to share his own experience about feeling angry, you could ask, "What might make a boy your age feel this way?" and allow him to talk about that emotion in a less personal way.

- With young children, you can use a puppet as a compassionate and sometimes funny character to respond with empathy and understanding, sometimes putting difficult emotions into words that may be hard to hear from a "real" person.

- For difficult emotions, you can engage all participants in talking about what a person—or the puppet character—could do to feel better at such times. It's often hard for children to think of ways to help themselves feel better when they are feeling distressed, so it is helpful to write down a list of these self-soothing techniques to keep on hand for times when they are needed.

- How long you play the Feelings Grab Bag depends on how long your child is engaged in it. The amount of time you spend talking about each emotion depends on the age of your children and their response. It is helpful to let your children set the pace, and to be sensitive to their cues about how much talk they can handle, especially about difficult emotions. Ideally, the game leads to a healthy discussion of their feelings about a variety of topics—not just divorce.

Feelings Telegram—Children often benefit from expressing their feelings through art and words to the most important people in their lives—their parents. You can use the Feelings Telegram technique that we use in young children's therapeutic groups. We often use a simple form to help children connect a feeling to a specific event or behavior, but they can also create telegrams on their own, just expressing how they feel. You can create your own telegrams for your children, too, expressing your feelings of love, pride, and joy, or appreciation for their acts of kindness or cooperation. Some parents have told me that they started a collection of telegram messages that they have kept for years.

Older children and teens may not want to talk openly about painful feelings. Sometimes they prefer to compartmentalize them, stashing them away in some mental drawer, so they can focus on school and activities. This can be an effective way for them to deal with upsetting feelings and refocus their attention on other important aspects of their lives. By recognizing these efforts to cope, you can fine-tune your ability to identify the right moments to deal with painful topics. Timing is everything when initiating conversations with older children and teens! Long drives in the car can provide opportunities for

MY FEELING TELEGRAM

TO: Dad

FROM: Kristen

MY FEELINGS ARE IMPORTANT. I CAN TELL YOU HOW I FEEL.
I CAN ALSO SHOW YOU HOW I FEEL IN A PICTURE. I WANT TO SHARE TWO
FEELINGS WITH YOU.

1. I FEEL Loved WHEN you tuck me in to bed

2. I FEEL special WHEN you play baby cub and Loin with me.

MY FEELING TELEGRAM

TO: MOM + DAD

FROM: JESSICA

MY FEELINGS ARE IMPORTANT. I CAN TELL YOU HOW I FEEL.
I CAN ALSO SHOW YOU HOW I FEEL IN A PICTURE. I WANT TO SHARE TWO
FEELINGS WITH YOU.

1. I FEEL BAD WHEN You FIGHT OVER THE CHEK

2. I FEEL HAPPY WHEN YOU TUCK ME iN

conversation that often feel more natural to teens than more formal face-to-face meetings to address concerns. By staying alert for natural opportunities and teaching moments, you will have greater success in opening conversations about your children's feelings.

You can help your older children identify and express their feelings in a variety of ways. In addition to leisurely, low-key conversations about the emotions reflected in books, movies, and music, you can encourage them to express their feelings through art, creative writing, music, interpretive dance, and other creative outlets. These can be therapeutic and, when shared, can lead to deeper understanding between you and your children.

Creative Writing is empowering for young people and can be a healing tool for understanding and dealing with complex emotions. Christine, age ten, had become especially angry, sullen, and withdrawn over the months that her parents were engaged in angry exchanges over their divorce agreement. She wrote this poem about divorce—then told the members of her support group that she "accidentally" left it on her mother's dresser!

> *Divorce*
> *Anger, fear, and worry sometimes turn to fury,*
> *And when this happens parents must*
> *Try not to turn to dust*
> *With anger, fear, and worry.*

Fortunately, Christine's mother was sensitive to the message her daughter was trying to convey—let's not let all this anger ruin our relationships and turn us all to dust. The poem became an important turning point for Christine and her family. Both of her parents responded to her poem with empathy and understanding. Most important, because she had helped them to see their behavior through her eyes, they became determined to resolve their conflict and keep their precious daughter free from its corrosive effects.

Writing can be a whole-family activity as well. In one shared writing experience, one person describes an experience—such as the first day of school—and identifies his feelings about it. The next person then writes her experience of the same event and her emotions about it. A similar activity is simply to put a single word for an emotion at the top of a page or family whiteboard, and let family members write about it and describe times when they experienced it. For the word "excited," for example, a child might write or draw a picture of Halloween or their birthday. Such activities can help children of all ages to develop their ability to identify and express a range of emotions, particularly important during a time of big family changes.

Family Fridge Newspaper: The Changing Times—Because life during and after divorce brings so many changes, a family "newspaper" can be a helpful way to encourage children to share their interests and feelings about what's going on in their lives. You can designate the refrigerator or a centrally located bulletin board as the place to post stories, poems, and cartoons to daily or weekly editions of a family newspaper. These items can be good ways for you to monitor changes and feelings and provide openings for you to talk about them with the author. Cartoons and funny stories that you and your children enjoy can add a daily dose of healthy laughter to share together.

Journals—both individual and shared between parents and children—can be another way of identifying and describing feelings at times when it is difficult to talk about them. There are a variety of ways in which journals can be used. They can provide a creative outlet for expressing a whole range of feelings and experiences.

For example, some parents find it helpful to start a shared journal or notebook with a child to open the way for ongoing communication about a variety of topics that otherwise might not surface openly in daily conversation. Issues about a parent's new partner, concerns about the future, friends, sexuality, and loyalty conflicts, as well as hopes, dreams, wishes, and feelings of accomplishment are the kinds of issues that may deepen communication through an exchange of writing.

Develop children's awareness of others' emotions—the roots of empathy. Empathy is an emotional cornerstone for healthy relationships. An empathetic response acknowledges another person's feelings, including painful or angry ones, and reflects caring for them. The art of empathy requires us to remain focused on how the other person is feeling, rather than ignoring or minimizing their emotions or losing focus on them and instead thinking about our own responses to them. During and after a divorce, when emotions play such a big part in everyone's life, having those feelings understood and accepted, and feeling the concern and care of others can promote the healing process.

You can help your children of all ages to become empathetic. You can begin during your children's early years when you teach them that they can learn about how someone is feeling by looking at them, listening to them, expressing concern for them, and asking them how they feel.

Children can learn to discern how others are feeling by observing their faces, gestures, and posture, and by listening attentively to their words and tone of voice. You can encourage them to be observant using some of the techniques for identifying feelings described earlier in this chapter. It can even become a kind of game—whenever you're in a situation where you can observe other people and talk about them without being overheard, you can engage your children in trying to understand what someone else is thinking and feeling, talking about the clues that lead you to your supposition.

You can help your children deepen their capacity for empathy by encouraging them to mentally put themselves in someone else's situation. Questions like, "If you were in your brother's place right now, how do you think you'd feel?" and "If what happened to Jeanne had happened to you, how would you be feeling?" can help them to imagine others' feelings caringly.

You can also encourage your children to ask about others directly and to express their observations about feelings. You may often make comments like, "You look kind of sad today, Buddy. How are you doing?" or "What a great smile! You sure look happy!" Children may need guidance and encouragement to begin making such caring observations and asking about others. Noticing their efforts and praising their kindness further promotes such empathetic behavior.

Children also learn how to develop empathy by experiencing it and observing it in the important people in their lives, especially their parents. They learn it by experience when they come home and announce, "I hate this stupid backpack!" and an empathetic parent responds, "Sounds like you're having a rough time. Tell me what's going on . . ." Such a response immediately acknowledges what the child is feeling at that moment and reflects understanding. This may make it easier for the child to get beyond the backpack to the more difficult issue. "I'm so tired of going back and forth and I have all this stuff to carry all the time. I just wish we all lived in the same house like we used to before you guys got divorced."

By contrast, reacting to the backpack outburst with "No you don't!" "We just bought it Saturday and you picked it out. You loved it!" "I don't like to hear you use the word 'hate,'" and other such responses that may easily slip out fail to reflect understanding of the child's feelings at that moment. Such comments do not model empathy or invite deeper conversation, but rather discourage the child from saying more.

Children also learn about empathy by watching their parents and others when they express their observations and support for a friend or family member in good times and in bad. "I hear the joy in your voice when you talk about your time with your kids," "It makes me sad to hear you so distressed," "How frustrating to have your computer crash after all that hard work you had done," and other such expressions demonstrate understanding and acceptance of others' emotions and concern for them as individuals.

Children's feelings may differ from those their parents experience, especially when it comes to divorce and changes in their family. Often it takes talking together for them to understand that their feelings are different from yours. It is very helpful for them to hear that although they may have different feelings and points of view from yours, you understand and respect their feelings, and you want to hear about them.

Teach children to manage strong emotions in healthy ways. Psychologists use the term "emotion regulation" to describe the ability to control impulses and effectively manage intense feelings. Mastering this fundamental skill is critical for social and emotional well-being and healthy relationships throughout life. In extreme cases, those who fail to develop this skill act on powerful emotional impulses that result in disastrous and destructive behaviors such as assault and other crimes of rage.

During and after a divorce, children are faced with unwanted, uncontrollable, and often unexpected life-altering experiences. Not surprisingly, they often grapple with intense emotions, and coping with them can be enormously challenging—even overwhelming. Learning to regulate their emotions is particularly important for children who have experienced major life changes over which they had no control. By learning strategies to deal with the upsetting new realities, they have a better chance of handling their strong emotions in healthy ways.

One of the most effective techniques for managing strong emotions is taking time to step back, breathe deeply, pause, and then think before reacting to a situation. Children can be taught this technique by visualizing a stoplight. The red light signifies intense emotion and time to "stop and think" before acting.

Once they "stop and think," children can learn to express their feelings using "I" statements rather than lashing out at someone else. "I am so angry right now" certainly expresses strong feelings, but no one is hurt by them. By contrast, name calling or physically lashing out and attacking another person only escalates problems. It is hard to be this objective in the heat of upsetting emotions, for adults as well as our children, but using the "stop and think" technique helps to make it possible. The phrase "say what you mean without being mean" can help us all remember to use "I" messages during those times when we run the risk of expressing anger in hurtful or damaging ways. Your children will benefit when you both model and teach them these techniques.

Here is how one set of parents helped their daughter learn to manage her strong emotions. Jane is furious at her younger sister for going into her room and taking her stuff. She is also angry about her parents' divorce and, consciously or not, has begun to take her frustration and anger out on her sister, a "safe" target. It might be tempting for her parents, who feel guilty about the divorce, to ignore Jane's aggressive and disrespectful way of treating her sister. But they realize that they will do Jane a disservice if they allow her to establish a pattern of displacing her anger and frustration in hostile and hurtful ways. Such behavior is harmful to relationships, and if it continues, this pattern will harm not only Jane's relationship with her sister, but will also jeopardize friendships and future intimate relationships.

So Jane's parents empathize with her frustration but set limits on how she expresses it. They encourage both their daughters to use "I" statements, such as "I'm really mad that you took my stuff without asking. I'd appreciate it if you would ask me first before you 'borrow' something."

In our children's groups and other evidence-based programs for children, we brainstorm "hot button" issues and teach children the skill of thinking through how they might respond when they're really angry, and then rate each response with the familiar face symbols:

☺ Makes the situation better.

☹ Makes the situation worse.

☺ Not sure it will make any difference, or need more
   time to test out and problem solve.

This game can easily be used at home. In a quiet, pleasant, unemotional time, you can talk with your children about how to evaluate their responses and make choices that will make the situation better.

This process of teaching children to stop, slow down, and think before responding has a positive physiological effect in the brain. Such a pattern of behavior calms the amygdala and helps to activate the prefrontal cortex, an area of the brain that controls reasoning and judgment. Thus it strengthens essential neural pathways for more rational thought, problem solving, and good judgment—critical skills that will last a lifetime.

Help children understand what they can realistically control: solvable versus unsolvable problems. Despite our best efforts, some problems cannot be solved because the circumstances are beyond our control. The concepts in the serenity prayer adopted by Alcoholics Anonymous provide guidance that can be helpful for children, too. The prayer asks for the serenity to accept the things we cannot change, the courage to change the things we can, and the wisdom to know the difference.

Especially following a divorce, it is important to help your children learn to differentiate between problems that they can control and those they cannot. Realistic perceptions of control are instrumental in helping children master the psychological task of disengaging from their parents' conflicts and redirecting their energies into age-appropriate activities. This understanding also helps children to learn that everyone has problems that are beyond their control—not just children, and not just children whose parents are divorcing or divorced. Even as they are undergoing big changes in their lives, this helps them to feel less isolated, and empowers them to focus on aspects of their lives over which they do have control. Kids are allowed to be kids, not little adults faced with solving complex problems they didn't create.

Numerous studies demonstrate the importance of being able to let

UNSOLVABLE	SOLVABLE PROBLEMS
· MOM + DADS DIVORCE	· WHAT TO TELL MY FRIENDS
· Their MARRIAGE PROBLEMS	· GETTING MY HOMEWORK DONE
	· MAKING NEW FRIENDS
	· DOING GOOD IN SCHOOL

go of uncontrollable problems or situations. Studies of learned help-lessness show what happens when we continue to try to control and change negative events that are completely beyond our control. Feelings of powerlessness, ineffectiveness, and failure take over, creating a perfect storm that often results in depression. Children are at risk for such feelings if they are put in situations in which they feel responsible for their parents' problems and strive to solve them, derailing them from their healthy developmental need to just be a child.

When children realize that that they do not have control in some important aspect of their lives, they may feel frustrated, angry, or sad that they cannot change the situation. They need help learning how to disengage from unsolvable problems and redirect their energy and focus on what they can control.

For example, six-year-old Jake was extremely unhappy about his parents' divorce and fervently wished for them to get back together. Whenever one parent came to pick him up at the other's house, he dawdled getting ready, hoping that would give them time to talk to each other. When that didn't seem to be working, he tried another tactic. This time, he would appear punctually, and with a big smile, invite his parents to sit down and talk with him. One time he even asked his mother to make brownies, his father's favorite, and when his dad appeared, he ceremoniously placed a platter of brownies in front of him, saying, "Look what Mom made for you!" These are certainly creative ideas, but Jake's belief that he could solve his parents' problems took a considerable toll. He was having trouble at school. He found it very difficult to concentrate, and he often wound up in the school nurse's and counselor's offices. Jake desperately needed help recognizing that his wishes for his parents' reconciliation, while certainly not abnormal, focused on an outcome well beyond his ability to control. Once he grasped this reality, he needed help learning how to disengage from those unsolvable problems and refocus his energy instead on what was within his control as a child.

One of the activities we use in our groups to engage children in learning to differentiate what they can and cannot control is the Red

Light–Green Light Game, which you can easily use at home with your children. The traffic light analogy teaches children and adolescents to stop and think about a problem and then determine whether it is within their control to solve it. Green means go ahead and try to solve it; yellow means proceed with caution, and red means stop; don't take this one on—this is not something they can solve.

In this game, the group is presented with a problem. Those who think they could solve it hold up a green light card, and explain why and how the problem could be solved. Those who think a problem is unsolvable hold up a red light and list their reasons why. This process often leads to a lively discussion in which children debate how much control they have over all aspects of their lives. They often come to realize that, except for their parents' divorce or decision to remarry, they can control a great many aspects of their lives. They can decide how to respond to their parents' decisions, and they can make choices about many other aspects of their lives. As one astute twelve-year-old said, "I didn't have any control over my parents' choices when they got divorced . . . but I've learned that I can choose to be happy now."

Teach children how to soothe themselves. Another important skill in managing emotional distress is the ability to self-soothe. Parents can teach children this set of skills, too, just as they teach "I" messages.

It begins by actively listening to what your children say about their feelings. It is not always easy to hear them say they feel hurt, angry, or worried, or that they miss their other parent. But listening is the first step in helping them find productive ways to feel better. The next step is to respond with empathy. Having done this, you can teach your children these fundamental skills to soothe themselves.

1. Help them learn how to reframe their thoughts in a positive way. Cognitive behavior therapy, which has proven very effective in treating anxiety-related problems, is based in part on the fact that much of how we feel depends on how we think about things. If we think about the worst possible outcome or continue to ruminate about our worries, anxiety increases. If, instead, we can manage to find more positive ways to think about a situation, we generally feel better and cope more effectively, and our anxiety decreases. You can help your children learn how to recast their worries and fears about the changes in their lives resulting from your divorce.

For example, here's how Marcy helped her seven-year-old son reframe his thoughts at a tough time. Derek came to her at bedtime one night and said tearfully, "I can't sleep. I really miss Dad. I was just thinking, what if I never got to see him again?" In his sadness, he had transformed missing his father into a dramatically oversized worry.

Marcy's response was full of understanding and empathy. "Oh, what a terrifying thought!" she began. "You really miss him when you haven't seen him for this long. It's hard to fall asleep when you have a lot of scary and uncomfortable feelings like that going on inside.

"But remember," she went on, "you're going to Dad's next week, and I know you guys will have a good time together. He's going to take you fishing, and I bet you and he will stop in and have cookies with Grandma, too." Here she helped Derek focus on the reality that he would see his dad soon, and helped to make that come alive in his mind by reminding him of the things he and his dad would do together.

2. Focus on what's within their control. You can help your children greatly by pointing out that they cannot change the reality of the divorce. But they *can* change how they choose to think about it, and how they choose to deal with it. Once children learn to identify uncontrollable circumstances, they can learn ways to help them disengage from those unsolvable problems and redirect their energies to aspects of their lives that are within their control, such as involvement in school and positive activities that promote their growth, development, and good health.

3. Help them think of ways to soothe painful feelings. In some cases, a situation that is causing children anxiety or difficult feelings becomes exaggerated in their minds. When they can look for and identify some positives within that situation, it becomes less ominous. At times, it may also be productive to guide children away from the overwhelming problem in their minds by breaking it down into manageable parts and developing a plan that will help to reduce their anxiety and soothe painful emotions.

Continuing with the example above, Marcy followed her comments about what Derek and his father would enjoy together by focusing on how to feel better at the moment. She said, "Right now, though, let's think about all the things we can do to help you feel better, so you can get a good night's sleep. What do you think would help?" She encouraged Derek to come up with his own ideas and added a few of her own. She suggested that he might like to call his dad to say good night. He liked that idea, and after he did that, he said he wanted to snuggle with his favorite stuffed rabbit and listen to some songs he liked. Marcy suggested that they read one of his favorite books together while they snuggled.

The next day, Marcy encouraged and helped Derek make a list of things that he finds enjoyable, soothing, and fun. They taped the list to his desk, so he could refer to it whenever he needed a reminder that his feelings could change, and he could take charge of changing them. She also encouraged Derek to think about some of the special things he and his dad enjoyed doing together. As she was guiding the conversation and the process, Marcy was helping Derek feel better in the face of big worries, and also showing him how to soothe himself in the future.

There are many resources that can help children soothe their difficult emotions. Some books are available on dealing with divorce, including a few written by children for children. Painting, drawing, playing with a beloved pet, listening to music, doing yoga, deep breathing, and engaging in physical exercise are all great ways to help children take charge of feeling better and relieving stress. When they develop these skills, children regain a sense of control over their lives and add to their self-confidence.

Replace damaging misconceptions with accurate understanding. As I have discussed throughout the book, helping children develop an age-appropriate understanding of family changes is essential for their healthy adjustment. For you as a parent, this means helping your children separate their own worst divorce-related fears from reality.

For example, five-year-old Natalie blamed herself for her parents' unhappy marriage and acrimonious divorce because she frequently wet the bed. As she lay in bed at night, she overheard her parents' loud, angry arguments. They fought about money, the condition of the house, her progress at kindergarten, and her dawdling. Natalie regressed in school, became depressed and lethargic, and lost interest in playing with her friends. She even refused to eat, saying that then there would be more money for their family if she didn't eat. Her misconceptions became so deeply ingrained that she wished she had never been born, believing her family would be happier and better off without her.

For children like Natalie, hearing their name over and over during heated arguments fuels their feelings of responsibility for the end of their parents' marriage and contributes to their own fears of abandonment. Children urgently need their parents and other caring adults to intervene and provide explanations about the conflict in their families that they can understand. A five-year-old child like Natalie needs a simple, clear explanation that she can understand. "These are grown-up problems between Mom and Dad, and you did not cause them in any way. Sometimes when you hear your name, it might seem like an argument is about you. But our problems are *not* because of you. It's our job as parents to solve our problems, and we promise to do that in a better way. Your job is to be a little girl and enjoy kindergarten, your friends, and all the things you like to do. One thing your Mom and Dad most agree on is how much we love you. No matter what, both of us will always take good care of you."

The important point here is that you can teach your children more productive ways of seeing family problems. Early and often, they need to hear the message that they did not cause the marital problems and cannot change the divorce, but they can change their feelings and aspects of their lives by how they think and what choices they make. The feeling of satisfaction that comes from learning effective coping skills can help them to develop optimism and positive thinking— essentials of resilience.

Use therapeutic storytelling to deal with difficult topics. Therapeutic storytelling is a nonthreatening and engaging process you can use to address your child's concerns. Using fictional characters, you can demonstrate effective ways to think about a situation, clarify misconceptions, disengage from an unsolvable problem, learn how to solve problems, teach effective ways of coping, and provide soothing and comfort to a distressed child. Since your child has an important role to play in the story, the process helps him develop his abilities to identify emotions, solve problems, soothe himself, and discover his own sense of hope and optimism.

Mental health professionals often use therapeutic storytelling with children who are struggling with difficult issues. It can be tailored for children from ages three through early elementary-school age. The technique can be used with just one adult and one child—plus the fictional characters—or with larger groups. For young children, it is often helpful to have a puppet, a favorite stuffed animal, or a doll as a prop to "play" the part of the primary character.

You invent the basic framework of a story that relates to your child's situation and play it out with your child. You have two roles to act out in the story—the primary fictional character and the narrator. Your child usually takes on the role of an interpreter or helper. The story is structured so that the primary fictional character talks about a problem that is much like one the child is experiencing, often expressing fears and worries that the child may keep hidden.

Here is an example of how therapeutic storytelling works.

The Story of the Turtle Family

❋

Parent (as narrator): One day Terry the Turtle walked down the mudflat moving very, very slowly—in fact, much more slowly than usual. Her friends noticed that Terry looked sad today. Why do you suppose she was so sad? (Allow child time to talk about reasons Terry might be sad.) Let's ask Terry why she looks so sad.

Parent (as Terry), to child: I just found out that my mommy and daddy turtle are getting a divorce. Do you know what that means? (This question provides the opportunity to be sure the child understands what divorce does—and does not—mean, and gives the parent a chance to clarify misconceptions.)

Parent (as narrator), to Terry: We can see you're really sad hearing about your mommy and daddy's divorce, Terry. You're right, divorce means that parents will live apart, in two separate homes.

Parent (as Terry): Yeah, they're going to live in two different houses, and I'm afraid that I won't ever see them anymore.

Parent (as narrator), to Terry: What a scary thought! What would make you think that, Terry?

Parent (as Terry): Well, since they don't want to be with each other anymore, I'm scared maybe they won't want to be with me either. Because . . . because I never clean my room like I'm supposed to, and that made them mad at each other and they started fighting, and now they're getting a divorce and it's all my fault.

Parent (as narrator), to child: Wow! Terry thinks that the divorce is her fault! She thinks since she heard her parents argue and she didn't clean her room, that she was the cause of the problems. What do you think? Do you think Terry really caused her parents' divorce, or did it just seem that way to her? (Allow time for child to talk about all the ways things can appear, and the feelings Terry might have in this situation.)

Parent (as narrator), to child: Sometimes, things can seem a certain way, but that's not really how they are. Terry is sad and worried because she already felt a little bad about not doing her chores, but then she heard her parents arguing and thought they were mad at each other because of her. But divorce is a grown-up problem, between the mom and dad. It's not anything that kids cause, and it was not Terry's fault.

Parent (as narrator), to Terry: Terry, I know it seemed to you that your mom and dad were arguing because of you, but what they were really arguing about was some other things—grown-up things. That

happens a lot with divorce. Parents have grown-up problems that
they can't fix. But the problems between them are not your fault. It
would be a really good idea to tell them about how you're feeling.
I'm one hundred percent sure they'll tell you what I just told you.

Parent (as Terry): Well . . . okay. I guess I could do that.

Parent (as narrator), to child: Meanwhile, I think Terry needs to feel
better. What do you think? Can you think of ways to help her feel
better right now? (Allow child time to come up with some ideas and
share them with Terry.)

Parent (as narrator) to Terry: Those sound like good ideas. What do you
think, Terry? Are there other things you especially like to do that
make you feel better?

Parent (as Terry): Well, I really like to sit on my special log in the pond
and sun myself. Sometimes it's just so pretty out there.

Parent (as narrator), to Terry: Well that sounds like a great thing to
do—to be in a peaceful spot outdoors on a sunny day. I'm glad you
have a special spot you can go to. I know this is a tough time for you,
Terry, but I also feel very sure you'll get through this and find ways
to be happy with both of your parents in both of your homes.

Parent (as narrator), to child: It's so nice that you could help Terry. You
gave her some good ideas and helped her to feel better. What a good
friend you are! I hope you will talk with your mom and me lots
and lots—especially if you're feeling sad or worried or scared, like
Terry was. Your mom and I both love you very much, and we will
always take good care of you. So even though we have grown-up
problems we can't solve and we're going to get divorced, like Terry's
parents, you don't have to worry about losing your special place in
our hearts.

Learn a problem-solving process. In the midst of deeply troubling
changes in our lives, sometimes our first instinct is to avoid the problem and the painful feelings associated with it. We may hope that

choosing not to think about them will make the painful feelings go away. Certainly there are times when it can be helpful to put emotions on hold for a while, because sometimes children are able to manage distressing feelings only in small doses. But research has proven that children benefit socially, emotionally, and academically by learning how to actively address their concerns and develop effective coping skills, including problem solving and positive thinking.

A number of studies related to emotional intelligence show that effective problem solving is directly linked to children's social, emotional, and psychological well-being, and to their school achievement. Teaching children how to think through a problem, generate a variety of potential solutions, consider the consequences of each option, and apply the best one are critical life skills. Problem-solving skills can be applied to any situation in children's lives, whether divorce-related or not. These pivotal skills build children's confidence and feelings of self-efficacy as they grow increasingly able to handle a broader range of situations and challenges. Practicing these skills activates and strengthens neural connections to the prefrontal cortex and hence develops rational thought and judgment.

Breaking problem solving into the five steps described below helps children learn the process. When you model them in your own life and talk about how you are making decisions, even young children can begin to absorb the concepts.

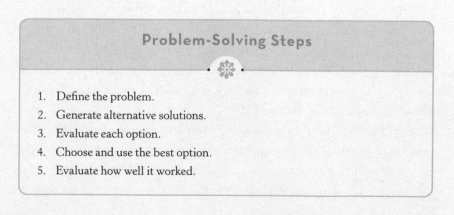

Problem-Solving Steps

1. Define the problem.
2. Generate alternative solutions.
3. Evaluate each option.
4. Choose and use the best option.
5. Evaluate how well it worked.

1. Define the problem. It may seem obvious that the first step is to identify, clarify, and understand the problem. But sometimes it is hard to distinguish between a problem and the feelings associated with it. For example, ten-year-old John complained, "It's just such a hassle being at two houses." This statement could be interpreted in different ways. Some parents might assume it has to do with something negative about the other parent. But it might mean many other things. It might mean that he feels the emotional turmoil of leaving a parent frequently. It might mean that he feels stressed about losing and forgetting things as he goes back and forth between his homes. It might mean that he sees the time and effort involved in going back and forth is depriving him of time with friends or a favorite activity. The most effective solution would depend on determining just what the problem was in John's mind.

2. Generate a variety of alternatives. In this process, it is important to begin by generating as many ideas as your child can think of, and not to evaluate them initially. It often helps to write these down so none are forgotten. You can coach your children on this part of the process, helping them think of a big variety of potential solutions. Sometimes children impulsively suggest solutions that parents immediately realize would have negative outcomes. There is great value in adding these to the list without any negative comment, in order to help children learn the next step.

In the example above, when John defined his problem as being worried about the possibility of losing and forgetting things, his parents asked him how many ways he could think of to solve that problem. He generated quite a list, including making a checklist every day, asking his older brother to be his manager, and even designing and installing a programmable robot at each of his parents' back doors to hand him everything he needed!

3. Consider the consequences of each alternative. Evaluating the potential solutions involves predicting the consequences. It can help children to hear the phrase "Stop and think" repeatedly, which helps them remember to step back from the emotions they may be feeling and think about what might happen if they chose this alternative. You can help them by asking questions like, "What would happen if you did that? Would it make things better, or would it make them worse?" Children can rate each option with ☺ or ☹. If they decide that the outcome would not be helpful, they can eliminate that choice and move on to other alternatives. In this step, it is also helpful to teach your child to anticipate and prepare for what might happen if their solution does not work as they expect it to.

4. Choose and use the best option. After your child has thought through the likely consequences of each option, you can encourage and coach her to decide on one that she foresees will have a good outcome—the one with the biggest ☺ next to it. At this point, it is often helpful to think through how to undertake the next steps in a way that will help to ensure success. For instance, if your child is worried about going to a friend's birthday party at a time when she is scheduled to be with her father, and she decides the best option is to call and talk with her father, it may help her if she plans what to say to him.

5. Evaluate the outcome. If the solution works well, point out your child's success and congratulate him! If it does not work so well, help him try to figure out why. Is a different solution required, or is it possible that the problem needs to be further clarified? Sometimes it takes several tries to realize that the initial definition of the problem might mask the true underlying issue. If the problem is accurately defined, then children can either come up with another solution to try now, or figure out what to do differently when a similar situation arises in the future. These two healthy outcomes— "Wow! It worked!" or "Looks like I need to try another solution"—are distinctly different from a sense of failure.

Children learn problem-solving skills through teaching and daily practice. While it is sometimes quicker and easier for you to solve a problem yourself than to teach the process, your children benefit by taking on problems appropriate to their developmental age. Through experience in problem solving, they gain confidence and an empowering sense of their own competence.

Here are two examples of the kinds of problems you can help your children learn to solve by encouraging them to think of several potential solutions, evaluate them, and decide which one they think will work best.

Example One: Your seven-year-old son calls home from school, upset because he forgot his lunch.

You: "Hmmm. Forgot your lunch, how frustrating. What are some ways we could solve that problem?"

Jeff: "You could bring me my lunch."

You: "There's one possible solution. Good start. What are some others?"

Jeff: "Well, maybe I could ask somebody to share their lunch with me. Or maybe I could ask the principal if I can get lunch at the cafeteria and pay tomorrow."

You: "Good! You've got three ideas. How do you think each of them might work out?"

Jeff: "Well, if I asked you to bring me my lunch, you might be too busy."

You: "You're right about that. If there's another solution, it would make my life easier today."

Jeff: "David usually has extra food and sometimes he throws a lot of his lunch away. I bet he would share with me."

You: "Sounds like a possibility. Do you and David generally get along pretty well?"

Jeff: "Yeah! We always play together at recess."

You: "Okay. So he probably wouldn't have a problem with your asking him. What about your third option?"

Jeff: "I could ask Ms. Marshall if I could charge my lunch, but I'm kind of scared to."

You: "Why is that, Pal?"

Jeff: "Well, last week James asked if he could charge his lunch, and she gave him a big lecture about responsibility."

You: "Does James usually have a problem with responsibility?"

Jeff: "Yeah. He forgets stuff all the time, so he's always in trouble."

You: "So maybe Ms. Marshall would be upset with you, or maybe not. That's hard to predict, isn't it?"

Jeff: "I suppose so. I don't think she'd be mad at me, but I don't know for sure."

You: "What do you think is the best solution?"

Jeff: "I think I'll ask David to let me have half of his sandwich and his fruit—he always throws his fruit out. I can get some water at the drinking fountain."

You: "That sounds like Plan A. If that doesn't work out for you, do you think asking Ms. Marshall about charging would be Plan B?"

Jeff: "I guess so."

You: "I'm proud of you, Son. You did a good job solving your problem. Tonight you can let me know how it went."

Example Two: Your thirteen-year-old daughter is supposed to spend Sunday with her father, but a friend has invited her to go to a major-league baseball game that day. Since she's a pitcher, she really wants to go to the ball game, but she does not want to hurt her dad's feelings.

You: "I'm so proud of you for being so sensitive of your father's feelings—that's really thoughtful of you. Now . . . let's think about how you could solve this dilemma."

Brianne: "Well, I guess I could just miss going to the game with Terri and watch it on TV with Dad . . . if it's broadcast here. Or I could just explain to Dad and ask him if we could spend the day together on Saturday instead of Sunday. You wouldn't mind, would you?"

You: "I wouldn't mind. I know both the game and seeing your father are important to you, and I'd still get to see you before and after the game on Sunday. Are there any other solutions you can think of?"

Brianne: "Maybe Terri's parents would let Dad go along if we paid for his ticket."

You: "Good. Anything else?"

Brianne: "I can't think of anything more."

You: "Okay, so how would you evaluate each of these solutions?"

Brianne: "If I miss going to the game and it isn't broadcast on TV, then I wouldn't get to see it at all. I'd really be bummed, and I might not be very good company for Dad—even though I'd try. I think he'd probably be okay with getting together on Saturday instead of Sunday if he doesn't already have plans. But it would be really cool if Terri's parents would let Dad come, too. He loves baseball as much as I do—and they do. Besides, I think they'd like each other. Dad has the same kind of crazy sense of humor that Terri's dad has."

You: "Sounds like you'd really like for it to work out to get Dad invited to the game. What do you need to do to see about making that happen?"

Brianne: "I'll call Terri's parents. . . . No, I'd better call Dad first and see whether he's okay with the idea before I call them. Then if he likes the idea, I can call them. And if he doesn't, then I can see whether he'd be willing to switch days. I guess I'd better ask him that what-if question, too—if Terri's folks don't think it will work out, would he still be willing to switch to Saturday."

You: "You're really good at solving problems! That's thinking on all cylinders! Go call your dad and then you'll know what to do next."

Although problems sometimes arise in the heat of an argument, this is not a time when children are motivated to learn about problem solving. The ideal time to help them learn this process is at a neutral time when no one is rushed, rather than in middle of emotional situation when no one can think clearly. That's not to say that they won't need strategies to deal with those emotional moments—they will.

But it's best for them to learn to anticipate those whenever possible and have options ready to put into play.

It takes some pressure off children to learn that their parents do not see themselves as perfect people or perfect problem solvers. Being candid about this is helpful, especially when children absorb their parents' healthy example of persistence in trying to solve problems, even when things do not always turn out as they might have wished. When our children see that we don't give up, and that we learn from our mistakes and keep trying, they see a healthy model of how to deal with life's challenges.

Practice hope and a positive outlook. It is logical to think that developing all of the resilience skills and particularly gaining self-confidence result in a sense of hope and a positive outlook on the future. Although developing these abilities does contribute to a positive frame of mind, we can also influence our other abilities by practicing finding the positives.

This is not to suggest that always glossing over problems or painful emotions with happy thoughts or fantasies is either healthy or helpful. Rather, it is important to identify what is genuinely positive even as we also acknowledge what is painful or difficult. Mastering a new skill, solving a difficult problem, making progress toward a goal—all of these are successes worthy of notice and celebration. You can help your children form this framework for their thinking by noticing and praising their achievements and efforts, finding and bringing focus to the bright spots in even very difficult situations, modeling this behavior in your own life, and of course, directly teaching and encouraging your children to find the genuine positives.

You can also help your children through your divorce by pointing out that their current situation, with all of its painful feelings, will not last forever. You can help them to imagine a more positive future and encourage a sense of hope that they will come through the tough times and look forward to better days ahead.

Here's how Doug helped his eight-year-old daughter during the particularly difficult months after her mother left. He acknowledged how sad Sallie was and how much she missed seeing her mom every day. But he also asked her to think about new realities and what she'd like life to be like in six months. Could she imagine settling into seeing her mom during the new schedule, and spending part of every weekend walking a different habitat and collecting leaves and wildflowers—something she and her ecologist mother both loved to do? Could she see herself and her new kitten sleeping in the bedroom that she and her mother had painted sky blue, just for her? Could she envision creating new traditions and keeping the routines she enjoyed with each of her parents? "Because all of that will happen," he told her. "It's starting to happen already. It's definitely different than it was before, but there will be good times."

One day he told her to get dressed up; they were going for a surprise treat. A touring production of the musical *Annie* had come to town, so Doug bought tickets and took Sallie to dinner and then to the theater. On the way home, they talked and talked. Annie and her friends surely did have "a hard-knock life," but long before Daddy Warbucks came into her life, she was making her own life better through hope. They sang, "The sun'll come out tomorrow . . ." again and again. They bought the album. And listened and sang some more.

On days when Doug could tell Sallie was feeling down, he was always ready to listen. "Want to tell me about it?" he'd ask. If she said yes, he put aside whatever he was doing and sat down to listen. If she said no, he'd smile and say, "That's okay, Kiddo. Just do me one favor. Think about what's on your mind, and then spin it, and see if you can find the spot where the sun could come out, and put a little polish on that spot."

While Sallie was going through her tough times, Doug was going through his own. But he practiced his own advice. When he was feeling down, he'd go in the bathroom, close the door, give his grief a little time, and sometimes take a warm shower. Then he'd look at himself in the mirror and remind himself of what he was grateful for—especially having Sallie in his life. Then he could smile again. He told Sallie about his own feel-better routine, and now and again he'd find himself locked out of the bathroom while Sallie practiced her feel-better routine and eventually emerged with a smile.

As Doug had hoped, in six months' time, the new routines had begun to take hold, Sallie was looking forward to her ecological walks with her mother, and they had developed some new routines that brought her and each of her parents closer together as they worked through developing hope and healing.

Foster development of your children's self-confidence. One of the ways you can help your children develop self-confidence is to help them identify and develop special talents and interests that they really enjoy. Knowing that they have some unique abilities and achievements gives children an added reason to feel good about themselves. These skills can also provide a healthy outlet for stress and a way to exercise some control over a part of their lives, both of which further contribute to children's sense of their own competence.

But self-confidence is a result of many factors. Taken together, all of the skills described in this chapter encourage and empower children to develop genuine feelings of self-efficacy—empathize with others, understand and manage their own emotions, cope with difficulties, understand what they can and cannot control, and effectively solve problems.

The Story of Adam

A few years ago I was facilitating a support group of ten- to twelve-year-olds who were at different points adjusting to their parents' divorce. One of the more challenging members of the group was eleven-year-old Adam. Like many children his age who faced similar situations, Adam was very angry and frustrated. His hair hung like a curtain over his eyes, and he brushed it aside only long enough to smirk at me as he slammed the door or banged his chair against the wall. His typical mode of expression was to yell.

Over the course of several weeks, the group worked on developing problem-solving skills, managing anger productively, and communicating with "I" messages, and we talked about using these strategies to make things better in some of their personal situations. Most of the group members were engaged and enthusiastic about the process. Everyone got a chance to share a problem, and then the group offered help in brainstorming solutions, role-playing communication skills, and developing a plan of action for solving their problems. Individuals then tested out their plan "live" with the real players and reported back to the group about how it worked. Everyone was eager to hear about the outcomes, and a feeling of eagerness filled the room.

Everyone except Adam, that is. He displayed a false bravado, with indifference and disdain as shields to protect his vulnerability. He was also disruptive, tossing spitballs, doing his best to disrupt the flow of group process, and generally making my job more difficult. Adam was not an easy convert to problem solving, nor was he an optimist who believed that things could get better. Quite the opposite.

But I am an optimist, especially when it comes to reaching kids like Adam. I did my best to engage him rather than do battle. I could see that he really did want to be part of the group. He never missed a session and always arrived early. I worked with the group to engage Adam, rather than "tell him to leave" as one of the kids suggested. My sense was that Adam had already experienced plenty of rejection and loss, so it was important to find a way to give him hope and keep him connected.

Two of the children who befriended Adam early on in the group encouraged him to share a problem that they could help him with. Adam was adamant. "No way! Nothing ever works with my mother. She's the supreme commander. I'm not even gonna bother." With a bit more encouragement, we got him to identify one thing that "kinda bugged" him; he insisted it was "really no big deal."

It was late May, and Father's Day was coming soon. Adam's dad lived out of state, and Adam really wanted to see him on Father's Day. "I sorta wanted to see my dad for Father's Day, but my mom said it's not my weekend—no can do. The Empress of the Universe has spoken!" For the first time, Adam opened up to the group.

We listened as he described his frequent battles with his mother and his inconsistent and infrequent contact with his dad. There had been so much anger that Adam wondered whether his parents even knew that he loved them. Sadness and loss were just below the angry surface of this child who had grown up too fast, with too many moves and losses. Although he tried to mask his feelings, it was clear that he wanted what all children want—to love and be loved by both parents.

We began to brainstorm potential solutions to Adam's problem. We wondered with him whether this was a solvable problem or one beyond his control. With the support of his peers, he decided that he would never know if the problem could be solved unless he tried. With this brave decision, the group began with renewed energy to help Adam figure out all the skills it would take for him to approach his mom in a new way. The first was for Adam to manage his impulse to yell or slam the door and find a more productive way to communicate. Then we encouraged him to acknowledge that in the past, he had said some things in anger that he didn't mean, and to apologize. Then we helped Adam practice how to ask for what he wanted in a calm and respectful way. Instead of attacking, blaming, or demanding, he learned to use "I" messages.

We took turns practicing these skills in a role play in which sometimes I was Adam and he was his mom. So he got a chance to show me how "mean" she could be, and my job, in the role of Adam, was to keep my cool and remember to take deep breaths and stick with his new problem-solving approach. He tested out how it would feel to say, "I'd like to talk to you about something important, Mom. Is this a good time?"

The group offered encouragement and honest feedback about various solutions. They all worked hard to generate alternative approaches and solutions. Adam even took notes that he kept on a tiny slip of paper in his pocket to remind him of his new skills. After a few sessions, Adam was ready to try his plan at home over the weekend.

When he came back to the group the next Monday, a change was evident. He arrived early, as usual, but with his shirt tucked in, hair out of eyes, and even a smile that replaced the familiar smirk. He looked happier and more confident—and more like a child than the tough wannabe adult he had been trying to project.

We eagerly asked him how it went, and he gave a thumbs-up sign. We were all eager to hear all the details, which Adam shared with pride. He had used a lot of the communication and problem-solving steps we had role-played, and remained respectful throughout. When he asked his mother if she had time to talk, she was caught off guard, and asked him, "What's wrong?" Adam had responded, "I know that I get really mad at you sometimes and say some terrible things, but I don't really mean them. I want you to know that I love you. On Mother's Day, it was important for me to be with you. But I love Dad, too, and it's really important to me to be with him on Father's Day. I hope we can work together, and I hope you'll help me find a solution to this problem. It would mean a lot to me, Mom." Adam's mom was stunned at first by the change in her son's approach to her—then overjoyed and grateful, and deeply moved to want to help him be with his dad.

When Adam described what had happened, there was a palpable change in the group. We all listened with rapt attention, and the students cheered when Adam announced that his mom agreed to contact his dad and work it out.

Adam did get to see his dad for Father's Day—and as a result, much more frequently thereafter. He even expressed his gratitude to his mother, and to all of us in the group, "for being there for me." The children shared a collective sense of triumph about Adam's success, and they all gained competence and confidence through their work together.

Even though these children could not change the reality of divorce, they now knew how to make better choices and control some aspects of their lives. Their new skills helped them to become more positive and optimistic about their lives and futures. Of course there will be other challenges and setbacks for Adam and all children, but with these skills to draw on, they are more confident, competent, resourceful and resilient.

Although Adam had the benefit of working through his problem and developing new skills in the context of a therapeutic group, you can adapt and use with your children much of what he learned and how he learned. Giving your child space and encouragement even when he is defiant, helping him learn to identify and clearly define a problem, developing a strategy and skills and support for his courage in using them, and ultimately celebrating his success are all practices that you can adopt. As Adam's story reveals, it often takes time and patience to help a child who is overloaded with feelings get to the point of being willing to open up and learn new approaches. But the result often pays dividends. Not only does your child solve an immediate problem, he also learns an array of skills that build his resilience and give him important lifelong tools.

I have told Adam's story and written this chapter with complete conviction that teaching children these skills really makes a difference for them. These principles are based on a wealth of research conducted over the years with children of varied ages and backgrounds. The overwhelming proof that these principles have an immediate and lasting impact on children's lives has been demonstrated by the thousands I have seen over the years in support groups and in my own clinical practice. I am convinced that you can use them to have the same kind of impact on your own child.

SEVEN

Emotionally Intelligent Parenting
Before, During, and After Divorce

Every family situation is unique, but there are many practices you can use or adapt to help your children through the difficult period surrounding your divorce and long after. Research on a broad range of families has identified behaviors and habits of parents that contribute to healthy family relationships; these same parenting behaviors and habits likewise help children adjust well after divorce.

Quality parenting—by both parents—is a proven source of resilience in children, including those whose parents divorce. This kind of parenting occurs in countless small, everyday interactions as well as times of crisis or big decisions. Communicating often and effectively, listening responsively, responding empathetically, managing conflict respectfully, establishing positive discipline and clear expectations for behavior, and affirming children's efforts and behaviors that reflect positive values are all part of quality parenting on a daily basis. Above all, repeatedly telling and showing children how much they are loved and reinforcing those words with physical affection make an enormous difference for children. These parenting practices form a foundation that makes it possible to work through the tough times together. When such parenting becomes habitual, the outcomes generally are strong and gratifying parent-child relationships and enhanced child well-being.

This chapter provides research-based information about positive parenting practices, and then offers clear, practical advice about how to provide emotionally intelligent parenting during and after a divorce. It is ideal if both parents agree to adopt these practices, but even if only one of you does so, your children will benefit.

How "Quality Parenting" Protects Children

Researchers define "quality parenting," or "authoritative parenting," as that characterized by emotional warmth and nurturance, effective discipline, and protection from ongoing conflict between parents. Quality parenting is one of the best predictors of children's adjustment when their parents are married, and it remains equally if not more important after divorce. Loving, authoritative parenting is strongly related to academic success, children's ability to manage their own behavior, reduced incidents of emotional difficulties, and increased long-term well-being. Whether in married or divorced families, good parenting is about the balance of two essential ingredients for raising healthy children: love and limits.

Based on these core pillars of parenting, child development researchers typically define different styles of parenting in four categories: authoritative, authoritarian, indulgent, and neglectful.

- An **authoritative** (quality) parenting style includes warmth, emotional support, effective discipline, and age-appropriate expectations for children. It is related to a number of positive outcomes for children, including those whose parents end their marriage.
- **Authoritarian** parenting is rigid, with strict discipline, but little warmth and emotional support. Children of authoritarian parents tend to be compliant in early years but may rebel during adolescence in response to being tightly controlled during their childhood.

- An **indulgent** parenting style allows children much freedom but lacks discipline, clear rules, and limits. Children need and want limits and feel more secure when they know the rules and what is expected of them. Children raised with lax discipline tend to be impulsive and less aware and respectful of other people's boundaries and needs.
- Children of **neglectful** parents who do not provide nurturing parenting or set limits for them suffer the most and tend to be overrepresented among those unfortunate children with the most serious problems.

Quality parenting is related to healthier relationships between children and parents. Of all the risk factors associated with divorce, disruptions in the relationships between parents and their children appear to have the greatest potential to affect children negatively in the long term.

Unfortunately, even when both divorced parents remain a part of their children's lives, many do not develop the strong, positive parent-child relationships so important to children's growth and development. Current research shows that weak emotional bonds between parents and children often result in a variety of negative long-term outcomes, including more psychological distress in adulthood, greater unhappiness, less life satisfaction, more symptoms of anxiety and depression, a diminished sense of personal control over their lives, and greater use of mental health services. Children who suffer the greatest emotional struggles are those who receive low-quality parenting from both parents who are in high conflict—a triple threat to children's mental health.

At a time when so much may seem beyond your control, it's especially important to remember what a powerful difference your own parenting behavior can make for your children, even if your former partner does not share your views, or is unable to parent effectively. By learning how to focus on the areas within your control and adopting many of the practices described in this chapter, you can build strong, positive relationships with your children and help them grow into confident, fulfilled adults.

Jessica—A Heartening Update

The story of Jessica, the young girl described in the introduction, had a more positive outcome because of her parents' dedicated efforts. With Jessica's permission, I showed her "miserable face" drawing to her parents and shared her description of "how all the good stuff has gone away since they separated, like how they used to snuggle me at night."

Both Paul and Carol were quiet at first, stunned by the depth of

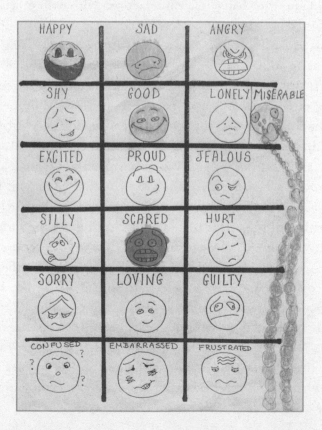

their daughter's sadness. Carol spoke first. "I never realized she was listening to my phone conversations. I thought she was in bed, and I do need some time to talk to friends. Paul has no problem with any of this because it's what he wanted."

Paul became defensive immediately and began to justify his reasons for the divorce. Even while they were trying to stay focused on Jessica's needs, how easy it was for them to slip back into old destructive patterns of communication. I pointed to Jessica's picture on the small chair next to us as a reminder of how much she needed them to parent her so that the "good stuff" could come back into her life again.

Carol and Paul responded with genuine concern and asked, "Where do we go from here?" Separately and together, both made a concerted effort to change their interactions with each other, Jessica, and her sister.

Carol was still juggling a busy, full-time job and caring for the girls three to four days a week. When she wasn't at the office, she frequently was online or checking her messages. She began to realize that her "busyness" was a way of avoiding her own painful emotions and undermining her fervent desire to be a good parent. After seeing Jessica's drawing and hearing her other daughter ask when *she* could get on Carol's calendar, Carol was determined to be more available and involved with her girls. When the children were with her, she stopped having prolonged phone conversations with her friends, and she waited until they were in bed before spending time online. She started having brief family meetings to talk with the children about how things were going, make plans for the week and the future, discuss concerns, and solve problems together. When the children's fighting got out of control and physical, Carol no longer just ignored it or yelled at them, but established clear, consistent rules and consequences. With coaching, she launched what she called her "campaign to catch them being good" and commented on their efforts to share toys, solve problems on their own, and help with chores around the house.

Paul instituted changes at his house, too. He made a concerted effort to leave his work at the office and ask the children what they would enjoy doing during their time with him, in addition to their regular schoolwork and extracurricular activities. Together, they developed a much-loved ritual of making their favorite dinners together and going to the Y to swim and play basketball on weekends. Both parents agreed to set consistent limits about the children's screen time and bedtimes and follow through on their responsibilities.

In addition, both parents recognized the importance of creating more one-on-one time with each of their children. Together, we modified the schedule in their parenting plan so that each child had some "alone" time with each parent every week, in addition to the times they spent together with each of them. Equally important, both parents made a firm commitment not to vent their anger and hostility about the other parent—even if they thought the children were asleep or otherwise unable to hear the comments. Thanks to Jessica's ability to express her distress and her parents' willingness to listen, both parents took care to safeguard bedtime rituals and her cherished "snuggle time" at night.

Carol and Paul also realized the need for better communication with their children. Since Jessica was more comfortable expressing herself through writing and drawing than talking, we developed a plan for them to connect with her and her sister through frequent, nonthreatening communication. They created a shared journal for each of the girls, in which they could draw pictures, write anything at all, and ask questions. Carol and Paul both wrote back, answering questions, offering thoughts, and gently asking their own questions. These journals turned into a safe, effective way to communicate all the way around, particularly because the children used them with both parents in both of their homes.

Before long, Jessica's drawings began to reflect a greater sense of security and well-being, her grades improved, and she began to smile more often. I grew to admire this family greatly. Because their deep love and concern for their children surpassed all other issues in their lives, and because they chose to learn new parenting skills and persist in applying them even during tough times, both parents formed strong relationships with their children. As a result, Jessica and her sister today are confident teenagers with good friends, optimism, positive plans for their future, and the assurance that both of their parents will remain a constant, loving presence in their lives.

Ten Emotionally Intelligent Parenting Practices That Promote Children's Well-Being

These days, you're likely to feel inundated with advice—much of it conflicting—on how to raise your children. New fads emerge regularly, and parents are given a handful of rules with the promise that following these will improve their children's self-esteem and/or make them smarter, happier, better behaved, or more successful in college and their future lives. All too often, these fail to include any discussion of the underlying relationship between parents and children, which is the vital foundation on which children's growth is built.

Research and clinical experience have shown that using these emotionally intelligent parenting practices can help your child not only survive the changes in your family but thrive immediately and over the long term.

1. Find Time, Make Time. In many families—including non-divorced families—even the most dedicated parenting is thwarted by the frantic busyness that characterizes both parents' and children's lives. One place to begin a new positive parenting effort is to declare supremacy over the calendar and find ways to reduce the number and frequency of activities that separate family members from one another.

With overcrowded schedules further complicated by arrangements to enable children to spend time with both parents, the calendar often assumes a kind of authority of its own, driving out the breathing room to just live and be. You will need determination, discipline, and

often collaboration to set priorities and decide which activities are most important—particularly when these compete with open space that may seem like wasted time or indolence in our culture. But clearing out space on the calendar is essential to establishing a meaningful family structure and opening up the time for the easy, open, ongoing communication essential to growing strong relationships.

2. Create One-on-One Time. As I discussed in chapter 4, one of the most important things you can do for your children is to create frequent, regular, pleasant occasions when you give your full attention to just one child. Such times provide opportunities for you to listen and observe carefully, to strengthen the bonds with your children, and to express your love, affection, and reassurance, as well as just to have fun being together. Creating such occasions does *not* mean lavishing children with special treats or gifts, but, rather, playing and sharing activities that bring you closer together. Your time and attention are the real gifts—the ones they will remember and cherish.

Reading together is a pleasant activity with multiple benefits that can be built into one-on-one time and daily routines. Studies show that reading to young children is one of the most important things a parent can do to ensure their success in school. Not only does reading benefit children's language development, which is the single strongest predictor of school success, it also strengthens emotional connections between parents and their children.

Play and other activities that children choose can be structured in ways that allow you and your child the opportunity to build closer emotional connections. For example, in working a puzzle or playing a game with your toddler or young child, it is best to let your child take the lead and then comment positively on his efforts and feelings, rather than tell him what to do, how to do it, or how to do it better. "It was hard to figure out those pieces to the puzzle, but you didn't give up. You figured it out. How proud you must feel!"

With an older child or teen, you might ask for "some time together—just the two of us" and offer a few options, letting her choose among those activities. Structuring the choices precludes a teen's making demands that may undermine the purpose of this time together or even strain your goodwill. Activities like going for a bike ride, playing a game together, or doing another activity focused on an interest you share are preferable to shopping sprees. Activities that create expectations for your wallet to open wide often dilute the real purpose of enjoying pleasurable, meaningful time together.

3. Establish New Family Rituals and Traditions. As a family is reconfigured, it is important to find activities that everyone enjoys and to create new rituals and traditions that convey the message that *we are still family.* If you and your children enjoy the natural world, regularly spending time together outdoors gives children a model of a healthy way to reduce stress as well as the enjoyment of time together in an environment you both cherish. Activities like hiking, camping, canoeing, riding bikes, doing crafts, cooking, and playing board games all promote interaction. New traditions, such as Paul's swimming-and-cooking nights with his children, send children a message that there are still many good things about their family and strengthen their bonds with their parents. Such activities help to normalize the new family configuration, reestablishing a sense of wholeness and connectedness. Designating a particular night of the week "Family

Fun Night" helps to create a tradition and routine that children look forward to and gives them a sense of secure family connections.

One parent recently told me that her thirteen-year-old son had invited some of his friends over to join in the family board games. As the evening unfolded, all of the boys relaxed, cracked jokes, and practically fell out of their chairs from laughing so hard. The mother was understandably delighted, seeing these young teens straddle childhood and adolescence in the safe structure of their relatively new family-night tradition. Such occasions provide building blocks that form a solid foundation for close and enduring relationships.

4. Express Appreciation and Gratitude. Mother Teresa said, "Kind words can be short and easy to speak but their echoes are truly endless." Research shows that healthy families—divorced or not—regularly incorporate genuine expressions of appreciation and encouragement for one another. The relatively new field of positive psychology highlights the value of expressions of gratitude in strengthening relationships and providing emotional benefits to those involved both in giving and in receiving the gratitude. Taking the time to notice and express appreciation for acts of kindness or consideration creates goodwill that fuels hope, optimism, and loving relationships.

Yet children often report that, in the aftermath of divorce, they "don't often hear much that's good" about themselves, and they yearn for recognition of what they are doing right. Once Carol realized how important this was to her daughters, she made a point of noticing and commenting on their positive attitudes and behaviors more frequently. Among her most touching comments to Jessica: "There are so many things about you that I love. I'm grateful that you had the courage to tell us how sad you were feeling so that we could figure out ways to make things better in our family." Such expressions surely help to promote hope, optimism, and healing.

Giving a heartfelt expression of gratitude is a skill that is enhanced with practice. The key is giving appreciations that stick like Velcro, instead of the quick "Hey, thanks!" that slips off like Teflon. Appreciations that stick are those that are genuine and specific and express how the person's actions made you feel. When Carol saw a cleaned-up family room, she said to Jessica, "I'm so grateful that you cleaned up the family room without my asking. I was so tired when I came home from work today, but when I saw that clean room, I felt so relieved and happy that it was done. Now we can use that time to do something fun together."

With comments like these, parents can help their children immensely by "catching them being good." Along with effective discipline and containing conflict, reinforcing children's positive behavior is a component of quality parenting with proven results.

Such positive attention is always important, but it is needed throughout a separation and divorce more than almost any other time in life. Children need their parents' attention and reassurance particularly because of the uncertainty in their lives. Giving children positive feedback helps to promote healthy behaviors and is far more effective than criticism or negative comments. By contrast, research has shown that children who experience continuous criticism either tune it out or begin to adjust their behavior to meet the negative expectations implied in critical comments. A valuable guide for healthy family relationships is to make five positive comments for every negative one.

You can help your children immensely by reinforcing their efforts and focusing less on outcomes. For example, you can offer encouragement by saying, "Good for you for hanging in there with those math problems. They were challenging, but you didn't give up. I like your persistence!" By contrast, if you praise only the good test score, the gold medal in track, or the flawless piano performance, this sends the message that you love your children for their accomplishments rather than for who they are. This sometimes backfires, making love feel conditional and resulting in children feeling pressured to succeed at all costs—or to just give up.

5. Convey Hope and Healing. In spite of the powerful emotions surrounding divorce, it is important that you communicate a positive sense of hope about the future to your child. A message such as "We've had some big changes in our family, but you still have two parents who love you, and we'll help each other get through this" acknowledges the difficulties but delivers real reassurance and hope. This approach also helps you come to terms with your divorce more readily, as it helps your children accept the family changes, feel more optimistic about the future, and worry less about you or their other parent. Unlike the child in chapter 1 who said, "I guess the divorce has made things better for Mom (or Dad), but not for me," children are able to develop a healthier viewpoint when you communicate positives. When you deliver authentic messages of hope and healing and follow up with behaviors that make these outcomes possible, you give your children some of the ingredients they need to grow up secure and confident.

6. Listen Beyond the Words and Respond with Empathy. "Active" listening is an invaluable skill that improves with practice. One way to open up communication is to signal its importance by setting aside other activities. This does not mean that you must yield to every interruption, particularly with young children who need to learn they cannot immediately command your attention every time they want something. But children notice when you are preoccupied, so it helps to send a signal that you are interested, ready to pay attention, and really listen. Putting down the newspaper, turning off the TV, or turning away from the computer and looking directly and affectionately at a child is an invitation to shared communication. These simple gestures say, "You are important to me. I want to hear what you have to say." Even though most daily conversations are not deep and serious, the pattern of easy and frequent interaction allows the big discussions to occur when they are needed.

A second aspect of active listening also encourages your children to open up. Remain neutral and nonjudgmental, yet let your children know you are listening. It is important to convey to your children that all of their feelings—even the most troubling and painful to hear—are acceptable, and that it is okay and important to express them.

Your instinct may be to always want to fix or remove such feelings. And so you might say, "Don't cry," or "Don't be sad." Although you may have the very best intentions in making such statements, children often interpret them as, "I don't want to know about your sadness." An important part of feeling loved and understood is having our feelings heard and accepted—not minimized or dismissed. Children find it far more comforting to have their feelings acknowledged sympathetically with a parent's gentle presence and kind response. "I'm sorry you're feeling so sad. I'm here to be with you because I care and always will love you."

One expression I hear often from children—"Divorce sucks!"—is particularly difficult for many parents to hear. This shorthand expression conveys a big bundle of emotions and feeds into the guilt and worry they already feel about the impact of their divorce on their children. Additionally, many parents strongly object to the word "sucks," making it even harder to respond to the underlying emotions.

But when you can set aside your own uncomfortable feelings and the impulse to correct the language, you may realize that your child has just given you an important opportunity to work through the painful emotions that underlie those explosive words. An empathetic, nonjudgmental response can be very helpful: "Divorce *is* hard. I know this isn't anything you would have chosen, and that's especially frustrating for you. I realize this is hard right now, and I wish it could be different." More than ever, at times when children's emotions explode in such expressions, they need hugs and reminders that they are deeply loved and always will be. Once children feel heard and understood, they are much more likely to engage in conversations and willing to solve problems.

7. Maintain Household Structure and Routines. As I've discussed elsewhere in this book, having consistent structure at home helps children to feel safer and more secure when their lives have just been turned topsy-turvy. Appropriate, regular bedtimes, meals together, and a limit on time spent in front of a TV or computer screen are all factors that have proven to positively influence grades and test scores, reduce the need for disciplinary actions, and foster better social and emotional adjustment.

Children sometimes have difficulty sleeping when they feel stressed, so establishing a regular bedtime and a ritual that helps them release their anxiety and go to sleep is particularly important. Getting enough sleep influences children's ability to perform their best in school, sports, music, and other activities. Equally important, sleep, along with good nutrition, is essential to maintaining good health— for you and your children.

Daily meals with the family gathered around the dinner table have become less frequent in our busy lives, yet studies repeatedly underscore the benefits of mealtime conversations and interactions that strengthen family bonds and create warm and lasting memories. Some studies even suggest that sharing family meals together helps to reduce the risk of drug use and precocious sexual activity in teens. Although it can be tough to schedule shared family meals around various activities, it is possible to limit other intrusions on this ritual, such as letting phone calls go to voice mail and turning off the TV. Lingering over a meal together not only fosters communication and family bonds, but also helps to develop important social skills that enable children to enter the adult world with greater confidence. Discussing highs and lows of the day at the dinner table, cuddling and reading together at bedtime, and even doing chores together can build a strong sense of family belonging.

Establishing household routines also means ensuring a structure for homework and other activities that enable children to develop their minds and talents. You can build in check-ins during homework time to set appropriate standards for the quality of your children's work, help with difficulties, and offer encouragement and support. By doing this, you communicate that their schoolwork is important.

Creating structure for the family includes not only managing the daily calendar, but also building in meaningful times for you and your children to communicate with one another and share affection. Physical affection is so important for children of all ages and is related to their physical and emotional well-being. Yet in the midst of stressful times, a time when children and adults most need it, affection easily slips away. Developing other special routines with each parent can be very helpful in the wake of divorce. For instance, taking your children to their favorite park on weekends creates a pleasant routine that they look forward to and a pressure-free way to connect.

8. *Point Out Resilience Role Models.* Like most of us, as children go through hard times, they find it deeply comforting and empowering to realize they are not alone. Discovering that there are people who have survived and even thrived through difficult times—whether the circumstances are exactly the same or not—can give hope to children who believe that their family's troubles are unique.

The stories of many successful public figures whose parents divorced or who overcame obstacles such as poverty, major illness, or profound life changes can serve as encouraging examples for children. Equally important, family and friends whom your child knows may be excellent models for resilience, and some may even be willing to share their experiences and the paths they took to feeling whole and pursuing their goals.

In many ways, *you* are the most important role model for your child. If your child sees you dealing with difficult times with hope and resilience, they are learning important life lessons. This does not mean that you never feel angry, sad, or depressed, but that you acknowledge these emotions and deal with them effectively. This means seeking support and help when needed, taking care of yourself physically, emotionally, and spiritually, and focusing on what is solvable and within your control to change for the better. Children learn through your example, and they also learn by talking with you about how you are trying to manage your differences peacefully, solve problems, and make aspects of family life better for them.

9. *Encourage Spiritual Experiences.* Many studies identify a faith-filled, spiritual orientation as an important component of strong families and well-adjusted youth. This includes a wide range of beliefs and experiences, including but not limited to participation in religious institutions. For many, belief in God or a higher power is a fundamental

source of spiritual strength. For others, spirituality may be found through meditation, appreciation of nature or the wider universe, involvement in compassionate outreach and charitable causes, or connecting with others in exploration of values and larger meaning in life.

Healthy families tend to be guided by an underlying moral compass, compassion for others, and a strong value system. Studies of adolescents show that the protective effects of spirituality include fewer risk-taking behaviors and greater regard for themselves and others. For many, me included, faith and spirituality provide a strong sense of meaning in life and an anchor during turbulent times.

With children who are old enough to deal with abstract concepts, it can be helpful to encourage them to think about a spiritual perspective or to reach out with compassion to those in need. Doing so helps to put their own situation in a larger context and feel connected to a spiritual being or a sense of the greater good, or both.

10. Engage in a Community. The link between social connectedness and children's well-being is well-established in research. Reaching out to become involved in supportive networks and community groups is especially important during divorce and other times of major life changes. Social connectedness—particularly in multigenerational communities of people who are committed to one another and the greater good—is highly correlated with positive child and youth development. The ancient African proverb that it takes a village to raise a child—in our terms, a healthy, resilient child—is well supported in research.

For parents who are reconfiguring their families, the implications are clear. Even though it may be tempting to withdraw, it is important to maintain a social structure for yourself and for your children. Family, circles of friends, school, church, and other networks of relationships are more important than ever. If these must change for any reason, it is important to replace them with other networks of people who can share in creating a community that provides love, support, and a value structure in nurturing you and your children.

Love and Limits: Creating Structure and Effective Discipline

As important as all of these emotionally intelligent parenting practices are to helping children thrive, equally critical are the practices of revealing love through empathetic support and maintaining structure and clear limits on behavior. Children thrive when they know they are loved, and they feel most safe and secure when they live within a consistent structure of guidelines and boundaries for their behavior—in other words, discipline. The root of the English word "discipline" is the Latin *disciplina*, which means "teaching" or "learning." This is the spirit of child-centered discipline that I encourage parents to adopt—one that teaches children what is expected of them and then holds them accountable to those standards.

Parents usually have and continually develop their own vocabulary of words and actions that express both love and limits. In the throes of a divorce, however, they are sometimes so overwhelmed by their own feelings that this vocabulary fades into the background.

I once read an article in a popular parenting magazine advocating that parents should tell their children they love them once a week, whether the parents think they need to hear it or not. I was astonished to think that something so essential to every adult and child—to hear that they are loved—would occur only once a week. In support groups and individual therapy sessions, I have heard too many children wonder about their essential lovability, question whether their parents would be happier if they had never been born, and cover deep insecurities about their own worth with drug use, sexual promiscuity, or other forms of rebellious behavior. Countless times, children in our various support groups have given this advice to parents: "Tell us you love us. Even if we act like we already know, please tell us again. We need to hear and feel it all the time." Their lives need to be filled with words and interactions that express affection, warmth, nurturing, encouragement, concern, listening, responsiveness, affirmation, and limits—all very real expressions of love.

The other face of parental love is caring enough to set clear expectations, limits, and consequences. When parents set firm ground rules requiring appropriate and respectful behavior and fulfillment of responsibilities, monitor their children's behavior, and provide consistent follow-through and enforcement, they provide a strong and loving structure that helps children and teens to feel loved and secure. As I've discussed, knowing how they are expected to behave gives children a sense of control over their own behavior. They feel a basic sense of trust and security, even as they learn new skills within a loving structure.

The period surrounding a divorce is sometimes made even more difficult for parents when their children behave in boldly defiant or unexpected new ways because of their own stress. Often, the intense feelings they do not know how to handle—sadness, grief, loss, anger, fear, jealousy—come out in totally inappropriate behaviors. If your children act out, you need to be very clear that although all of their feelings are acceptable, all behaviors are not. Any behavior that has the potential to hurt the child himself, another person, or an animal, or to damage property, is completely unacceptable and must be stopped. Likewise, swearing and hateful words are disrespectful of others and will ultimately add to a child's problems.

Using authoritative parenting, you can help your children by listening and accepting the feelings underlying their actions at the same time that you set firm limits on unacceptable behavior. "I know you are sad and angry about all the changes in your life, but it is not okay to take out your feelings by hitting your brother (or throwing the remote, or swearing at me)." The combination of loving understanding and insistence on living by clear rules is the most powerful and effective means of raising children to become responsible, confident, and secure.

Why Is Limit Setting So Important Before, During, and After Divorce?

There are many negative consequences for children who grow up without discipline, not the least of which are their own deep-seated fears that their parents do not believe they are capable of good behavior and that no one cares enough to pay attention and demand their best. As one anxious child commented to me about a parent who was extremely lax with her, "All she ever says is 'I guess' when I ask if I can do something. It's like she doesn't even have the word 'no' in her vocabulary." Other consequences are, of course, that children get into trouble at school, are rejected by their peers and adults, and ultimately behave in ways that may be dangerous to their health or well-being.

Research shows that, in the midst of family upheaval and stress, one parenting practice that often declines is prompt and effective discipline to correct children's inappropriate behavior. Sometimes parents feel guilty that their children are hurting and are understandably reluctant to add to their distress. They worry that authoritative discipline will do just that. It is particularly difficult for parents who believe they are cast in the role of "bad guy," while the other gets to be the "fun guy." While these are painful situations for conscientious parents, all of the evidence shows that those who consistently provide both love and limits, rather than acting like a buddy or a confidante, give their children the lifelong gift of learning how to manage strong emotions and assume responsibility. Home is the primary—and sometimes the only—place where children learn a model of self-control, develop ethics and values, and are given the ground rules for responsible living. Failing to provide those critical abilities and develop a code of values leaves children without a moral compass and rudder to navigate their lives.

Consistent discipline throughout the divorce process is particularly important for several reasons. First, given the uncertainties surrounding their parents' divorce, children often feel that their lives are out of control. Not surprisingly, they sometimes find it more difficult than usual to manage their emotions, and they act out in a variety of inappropriate ways. When their behavior pushes acceptable limits, they become even more fearful, anxious, and insecure, and these feelings are magnified when their parents fail to step in and take control. Children seldom admit to wanting more structure and discipline, but misbehavior is often a plea for parents to set limits and insist that their children adhere to them.

A second reason for maintaining discipline is that children's inappropriate behavior ultimately results in negative responses. The discipline or criticism they receive from teachers, friends' parents, and others in authority can feel humiliating. Worse, if they are excluded from situations because of behavior problems, they can become increasingly isolated and worry that they may be permanently excluded or abandoned. In the worst cases, youths and teens who seriously flaunt the rules become—and begin to see themselves as—troublemakers, always on the wrong side of authority. The consequences for them can be dire. While some may appear to shrug off threats of rehabilitation or jail terms, most of these individuals are deeply troubled and unhappy.

Children's misbehavior has another undesirable consequence: It erodes parents' own positive feelings about them, and this, too, comes back to impact the children. Although continuing to love their children despite behavioral problems, parents often feel disappointed, angry, frustrated, and powerless in these situations. These are miserable feelings for parents to add to those they already feel in connection with their divorce, and they also leave children further alone and adrift from what once was their family.

Setting Limits with Structured Choices

One technique that is particularly effective in setting limits is providing children with structured choices. This approach helps to prevent power struggles by giving children age-appropriate options and the power to make a decision. This structured-choice process fosters children's sense of control during a time when they often feel powerless over family changes, and it largely precludes situations in which children make and stubbornly cling to unreasonable demands. Structured choices are not about major life decisions, but day-to-day details, within reason. Here are some examples, with their underlying messages for engaging the cooperation of young children:

"Let's see. Green pajamas tonight or red ones? You decide." The parent's underlying message: It's time for bed and you will sleep in pajamas, not daytime clothes.

"Okay. Brush your teeth first or wash your hands first? You choose." The message: These are bedtime routines.

"Bath or shower? Bubbles or no bubbles? You decide." The message: You must get clean.

"Will you be turning off your light after you finish reading your book, or do you want me to come back in fifteen minutes to turn it off?" The message: Reading time is limited; the light must be turned off in fifteen minutes.

In establishing choices for young children, it is important to make the options simple, as they are easily overwhelmed by too much freedom, too many choices, and lack of structure. At age five, our daughter Kristen showed why structured choices work so well. We were in a restaurant, and the waitress asked whether the children wanted dessert. She then described all the possibilities for a fantastic ice cream sundae: various toppings and candies and nuts and whipped cream and cherries. As Kristen's eyes grew wider in delicious anticipation, I could see she was overwhelmed by too many choices. How could she possibly decide among all these wonders? When I leaned over and suggested that she just choose one or two toppings, relief crossed her face, and our little girl actually said, "Thank you for making the limit."

Note: Do *not* expect your adolescent to thank you for setting limits. Ours never did! Nonetheless, the use of structured choices is effective with older children, too. With teens' growing need for autonomy and independence, structured choices respect their need to make some decisions, while making it clear that they have responsibilities. Chores, time frames, and the sequence of activities all provide opportunities for choices without undermining the essential requirements. Here are some examples:

"Are you going to change the cat litter before you start your homework or after?" The message: Both homework and chores need to be done.

"Are you going to do your math homework at Dad's or skip the movie and do it when you get home tomorrow?" The message: Homework will be done on time.

Structured choices can be a very effective way of engaging cooperation for daily routines, too. For example, one afternoon I had to pick up our daughter from school. I was in a hurry to leave, but our young son didn't want to leave the comfort of his home and toys and go out in the cold. Already late and clearly needing to leave, I noticed our cat, Puff, curled up on a nearby chair. I said to my son, "We need to leave now. Do you want to go get in the car with Puff, or without him?" He was surprised and delighted at the prospect of bringing the cat along for the ride, and I've never seen a child move so quickly! (In Puff's best interests, we kept his role in structured choices to a minimum!)

Even with skilled efforts to redirect and encourage cooperation, there are, of course, times when stronger limits and consequences need to be set on aggressive or inappropriate behavior, while teaching children constructive ways to express emotions.

One such technique that therapists and parents have used successfully is a five-step process that accepts the child's feelings while firmly setting limits on inappropriate behavior.

1. Acknowledge and reflect the child's feelings.
2. State the limit.
3. Provide acceptable alternative ways for the child to deal with his emotions.

4. Restate the appropriate behavior and the consequences for not following the rule.
5. Reflect the child's feelings about the limit.

Here's how it works. Five-year-old Jason is busy building with blocks when his three-year-old sister comes by and knocks over his tower. Jason jumps up, crying, and throws some of the blocks at his sister. His mother, Ann, knows that Jason has been struggling with the changes in his life since the separation and has been misbehaving more frequently. Although she is tired and feeling guilty about initiating the separation, she realizes it would be a mistake to overlook Jason's misbehavior. Ann uses the approach to discipline described above.

"Jason, I see that you're really mad at your sister for knocking over your tower." (She acknowledges his feelings.)

"But blocks are for building, NOT for throwing. They could hurt someone." (She firmly states the rule and sets a limit on the behavior.)

"You can tell your sister in words how frustrated and mad you feel, or you can draw a picture to show how you feel." (She suggests an alternative, acceptable behavior.)

"Blocks are not for throwing. If they get thrown again, they will be put away for today." (She states the consequence as she restates the rule.)

(If Jason cries and complains) "I understand you don't like the rule, but it's not going to change. (She reflects his feelings about the limit.)

Following through with the consequence is often difficult, but it is an essential part of the structure that helps children learn what is acceptable, find ways to manage their behavior, and ultimately to feel secure in the knowledge that their parents love and respect them enough to insist on their better behavior. Inconsistent discipline has the unintended effect of increasing children's negative behaviors. If they learn that they can sometimes get their way by crying and acting up, they are far more likely to repeat those behaviors. Whenever it's possible for parents to establish similar general expectations for children's behavior in both homes, it reduces their difficulties in dealing with major differences between their two worlds.

Bridging the Gap Between Two Separate Worlds: Effective Coparenting

"It's weird," said nineteen-year-old Amanda in one of our therapy sessions. "For as long as I can remember, I've been keeping life with my mom completely separate from life with my dad. So when I went to Mom's family reunion last week, I felt like I had to keep half of my life a secret—the half with Dad and his new family. I can hardly bear to think about my college graduation when both sides come together." From an early age, Amanda had worked hard to master the goal of keeping her two worlds separate. Now, as a young adult, she not only struggles with how to integrate these vastly different parts of her life, but also with questions about her own identity.

In *Between Two Worlds*, author Elizabeth Marquardt describes what I have heard children of all ages express repeatedly: the feeling that they must compartmentalize their lives into two completely separate and distinct realities. Her survey of fifteen hundred young men and women documented some marked differences between those who grew up with divorced parents and those who grew up in homes with continuously married parents. Among these differences is the sense that children who grow up in divorced families are "little adults" who often feel compelled to keep secrets that are not their own. These are huge burdens for young adults and can have lifelong repercussions.

You can help your children with this aspect of divorce by working to build bridges that connect the two separate portions of your children's lives. The first step is to acknowledge the two different worlds and deal with the feelings children have about going back and forth. Then, to the extent possible, both you and their other parent need to support their healthy relationship with the other parent and never bad-mouth him or her in front of your child. This can be particularly difficult if you're the one who's been "left," and it may be tempting to align with children who may also feel that they have been "left." Children never benefit by feeling rejected, however, so the most helpful approach is for you to reassure them that both of their parents love them, and if it is safe, to do everything in your power to help ensure that your children have a positive relationship with their other parent.

Maintaining a respectful, courteous attitude when you and your former spouse attend your children's events together is another important way that you can help your children bridge the gap between their two worlds. When you can maintain a professional and respectful attitude toward one another as you attend your children's school activities, sports events, recitals, and other special occasions, you spare them the agony of deciding which side of the room to go to first, or which parent to greet first.

Supporting your children's time with their other parent is sometimes challenging but important. Keeping lines of communication open through nonjudgmental conversations about your children's time with their other parent is helpful as long as it doesn't slip into prying, interrogating, or asking them to keep or betray secrets, all of which would cause them further pain and sadness. It is most helpful if both you and your former spouse consistently reassure the child of your own love, and whenever possible, also of the love of their other parent. Ten-year-old Allison's drawing of an imagined bridge between her parents is decorated with hearts and flowers—symbolic of her comfort and ease in going back and forth, thanks to her parents' dedicated efforts to bridge her two worlds.

You can also help to close the gap between your children's two homes by establishing similar rules and limits at both households and comparable consequences when your children step outside the bounds. Communicating about important aspects of your children's lives, including discipline, helps to smooth their transitions and build a bridge between homes with consistent parenting. The ideal, of course,

is to focus on positive ways to set and communicate expectations and reinforce children's healthy adjustment, rather than to concentrate on their potential misbehavior and negative consequences.

Parenting in this collaborative way is often challenging for former partners, but it can and does happen. Although it takes a concerted effort and commitment, many couples I've known work hard to make parenting their top priority and find ways to agree about the most important responsibility in both of their lives—their children.

And as with other aspects of the new family configuration, paying close attention both to children's words and to their unspoken behaviors enables you to help your children with the gap between their separate worlds. When they come home from a visit with the other parent visibly upset, or when they become withdrawn or exhibit other troubling changes in habits or behaviors, it is important to tune in to them and encourage them to talk about their feelings—when they are ready.

It is normal for children to need some time to readjust, and they may feel out of sorts, tired, or irritable at first. It can be emotionally taxing for them to deal with all their mixed feelings about leaving one parent, and even if they are happy to see the other, making the switch still may stir up feelings of loss and sadness. It's not surprising that children often need some "downtime" to transition from one home to the other. Give them some space—and perhaps a snack—before trying to engage them in conversation.

If your child repeatedly comes home in distress, it may be necessary to find appropriate professional help for them. While it is important not to place blame and jump to the conclusion that a child's distress is caused by their other parent, if a child's stress continues unabated, it is a sign that you need to pay attention and find ways to ease it. Without interrogating your child, you can help them by thoughtfully commenting on how unhappy they seem, and then listening carefully to how they are feeling. It may be helpful for both parents to consult with a mental health professional who can talk first with your child, and later with you and your former partner to provide suggestions on how both of you can best support your child. It may mean making some changes to the schedule, or perhaps just minor adjustments that could make a world of difference for your child. The important message to your child is that his parents are paying attention—and they care.

Advice from Children to Parents

In the groups I have worked with, I am always impressed with children's insights. Often, we talk about what advice they would give to parents, and they always have a lot to say! Not surprisingly, throughout the changes in their families, their advice is generally aligned with the principles of emotionally intelligent parenting. Here are some points that children make frequently:

- **"Tell us what we did right."** Children often say that they seldom hear comments on what they do right. You give your children a lasting gift when you consistently and frequently point out their strengths, appreciate their good deeds, notice their efforts, applaud their successes, and reassure them of your unconditional love for them.

- **"Be honest with us. Tell us if you're getting a divorce, but please spare us the gory details."** Although learning that their parents will divorce is painful for children, it is important for them to understand the changes that will affect their lives. Because they love both parents, they find it exceedingly difficult to hear the details of a parent's infidelity or character flaws. They do need some age-appropriate explanations, however.

- **"Don't use us as bullets. Don't fight in front of us. Don't say, 'Your dad is an idiot.' Don't ask us if Mom is dating."** Among the most difficult situations children experience is to hear one parent make negative comments about the other or treat the other disrespectfully. Children are keenly aware that they are part of two parents, and having one parent denigrated makes them feel that half of them is bad, too.

  It is most helpful if you not only avoid saying negative things to or about the other, but actively convey messages about that parent's positive qualities, especially those that the child has inherited or learned from a parent. Above all, resist the temptation to ask your child about your former partner's personal life—it is one of children's most dreaded dilemmas.

- **"Let us know that it's okay to love both of you. Don't make us choose between the two of you."** In the wake of a divorce, children often feel isolated and unsure about what they can say to each parent. Sometimes, in the midst of pain and conflict, parents unwittingly place their children in the middle of their fight. The children may frequently overhear negative comments about the other parent, or observe an icy silence, a cold war between the two people they love most. The result is that children feel extremely torn, unhappy, insecure, and often angry at one or both parents. In other situations, parents may unconsciously imply that the other parent is not worthy of the children's love.

- **"I can't afford to buy you all the toys like your father can, but I show you my love through the way I make a real home for you."** Children can read between the lines, and what they hear their mother saying is "I earn your love, but your father just tries to buy it." Such statements are confusing and often quite painful for children.

- **"Don't give us everything we want just to get us to like you more than our other parent."** Children are very astute, and they recognize bribery for what it is. Although they may take full advantage of parents' guilt by asking for or even demanding clothes, toys, and treats, they are actually much more comfortable when you set limits. There is no substitute for quality time spent with children and loving, thoughtful attention to what is going on in their lives. These are what children really crave from both parents and what will ultimately win their respect.

- **"Look at your divorce through our eyes, too."** Usually, children are acutely aware of their parents' pain and struggles before, during, and after a divorce, and they often want to protect their parents from their own feelings about it. But they are greatly relieved when their parents acknowledge that divorce is hard on everyone in the family, and that it can mean big changes and difficult challenges for the children, too. Parents can help their children by both noticing how the children are feeling about the changes in their lives and creating an atmosphere that allows them to be open about their feelings and worries.

- **"Let us know that you love us. Even if we act like we already know, tell us again."** Because divorce creates such uncertainty for children, they need frequent reassurance that their parents love them. This advice from children is very telling—"even if we act like we already know" indicates that despite the bravado children may display, they are greatly reassured to hear this all-important message from their parents over and over again.

Although you cannot control the behavior or the choices of your former partner, you do have control over one factor of utmost importance in shaping your children's lives—the quality of family life you create through your own parenting. You give your child a great gift when you nurture a warm, close parenting relationship with your children—one in which you provide both abundant love and safe, secure limits.

EIGHT

. . . .

New Relationships, Dating, and Remarriage: How the Children See Them

Wedding Day—The Bride's Perspective. Tina was radiant. Her wedding day dawned warm and sunny. She hoped the beautiful day was a good omen. She'd had some trepidation about getting remarried, but overall, she thought this would be a wonderful fresh start, full of the promise of love, companionship, security, and stability—a complete change from her unhappy first marriage, its difficult end last year, and the uncertainties that divorce had created.

She had met Richard at the health club just as her divorce was being finalized. He was warm, affectionate, witty, and handsome to boot. In seeking her out, Richard had made her feel desirable and cherished in ways that she had not experienced in many years. He was a good father to his two children and very kind to her eight-year-old son, Marcus. He took the time to coach him on his batting and cheer him on at his Little League games. That was very important to Tina. She loved her son deeply and worked hard to be a good parent. But since the divorce, she found it was tough to balance meeting the obligations of her demanding job, running the household, and giving Marcus the attention she knew he needed. In the past several months, his grades had dropped, and he had become uncharacteristically sullen and disrespectful, occasionally even erupting into bouts of rage.

Tina was worried about him. She hoped that having a man in the house would be good for Marcus, especially because Richard was so kind to him, even when he was unresponsive.

She was anxious for Marcus to feel a part of her wedding and the start of this new family life, so she had given him a special role. He was to be the ring bearer. How sweet he looked in his tuxedo, his curly hair shining. But he seemed pensive now, and Tina wondered what was going through his mind.

Wedding Day—Her Son's Perspective. Marcus sat hunched in his chair, all dressed up in silly, uncomfortable clothes, fidgeting with the pillow that held his mom's and Richard's new wedding rings. "How weird is this?" he thought to himself. "How many kids go to their mother's wedding?" She was supposed to be with his father, not some other guy. This whole wedding business felt just plain wrong to him. As he sat there, Marcus tried to think of ways he could stop this marriage from happening. Maybe he could throw the rings down the toilet. Maybe he could just stand up and shout "NO!" during the ceremony. Maybe he could fake a life-threatening illness and his mom would have to take him to the hospital. Maybe. . . . His mind was whirling with possibilities.

His parents' divorce had come as a complete shock to Marcus. They never fought, and it seemed like they got along as well as any of his friends' parents—better than some. Since his dad had moved out, Marcus missed him a lot. Like his mom, his dad worked long hours, so they did not have much time together. He also missed the way life had been before, with both parents at the dinner table and both of them there to read with him at bedtime. Going back and forth between his dad's apartment and his mom's house still felt very strange and annoying to him. He always felt off balance—never completely sure of where he was supposed to be and what he was supposed to have with him. All of the old routines were gone, and even meals were different now—more boring. Both of his parents seemed to worry about money now, too. What was happening? Were they going to be poor?

Now here was Richard, trying to take the place that belonged to his dad. Who did he think he was, anyway? Why, he was a stranger. Marcus guessed he wasn't a stranger to his mom, though. She was always snuggling up to Richard, all smiles and dewy-eyed. Sometimes he brought his kids over, and then his mom made a big fuss over them, making their favorite fried chicken dinner and baking cookies. She never made cookies just for him anymore. She was happy, he guessed, and he was glad about that. But as for himself, he just felt alone and out of sorts, "all discombobulated," as his dad said. And what about his poor dad, all alone in his little apartment? What could he do to stop this wedding and get his dad back home, where he belonged, Marcus wondered.

Remarriage—Expectations and Outcomes

The way Tina viewed her wedding day and the way her son saw it are typical of the dramatically differing perspectives parents and children often have about new relationships and remarriages. Particularly after the pain of ending a marriage, it is natural for adults to want to feel loved, desirable, and passionate again. New relationships and new love are a welcome source of excitement and exhilaration. They represent a chance to start over. These hopes and dreams help to ease the hurt, sorrow, and anger that have often consumed too much of their lives recently.

From her son's perspective, though, his mother's remarriage meant more changes to get used to and the loss of a dream that his parents would get back together again. It's not that Marcus is mean or selfish, or that he doesn't want his mom to be happy. But like most children faced with parents' new partners, Marcus has mixed emotions. He loves his mom, and he certainly likes it better when she is smiling and happy instead of crying and in a bad mood. At the same time he wishes it could be *his* dad standing next to her, both of them smiling and happy together.

He worries about what all these changes will mean for him. Is Richard going to try to take his dad's place? Will Richard try to tell him what to do and boss him around? Will he still be as nice to his mother once the wedding is over? And what about having to share his house, his stuff, and his mom with Richard's kids? Richard seems like a nice enough guy, and sometimes Marcus has a good time with him, but then he feels a little guilty and disloyal to his dad, who doesn't have a new relationship. Sometimes Marcus wonders, what if I really start to like this guy and he and Mom end up getting a divorce and I have to go through all that again? Marcus is filled with so many conflicting emotions that he cannot even begin to tell his mother how he feels. His mom keeps telling him how exciting the wedding will be, and how much fun he will have. While there may be some fun and excitement, his feelings are all tangled up, with happiness and sorrow and anger all rumbling around inside him.

In contrast to children's complicated feelings about their parents' remarriage, adults have many compelling reasons to become involved in new relationships after divorce. Mutual love and respect, companionship, passion, intimacy, economic advantages, and someone to share the demands of raising a family are some of the many reasons that so many people enter new relationships within the first few years after a breakup. After the turmoil, sadness, and loss of a divorce, the chance for a new loving relationship can be a healthy step toward getting life back on track. Filled with the promise of hope for a new start, couples see remarriage as a way to enhance their lives with a new partner and form deep loving bonds with a new family composition. Concerned parents hope that their children will share these dreams.

It is not at all surprising that three out of four adults remarry after divorce. Even with all the hopes and positive potential, however, remarriage requires enormous adjustments for adults as well as children, and poses many risks. In *For Better or for Worse: Divorce Reconsidered*, E. Mavis Hetherington and John Kelly report results of nearly three decades of research from Hetherington's Virginia Longitudinal Study of Divorce and Remarriage involving 1,400 families. These studies show that in the early years of remarriage, stress levels are equal to what couples experience during the early stage of divorce, and three times greater than in non-divorced families. As stressful as remarriage is without children, it is even more so when children are involved. Forging new family relationships is very challenging. Remarried couples with children rate the children as the number one cause of conflict between them.

While the challenges are well documented, research also shows that stepfamilies typically experience important positive changes as well. Remarriage is the quickest way out of poverty for women, so many reconfigured families enjoy an improved standard of living, including vacations and other benefits that often are lost when a marriage ends. New couples experience emotional improvements as well. Depression and loneliness decline, and their social lives get better. Even with the challenges, couples in the early years of remarriage report being happier with their marriage than couples in longer established first marriages, although this satisfaction often deteriorates rapidly.

Despite couples' positive feelings early in remarriage, however, divorce rates are higher in remarriage than in first marriages—60 percent, as opposed to approximately 50 percent of first marriages— and higher still when one or both partners have children. These relationships also result in a greater number and severity of problems in children's adjustment.

The causes are not surprising. Old patterns of behavior, unrealistic expectations, low tolerance for dissatisfaction, troubled family history, poor relationship skills, and the complications of raising stepchildren all contribute to marital problems and often the end of these marriages. Even for couples deeply in love, building and sustaining a strong marital relationship within a stepfamily can be rewarding but also challenging.

Children's Perspective on a New Relationship

As Marcus's story reveals, a parent's new relationship or remarriage looks very different from children's eyes than it does from the adult's. In the safety of a therapist's playroom or a support group, children often reveal feelings about their parents' dates and new partners that they cannot or will not share with their parents. Although the details of their situations differ greatly, one theme is consistent: New partners and new relationships represent a huge adjustment for children—*another* huge adjustment, on top of all those that occurred because of their parents' divorce.

Parents often unwittingly underestimate the magnitude of this adjustment for their children, in part because their experiences and needs are so different from theirs, and in part because children have such a hard time revealing their conflicting feelings and fears. Children's needs are substantially different from those of their parents, sometimes even opposite from theirs. While their parents crave new love, children need reassurance that the "old" love of their parents is secure and lasting.

The feelings one group of vocal ten- to twelve-year-olds expressed were particularly revealing. One day, no matter what the topic, they kept coming back to their parents' new "friends." At one point, a flood of vivid, acerbic comments came pouring out.

"Ewww! She's so weird. She acts like she's going to be nice at first, but really, she's just mean and nasty."

"Yeah, my mom's boyfriend thinks he owns the place now, like he's boss just because he's going out with my mom. He tries to tell us what to do, but he's nothing to us. He can't handle it when he doesn't get his way."

"It's the same with my dad's girlfriend. She always has to be right next to him, as if she owns him. She's always hoggin' his attention. Why does *she* always get to sit next to him in the front seat?"

"When my dad's new wife moved in, she changed everything. She painted the living room this ugly color—I mean it really makes me gag! And she brought her fancy furniture and now we can't even sit in it. Like we're not clean enough to sit on her precious sofa and chairs. And why does she always get to sit next to my dad on the couch? I used to be able to sit next to him during a movie!"

"My mom's boyfriend comes over for dinner all the time, and she makes him barbecued ribs and homemade pies. He just sits there and hogs it all down. But when we ask for cookies, she says she doesn't have time to bake."

They went on and on, eagerly adding to the litany of complaints. Their comments were full of passion, conviction, and emotion—and not one was flattering. As a stepmother of four children myself, I was especially interested in the intensity of their reactions and wondered about how universal such feelings might be!

Finally there was a pause, and I took the opportunity to speak. "You know, as I listen to how much you don't like your parents' new partners—how mean and nasty they sound—I wonder how it is that all of your parents chose to be with people that you really don't like." They giggled and shifted in their seats. I went on, "When we have such strong feelings on the outside, there are usually some other, equally strong feelings inside that we don't show or talk about. You know, the group is a safe place to do that."

Silence fell over the group for a moment, and then eleven-year-old Josh quietly commented, "Yeah, I'm afraid my dad loves his new girl-friend more now than he loves me." Nods of agreement went around the room, as if a deep and closely guarded secret had finally been released. Their relief was palpable. Slowly, one by one, they began to describe their parents' enthusiasm for their new relationships, and the sharp contrast they saw in their parents' behavior with them. "My mom always sounds so happy when she picks up the phone and it's her boyfriend," said one girl. "She never sounds that happy when she calls me from work to see if I've done my homework. Mostly she's just yellin' at me for not having it done yet."

Often, children are still struggling with all the changes in their lives and grieving for the loss of their family. As with Marcus, many children take a long time to give up their dream of reuniting their parents. The new relationship makes the end of their parents' marriage suddenly very real, shattering their dream that their parents may one day reunite. When a parent chooses a new partner, children often feel overwhelmed by another huge, unsettling change in their lives. They often feel resentful of someone who is taking the place of a beloved parent in their family.

Many also experience what I have come to call "fear of replacement," a deep worry of losing their special place in their parent's heart and in the family. From their perspective, a new partner captivates their parent's attention and pulls her away from them. Children's fear of replacement is often magnified when new partners bring their own children into a relationship. As six-year-old Deniqua said, "Dad picks us kids up and says, 'How are you guys?' But when he sees his girl-friend's daughter, he throws her up in the air like he used to do with us. Now we don't even get as many hugs as we used to."

This fear was even greater for ten-year-old-Jacob. When his dad remarried, the house was reconfigured to accommodate his new wife and her children. Soon afterward, I noticed that Jacob seemed very tired. "Yeah," he said. "I have to sleep in the basement now because my dad's new wife and kids moved in with us. Every time someone walks around upstairs, the floor creaks and it wakes me up. It's kind of scary and really hard to sleep." Then he added quietly, "I always thought basements were where people put things that they don't want anymore." His physical displacement gravely underscored his fear that he no longer had a place of importance in his dad's life.

For young children who have grown accustomed to sharing a bed with their parent, being sent off to their own bed while a new partner sleeps with their parent is especially jarring. Although they rarely have the words to express it, they experience that loss of physical closeness and comfort as a loss of security and feel replaced by someone who appears to hold higher value to their parent.

The forecast for stepfamilies is not all cloudy, however. Although many children are wary or resentful of a new stepparent and the uncertainty of life in a stepfamily, only about 25 percent of children in stepfather families are overtly resistant—most of them girls. From a girl's perspective, a stepfather may seem like an interloper, especially if she enjoys a very close relationship with her mother—a relationship she sees as *her* territory. Boys are more likely to accept a stepfather, happy to have a male presence in their home with their mothers. Over time, children's resistance subsides, especially when they have been prepared for the new marriage and have had time to build a relationship of their own with their stepfather. If the marriage is solid and the stepfather is supportive, children are far more likely to see the relationship and remarriage as positive. When a new relationship contributes to their parent's well-being and children see it as an enduring, stabilizing force in the family, they are far more likely to understand and appreciate the benefits of remarriage.

Dynamics between stepmothers and children are often more complicated, especially if these women stay at home caring for stepchildren and take on the role of the primary disciplinarian. Stepmothers in such situations have huge challenges. Those who use the effective combination of warmth, sensitivity, patience, and parenting skills and *never* criticize the stepchildren's mother reap the rewards of more positive relationships with them. Children in these circumstances end up feeling safer and cared for as a result of the extra love, authoritative guidance, and support. Research shows that good relationships between stepmothers and stepchildren are more likely when stepmothers and biological mothers are not in conflict and fathers are actively involved and supportive of their wife's reasonable efforts to set limits with his children.

Realistic and Unrealistic Expectations for Remarriage

As they contemplate remarriage, most parents look forward to a committed relationship that offers lasting benefits for them and their children. Yet the challenges and adjustments are considerable for children and their parents, and unrealistic expectations can result not only in serious disappointment but also in resentment and feelings of failure. For this reason, it is wise for parents to thoughtfully examine their expectations and consider whether they are heavily coated in stardust or based on a realistic appraisal of what lies ahead.

These are some common expectations that fall into the category of wishful thinking rather than reality.

Instant love all around. One of the most pervasive and unproductive beliefs couples hold about remarriage is that their new stepfamily will be the equivalent of their original family. They foresee quick adjustment and imagine instant love resulting in close bonds between stepparents and stepchildren. Such unrealistic expectations can only lead to disappointment and resentment. New spouses and siblings often feel more like indifferent roommates than family members. For some children, especially girls in early adolescence, adjustment to life in a stepfamily is often as great as, if not greater than, their adjustment to the divorce.

It is more realistic to anticipate a long period of adjustment, understanding that solid relationships take time to form. Unlike parents and children in an original nuclear family, stepparents and stepchildren do not have the benefit of attachment bonds that originate at birth and are nurtured daily from then on. It takes a long time for stepparents to establish trust with children with whom they have no shared history.

Research has shown that it takes a substantial amount of time— sometimes three to five years—for everyone to adjust, and the first several years may be quite turbulent. The greatest risk of divorce in remarriages is during the first five years. The general course of family life in a stepfamily is some disorganization and turbulence during the first two years, with stabilization developing during the next three. Children's behaviors have an important influence on the marital relationship in stepfamilies, and tensions between children and stepparents are frequent. Given all these major adjustments, it is not surprising that children in stepfamilies are more likely to have more social and emotional problems than children in continuously married families.

The same kind of family. Another common misperception is that a newly composed stepfamily will operate just like the original nuclear family. Stepfamily relationships require particular care, time, and cultivation. Parents are not interchangeable characters playing roles that children will relate to with equal connection and emotion. Although stepchildren and stepparents eventually may develop a close relationship, it is unlikely—and should not be expected—that it will be the same kind of bond that children have with their parents.

Children are concerned with how the new family formation will affect them and their relationship with both of their parents. Often they continue to worry that developing a positive relationship with a new stepparent makes them disloyal to a parent they love. I've heard many children echo the allegiance of Ben, the young boy in the movie *Stepmom*: "I'll hate her if you want me to, Mom." Sometimes such loyalty conflicts are fueled by competition between a stepparent and a child's biological or adoptive parent—a situation that is unfortunately all too common after divorce and that undermines the progress of developing stepfamily relationships.

New partners: parents' happiness = children's happiness. Divorced adults get to choose their new partner. For their children, it is an arranged marriage. As one young teen pointed out, "Here is this person that I share my dad, my home, even my bathroom with. I didn't have a choice. If it weren't for Dad, I never would have even known her."

Although most children don't reveal such feelings to parents, they often view a new person as an intruder moving into their territory. Particularly if the relationship develops quickly, children feel the sharp contrast between the close, loving relationship their parent shares with this other person, and their own undeveloped and tenuous relationship with someone who still seems largely like a stranger.

Remarriage as rescue. Remarriage often seems like the best solution to ending the pain of an unhappy first marriage, the ordeal of divorce, and the stress of caring for children alone. It is an appealing fantasy—but it is not necessarily a solution. Solid marriages are built on much more than the desire to escape past or current difficulties.

When children are involved, the challenges are greater and the stakes higher. The considerations for successful remarriage include not only a strong and loving commitment between adults but also a clear-sighted understanding of what it will mean to share family life with children, making the children's needs a high priority, and taking the time to prepare children for the changes.

Remarriage with Families: Skills and Strategies for Success

Given the statistics, the negative stereotypes of stepparents in folktales, and all the stresses associated with remarriage, it may sound like step-families are doomed to failure—that the risk is not worth the gamble. But as millions of happily remarried couples can attest, learning from a prior marriage and not repeating the same mistakes and patterns help to make it a risk well worth taking. Remarriage is an opportunity to build strong loving relationships that can provide lasting benefits and a new way of life for parents and their children, perhaps in ways they may have never imagined. Fortunately, there are guidelines that can help to stack the deck for success. A solid body of research reveals factors that impact the likelihood for success in remarriage and happiness for all members of the newly formed family. In recognition of the importance of supporting healthy stepfamily relationships, new interventions and education programs are being developed to strengthen and support remarriage that focus on skills for healthy strong relationships in remarriage and stepfamilies. Many of these are at the heart of any good relationship. Some are specific to remarriage and blended families.

Fundamental marital success factors. Since many resources on each of these topics are available, this section provides only a list with brief descriptions. If you recognize any of these as an area of your life that would benefit from improvement, I encourage you to seek out books, workshops, and professionals to help you strengthen your skills for developing a satisfying and lasting new relationship.

Communication. In all healthy marriages, strong communication is essential. Couples in successful remarriages talk frequently and openly, and the need to do so is great, since every member of the family has a different history prior to the formation of the new family, and likely a different set of feelings about it. Remarried couples benefit as a couple and bring effective guidance to their family by candidly discussing their perceptions of problems, trying to understand each other's viewpoints, and solving problems together.

Skills that promote friendship, emotional intimacy, and bonding as a couple. Remarried couples may benefit from developing their relationship even more diligently than couples in first marriages. With the added stresses of stepchildren and a history of marital difficulties, they need to attend to creating a solid bond between themselves. This is cultivated through words and behaviors that express caring, nurturing, affection, and appreciation. Willingness to disclose intimate information is another important element that communicates trust and the unique bond between two individuals.

Time together as a couple. Remarried couples with children have the added challenge of finding time for themselves in households with the added pressure of stepparent-stepchild relationships. It is important to invest in your own relationship, because that will be a source of strength in your blended family, benefiting your children as well as yourselves. This requires balancing your children's needs with yours as a couple. Many couples find it beneficial to seek professional help for additional support—even before they remarry.

Effective management of conflict, anger, and stress. Couples in healthy remarriages seek to understand problems from their spouse's point of view, with empathy. Beyond this, they are able to regulate their own strong emotions and deal with anger, stress, and conflict in healthy, productive ways.

Additional Factors That Impact Success in Stepfamilies. One of the fundamentals of success for merging families is understanding the importance of the stepchild-stepparent relationship and its influence on the marital relationship. Because parents have strong bonds with their own children, they instinctively are protective of them. A parent's desire to be seen as a "good parent" may contribute to defensiveness and denial, and vulnerability to feeling hurt by a new partner's criticism. These complicated emotions, plus hurt feelings or problems between a stepparent and stepchild, can easily undermine a remarriage. The need for stepparents and stepchildren to develop positive relationships is critical to the new family's success.

Here are some of the factors that can influence it.

Children's ages. How old children are at the time of their parent's remarriage has a major effect on the nature of the relationship between the stepparent and stepchild, and thus on the marital relationship itself. The younger the children are, the more likely they are to accept new stepparents and form a greater connection with them. By contrast, it is much more difficult for adolescents to adjust to the realities of a parent's remarriage and form new relationships with stepparents. Some research suggests that the best period of time for remarriage is before the child's tenth birthday, or after their sixteenth. It is also important for couples with adolescents to have a realistic understanding that stepsiblings may have a positive relationship but not necessarily develop strong and emotionally close bonds, at least not initially. As with their stepparents, children do not choose their stepsiblings, they simply acquire those who show up with their new stepparent. Even the kindest and most flexible children are bound to feel like strangers for a while, and may never develop a close relationship.

Realistic expectations. Stepfamilies fare better when they have realistic expectations for the new relationships. Healthy stepfamily relationships—between stepparents and stepchildren, and among stepchildren—develop very slowly, and some relationships take more time than others to form. There is no instant love, immediate attachment, or quick fixes. In general, the most effective way to develop close connections and healthy relationships is through one-on-one interactions rather than an entire family unit.

Proceeding slowly. For new stepparents, it is best to extend support and friendship to stepchildren, with behaviors that show concern and empathy for the children and their feelings, and interest in their lives. While this may seem like a minimal parenting role at first, going slowly gives new stepchildren time to get to know their stepparents as other adults who care about them. In this way, they will learn to trust that they are truly available to them as a resource and support. Efforts to move too quickly into the role of a parent can easily backfire. It is easier to become closer if you've gone too slowly than to back off if you've been too intrusive and come on too strong too soon. Stepparents who are disengaged, have little or no interaction with their stepchildren, or step in with punitive discipline too quickly will find it much harder to build a positive relationship than those who take positive steps to develop the relationship gradually, building trust and goodwill in the process.

Sometimes, despite stepparents' best efforts, children and teens are not responsive to their attempts to reach out to them. There can be a variety of reasons for their resistance, including resistance to change, worry about feeling disloyal to their other parent, temporary adolescent rebellion, and negative perceptions of a stepparent—especially if they think the stepparent is trying to replace their biological parent. So it is wisest to nurture the relationship over time. Patience and compassion usually reap rewards in the long run.

Definition of parenting roles. One of the greatest gifts that stepparents can give their new spouses is to support their healthy relationship with their children. Stepparents can offer valuable support for their partner's effective parenting, but it is best not to step in immediately as a disciplinarian. Negotiating parenting roles—especially the responsibilities for discipline and the nature of support offered—and working toward consensus on household rules have been shown to have a big impact on the success of merged families. As with all healthy relationships, being open to new ideas and approaching issues with flexibility enhances the marital relationship.

Consistency in creating and applying rules. Children have built-in radar to detect parents' favoritism in families—especially stepfamilies. So it is very important to develop rules that can be applied equally to every family member and to be consistent in applying them. This may be especially challenging because differences in rules and discipline practices have been established before the families were merged, and old habits may linger. So stepparents need to be on the lookout for any preferential treatment—you can be sure children are watching—and this could become the source of unspoken resentment. Even if it's unintended, it still hurts relationships. Tensions between and among stepchildren can accumulate and spill over in a "percolator effect," especially in response to perceived inequities.

Maintaining positive coparenting relationships. The quality of the coparenting relationship with former partners has a definite impact on new marriages. Remarriages fare better when parenting relationships with former partners are respectful, cooperative, and businesslike, with clear boundaries. Strife between former partners, particularly in regard to parenting issues, spills over into remarriages, adding to the challenges of forming a new family. Everyone benefits when relationships between former partners are respectful and reasonably polite.

Managing conflict productively. Conflict involving stepparents and stepchildren can quickly erode the quality of the marital relationship, so it is critical to manage disagreements, hurt feelings, and other sources of conflict between them. It might be tempting to avoid conflict, hoping it will go away, but often the opposite happens, and the result is that hurt and resentment accumulate. In first marriages, the relationship between the couple sets the foundation and tone for family life. In stepfamilies, relationships between stepparents and stepchildren have a strong influence on the quality of family life.

Anticipating changes in living arrangements. Children's residential arrangements are likely to change over time. Remarried couples can best handle these changes if they anticipate their happening and prepare for them by communicating about roles and expectations. Often adolescents or preadolescents will ask to live with their other parent for a while. This occurs most often with adolescent boys who live with their mothers and yearn for closer contact with their fathers. This can be difficult for residential parents to accept, but it is often an opportunity for children to strengthen a relationship with a parent with whom they need a closer connection. Parents who listen carefully and respond with understanding and empathy to this request demonstrate to children that their feelings matter. When handled carefully, such changes can provide opportunities for growth and deeper, more meaningful relationships for the entire family.

Planning finances in advance. Money is a major source of arguments in marriages, so it is wise to negotiate and understand financial arrangements before remarrying. Having discussions and coming to an agreement about how children's needs will be met, and whether finances will be dealt with from separate accounts or a single pot of family funds helps to prevent conflict. There is no one solution that works best for everyone. Research shows that it is the extent to which couples agree on a financial plan that matters most in remarriages, rather than any particular financial plan.

Enlisting extended family. Developmental psychologist Dr. Urie Bronfenbrenner believed that all children need someone in their life who's crazy about them. Grandparents, aunts, uncles, and even close family friends can fill that special role. When families merge, these loving adults play important roles in helping to foster the growth of stepfamily relationships. They can help to bridge any distance between children and stepparents by providing a listening ear, responding with empathy, and taking time to share activities that nourish their relationship. They can also help greatly by what they do not do—by never demeaning either parent or a stepparent. Instead, they can provide a safe haven, listening to children's feelings and experiences, asking about all of these people who are important in their lives, and letting them know they are loved and valued.

Paving the Way—When and How to Prepare Children for New Relationships and Remarriage

The Big Message: Proceed slowly and prepare yourself and your children very well.

When I work with parents who are becoming involved in a new relationship, I strongly urge them to proceed slowly and with caution—at least when it comes to involving their children. It's difficult at times to tell someone who has been through the pain of divorce to put off bringing a new love into their homes and their children's lives. I do so because undertaking a new relationship slowly is in their own best interest, as a large and compelling body of research demonstrates.

But equally important, I do so as a spokesperson on behalf of their children. As you have read throughout this book, divorce has a large—sometimes monumental—impact on children. They need careful preparation for every major change in their lives, and divorce is not just a single event, but a series of big changes, each of which has a profound impact on them. At all ages, children need careful preparation and time to adjust. Preteens and adolescents need even more time than younger children. Bringing a new person to your dinner table, to your bedroom, or into your life as a spouse and into theirs as a stepparent is an adjustment for children at any time. Doing so too quickly after a divorce can send them reeling.

Healthy new relationships are a positive step forward after a divorce, but give yourself the gift of time when choosing a new partner. In the desire to feel loved, desirable, and happy again, newly single parents are very vulnerable, and their children are even more so. Going slowly, choosing carefully, and preparing yourself, your children, and your future partner pay off enormously in the quality of family life you can eventually enjoy over a lifetime together.

Twelve Strong Recommendations

1. Thoroughly end one relationship before you begin another— carefully. Make sure your divorce is settled not just legally, but emotionally, too. Take care of yourself emotionally so that when you meet a potential new partner you can forge a new relationship as a reasonably whole and confident individual, not one who feels broken and wounded, in need of a healer or caretaker. Generally, it takes *at least one and a half to two years* to work through the emotional and financial issues surrounding a divorce and be well enough prepared to undertake all that a new relationship requires in order to become sustained and mutually rewarding.

2. Take care to tend and maintain healthy relationships with your children after your divorce. Their need for your love and help in adjusting to changes is especially great at this time. In maintaining strong relationships with them, you ensure that they feel secure in the knowledge of your strong connection, so when a new relationship comes along that is right for you, your children remain confident of their special place in your heart.

3. When you feel ready to date, go slowly. Introduce your children to the idea that you will be meeting new friends. Give them

time to prepare for the possibility before it becomes a reality. Ask them how they feel and allow them to ask questions, listening for the meaning behind their questions. Often what children really want to know is whether you will continue to love and care for them if you have someone new in your life.

4. Continue to talk with your children about the divorce and the changes in their lives, checking in frequently to see how they're feeling about "stuff in general" and changes in the family specifically. For a long time, children grapple with no longer having two parents together. They need time to adjust to this loss before they adjust to a significant new person in their lives.

5. Get to know a potential partner well as a friend and confidante, as well as a lover. If you are considering him or her as a life partner, explore thoroughly whether this person shares your commitment and values as a parent. Consider not only whether this individual will be a good partner for you, but equally important, whether he or she will be a good stepparent for your children. Make sure that he or she understands that your children are a priority in your life, and is very willing to support your important role as a parent.

6. When you are ready for an intimate relationship, do not bring your date into your home when your children are present. Arrange to meet during a time when your children are away from your home, not when they are with you. It is very unsettling for children to meet a stranger in the bathroom or at the breakfast table. And having casual sexual relationships with one or more individuals sets an example for preteens and adolescents that most parents would not want them to follow.

7. Eventually, if and when you meet the right person and agree to enter a committed relationship, tell your former partner before telling your children. In so doing, you protect the children from having to keep a secret from their other parent. You also ensure that your children's other parent does not hear the news from them before they hear it from you. Your ongoing

relationship as parents for your children benefits from the respect this demonstrates.

8. Make early meetings between children and potential partners brief and casual, preferably in a child-friendly setting such as a park. Children need to get to know them gradually over time and form their own impressions. In these early meetings, avoid showing physical affection. It comes as a real shock to see a parent as a romantic partner to someone they don't know.

9. Arrange for your child to spend significantly more time with the person when you think it likely your relationship will be long term. Then, prepare your children before you bring your prospective partner to meet them. Explain your relationship in age-appropriate terms—with young children initially as "a new friend." Avoid "selling" the individual to them, expounding on their good qualities or setting up an expectation that the children will like him or her. Introduce the person by name, not as a relative—that adds to confusion for young children and may seem false to older ones.

10. Understand that children have fears about what a new person in your life will mean for them and their relationship with you. They worry that they will lose your love, time with you, and even available family resources. Reassure them and demonstrate that they will never lose the special place you have for them in your heart. Act on your words by keeping time with your children a priority when they are with you, especially during the first year following your separation.

11. Set aside regular one-on-one time with each child. Keep dating and parenting separate. If children feel pushed aside or ignored when you are with another person, they feel resentful—a feeling that is likely to last and undermine a future partnership.

12. If you plan to marry someone with whom you've had an affair, recognize that your children (and your former partner) will see that individual as responsible for the breakup of your marriage. Their feelings and acceptance of your new relationship are very

likely to be complicated and colored by these circumstances, even if they like the individual.

Keeping all these recommendations to guide you, remember that a solid loving relationship with someone who shares your dreams and values can add stability to life for you and your children. New relationships all take time, care, and patience but can be well worth the wait and the effort in the long run.

Moving Forward as a New Family

Beginning a new life with a new partner and forming a stepfamily are full of promise. I am happy to report that I've seen many reconfigured families ultimately find deeply satisfying rewards in their new relationships. Their success, however, is based on continuously, conscientiously, and lovingly working at these relationships.

Unfortunately, a new marriage and family life do not mean that all of the challenges and adjustments are behind you. Children's adjustments are usually greater than those their parents face. Remarriage is a major transition for them—especially for adolescent girls—and they may continue to experience loss and stress for some time after the new family has been formed. Patience, empathy, and quality parenting are all needed to help them adjust.

There are a number of things that parents and stepparents can do to help the new step relationships form and gel. For starters, letting children decide what to call the new adult in their lives gives them some sense of control and comfort in a situation that has potential to cause guilt or discomfort. Insisting that they call a stepparent Mom or Dad or another name that they feel belongs to their parent may make them feel disloyal and resentful. A first name or a respectful, agreed-upon nickname is a more comfortable choice. Seven-year-old Jeff chose to call his new stepfather Bear—a fond nickname that came from a game they played together when they were first getting acquainted. Bear was the name that family and friends soon adopted and stuck with, even after Jeff's father disappeared and Jeff began calling his stepfather Dad.

New family routines, traditions, and rituals are likely to help a blended family develop a sense of shared interest and mutual satisfaction, especially if children have some choice in them. Soliciting their ideas and encouraging their input and suggestions helps to create the glue that helps to stick families together. Celebrations become more memorable and meaningful when children and teens have a role in planning them.

Sometimes the most important roles stepparents play are those of peacemaker and stress reducer. There are many ways to accomplish this. New stepparents do their partners and their children a great service by helping to contain conflict between former partners and doing their best to promote positive relationships between children and their parents. They can foster these relationships by supporting children's need for both parents' presence at events that are important to them—soccer matches, school plays, and certainly graduations and weddings—without fear of conflict or icy silence.

Ensuring that major events in a child's life are celebrated with love and joy, and not tainted by conflict between and among parents, is another important way that parents and stepparents can smooth life for children and strengthen family bonds. Major events such as bar mitzvahs and bat mitzvahs, first communions, graduations, and weddings require extra sensitivity and care so that children—even as adults—are not put in awkward positions and loyalty conflicts.

Over time—and it does take time!—when there are reasonably positive relationships between parents, former partners, and stepparents, stepfamilies can provide children with additional caring adults in their lives to provide support, role models, guidance, and love. Children with supportive stepfamily relationships often comment that they have the benefit of knowing there are more people who love and care about them. "My stepdad, Barry, is like a favorite uncle, best friend, and mentor, all rolled into one lovable teddy bear," says Diana, age nineteen. "My mom is so much happier now with him in her life. I don't worry about her as much as I did before she got married again. And I feel better about going off to college, knowing that she and my little sister are going to be okay without me."

More than anything else, parents' and stepparents' constant commitment to give children loving attention and provide high-quality parenting will help children to grow up confident and secure. This does not mean that they will escape all of the painful feelings or difficult times that are a part of nearly every divorce. But with support and preparation, they can come through the changes with remarkable resilience. And while these stepfamilies, like all families, will face their own unique challenges, the benefits can far outweigh the obstacles.

Proof of the Possibilities: The Story of Ryan, Rebecca, and Mindy

Like so many other life changes, when remarriage is handled thoughtfully, with care and judgment and preparation, children can and do thrive. I found one particularly vivid example in a serendipitous encounter with a caring divorced father I met on a three-and-a-half-hour flight. I was working on this book, he asked about it, and we spent the entire flight talking about how parents can nurture their children through the passages of divorce and remarriage with resilience.

Ryan was planning to remarry but felt very concerned about his eight-year-old daughter, Rebecca. He is a very successful professional, but it was clear that Ryan saw his most important job as being a good dad to Rebecca. It was very important to him that his sweet little girl feel secure in the knowledge of her parents' love for her, despite their divorce. Ryan had taken great care to nurture and maintain a close relationship with Rebecca. Now, as he contemplated his upcoming marriage to Mindy, he was concerned about how it would affect his daughter. Especially because they had such a close relationship, he worried that she might feel pushed aside, less important than she once was. This sensitive, deeply caring dad was tuning in to his daughter's underlying fears about this new relationship in the life of her beloved parent.

We talked about how he might talk with her to prepare her for the changes, and how he could reassure her of his deep, abiding love for her. Ryan later reported that he went home and had a tender heart-to-heart talk with his daughter. They talked about their closeness, their love for one another, and how much neither of them ever wanted that to change. Tears were shed and hugs exchanged as they acknowledged their fears of the unknown, and particularly of anything ever coming between them. Ryan reassured Rebecca that although there would be changes in their family, there would be some good changes, and she would have a special place in his heart forever. They vowed to keep their special "talk time" when they could ask and tell each other anything. It was an emotional night for both of them, to be sure.

Ryan wondered how Rebecca would feel the next morning. Exhausted from staying up late? Sad and angry at the realization that her parents would not get back together, and at having to cope with

so many changes in her life? He awoke to find her happily drawing at the kitchen table. "Look, Daddy!" she exclaimed, "I drew a picture of all of us—you, Mindy, and me—all together, celebrating your wedding."

Rebecca's drawing reveals the joy and understanding that can come from talking with our children about their feelings and the changes in their lives, and the power of love to see us through to a brighter side. Ryan and Mindy married the next summer. Rebecca's beautiful drawing was reproduced on the cover of their wedding announcement. I'm happy to report that Rebecca and all of her family are thriving and enjoying life. When she celebrated her ninth birthday, her mom, dad, stepmom, and best friends were all at her party. Such new beginnings and happy endings are indeed possible.

NINE

Life After Divorce:
Real Possibilities for Success

As I write this final chapter, I think about all the children and families whose stories are told in this book. Their initial feelings and challenges are similar in many ways, but what happens to them varies greatly. The diversity of children's outcomes is well established in research. Some struggle with the fallout from divorce throughout their lives. Others, like Jessica, may have a host of distressing feelings and adjustment problems in the early stages, but come through the multiple changes to their lives with remarkable strength and resilience.

The most rewarding part of my work over the years has been witnessing children and adolescents who come through their parents' divorce not just surviving, but thriving in all aspects of their lives. Their success is testimony to the power of quality parenting and loving parent-child relationships—all effected by diligent parents, even as they deal with their own powerful emotions.

Sadly, the stories of children who are deeply affected by divorce are all too common. Your children do not have to be among these, and I hope the perspectives and strategies in this book help you to better understand what your children are experiencing and how to provide the kind of parenting they need in order to thrive in the long term. Like all families, you and your children will face challenges—sometimes very difficult ones—but I hope the information in these chapters helps to bolster your success in dealing with them.

This final chapter tells the stories of three families who ultimately succeeded in the aftermath of divorce. All experienced their fair share of difficult challenges and painful emotions. Some initially were entrenched in bitter conflict. Nonetheless, they all got through their difficulties because the parents were determined to put their children first, and they acted on that determination each day. Among the other factors that ultimately added stability and support for the children were the loving and attentive new stepparents who came into their lives several years after the divorces. These are real stories, not happily-ever-after divorce fairy tales. They are the stories of people who confronted their challenges, not with perfection, but with the courage do their best through the ups and downs of family changes.

The Story of Melissa, Steve, Meg, and Sam

Melissa and Steve had been married ten years when they came to the agonizing decision to end their marriage. Although Steve did not want the divorce, he recognized that their marital relationship had been in trouble for a long time, despite their efforts to save it. They contacted me early in the process of their separation to ask how to prepare their children for their separation and how to reduce its impact on them. The pain they both felt was evident in their words and posture. Melissa was overcome with feelings of grief and guilt because she initiated the divorce. Steve, who had been an involved and loving stay-at-home dad, was devastated by the loss of family life as it had been, and he, too, was grieving—and angry.

Despite their emotions, which at times were overwhelming, both worked hard to contain their anger, grief, and conflict when they were with their children. During and after their separation, they dealt with their feelings through therapy and with trusted family and friends. In this way, they were better able to provide the attentive parenting their children urgently needed. When they established the new schedule, both parents listened carefully to their children and paid attention to how they were feeling and adjusting. When the inevitable happened and the children acted up, these authoritative parents set limits on their unacceptable behaviors, providing the guidance and discipline that their children needed to feel secure.

Because the divorce changed their financial situation, Steve had to earn an income, and he searched for a job locally. When he could not find one in his field, he made the difficult decision to move out of town. Concerned about yet another loss for their children, Steve and Melissa worked out a parenting plan of joint legal custody, with the children regularly spending time on alternate weekends and school breaks with Steve in his new home 150 miles away. Melissa realized that having their dad so far away added to the loss the children felt, and she went the distance—literally—to support their time with him. When Steve had to work too late on Fridays to make the round trip, Melissa drove halfway so the children could still have two weekend nights with their dad. The drives turned out to provide good transitions between homes because they allowed plenty of time for the children to talk with the driving parent about their feelings and challenges, and for the parents to listen and help.

Although this summary may make it seem like their adjustments came smoothly, in reality, Melissa and Steve's relationship was very rocky during the first year and a half and, like all families, they continued to face their share of challenges after that. During the first year after their separation, their children showed signs of anxiety, which diminished with therapy, plenty of loving reassurance, and quality parenting. Both parents eventually became involved in new relationships, but they waited to initiate them, and then proceeded slowly, with a great deal of concern for their children's adjustment. Both chose supportive new partners who were committed to providing quality parenting for both their own children and their stepchildren.

As I worked with this family, I could see that they had the ingredients for successfully navigating the changes in their family. Although the marriage had dissolved, Steve and Melissa's parenting relationship had not, nor had the loving, secure bonds between both parents and their children. Their efforts paid off in two healthy, well-adjusted children who are now thriving in every way. Sam, at five, was a curious, verbal child, so he worked through his adjustment with heartfelt questions and surprisingly sustained conversations. Meg, who was eight at the time of the separation, used art as a way of expressing her feelings. "What really helped me was drawing. I could always use the colors as emotions. Talking is sometimes hard because feelings about divorce can't always be put into words." Among those feelings, fortunately, were hope and optimism for the future, as reflected in her drawing of a joyfully colored heart with wings that allowed it to soar.

Seven years have passed since Steve and Melissa's divorce, and I recently followed up with the children to see how they were faring. Meg is still using art to express her feelings, and perhaps because she has had so much practice, she is now a talented young artist. Even now, she still has some struggles with the changes resulting from the divorce, but she always manages to find positives amid the negatives. "I still have trouble with the distance to my dad's house. All the traveling is kind of hard, but I really want to see him, so in the end, the traveling is totally worth it," she says. Another manifestation of her positive attitude is reflected in her view of her living situation. "It's really hard when all my friends have parents that are married to each other, but then I think about how I get to have two houses, two parents, and two stepparents, so there are some advantages."

Her overall adjustment is evident in her acceptance of the situation and her genuine pleasure in realizing that both of her parents are happier now. "Sometimes, you have to think about the positive things about your parents' divorce. I have to think about how my parents are probably much happier now than they would be if they had tried to stay together." She adds, as important advice to other children, "And, never, ever blame yourself, because there is nothing you could possibly do to change anything."

Meg's words mirror the research on risk and resilience related to children's outcomes after divorce. She understands that the divorce was due to irreconcilable differences between her parents and accepts that these issues are beyond her control. She continues to cope with her feelings very effectively by expressing them through art and talking with people she trusts. Perhaps most important, Meg continues to have close, loving relationships with both of her parents and with her stepparents, too—something they all have worked very hard to ensure. Her positive outlook continues to infuse her day-to-day life with hope and optimism.

Sam, now eleven, has his own unique perspective on the ingredients that have been essential to his resilience. "It helped me when I was sad or upset to talk to my mom. Sometimes I couldn't find the words I wanted, but reading some books really helped me. I cried a little, but after that I always felt better.

"I asked my mom and dad a lot of questions about why they got divorced, and that helped. They never got mad at me for asking questions. Sometimes it helped me to have my mom talk to my dad about the things I didn't like about him moving away. She taught me how to say what I needed, and now I tell him how I feel. It helped me that most everything else in my life stayed the same."

Echoing the hopes of millions of children, he adds, "I like that my mom and dad say nice things about each other. It was hard at first, but I am happy and my family is happy, so it is good. I have good friends and I love my family. And they love me."

Like his sister's comments, Sam's words also mirror several factors that have been proven to influence children's well-being before, during, and after divorce. He had help learning to identify and express his strong and varied emotions to parents who listened. The knowledge that his parents can still see the good in each other clearly helps him to feel secure. He points out the stabilizing effect of the family and friends who have remained constant in his life, even in the midst of major family changes. The collective efforts and support of Sam's parents, stepparents, grandparents, extended family, friends, and other supportive adults have resulted in his feeling secure in the knowledge that he is loved—and he returns that love.

Because of the thoughtful effort that Steve and Melissa have put into loving, attentive parenting, Meg and Sam are thriving. I'm confident they will continue to do so.

The Story of Kate, Michael, and Noah

Kate and Michael's story is more complicated. They were so bitter and vitriolic that it seemed impossible they could ever resolve their differences enough to cooperate as parents. Theirs began as one of the worst divorce horror stories, with shouting matches in front of their son, false accusations, orders of protection, and acrimonious litigation. When I first met with them, they were embroiled in a hotly contested battle for custody of seven-year-old Noah, and both were fierce warriors. Both retained lawyers known for aggressiveness, and the combat continued to escalate.

Not surprisingly, in the midst of all this conflict, Noah reacted the way children under stress are known to do. His grades slipped considerably, his teacher complained about his disruptive behavior at school,

and he became increasingly disrespectful and uncooperative toward his parents—a disturbing new set of behaviors. Through his actions, this unhappy child was sending an SOS to his parents and anyone who would listen—help! In an early session, I asked him to draw a picture of his family. The result was extremely telling. He drew a scene labeled "World War III," with Fort Mom and Fort Dad pointing pistols at each other and Noah himself caught in the crossfire. As he drew, he repeated over and over again, "All the fighting is killing me!"

Although Kate and Michael were fully entrenched in their battle, they shared a deep love for their son and the fear that they would lose him. As we worked together, it became clear that fear was the driving force for much of their warriorlike behavior. Both parents had the same serious misconception—that there had to be a "winner" and a "loser" in the parenting of their son. Yet what Noah wanted was to have time with both of his parents, and not to have anyone in court ask him to choose one over the other. Most of all, what this child wanted was an end to the hostilities that had taken over his family. He needed for his parents to be civil toward each other, at the very least.

It took several meetings with Kate and Michael before they began to realize how they could both be a part of their son's life and to understand that their ongoing conflict was tantamount to continuous exposure to a virulent toxin, seriously jeopardizing his healthy development. My words seemed to have little influence on dampening their animosity toward each other. But when I showed them several drawings Noah had made—including "World War III" with him caught in their crossfire—both Kate and Michael were immediately overcome with anguish and remorse at their own role in causing their son's misery.

From that point forward, there was a distinct change in our meetings. With their growing awareness that all the fighting was making things worse for everyone and that their beloved only son was moving further away from them, Kate and Michael were finally ready to change their behavior.

The business model of a mission, goals, success, and the respectful relationships required to achieve them resonated with them. Michael, a successful entrepreneur, especially responded to the comparison of their coparenting relationship with that of business partners in a multimillion-dollar enterprise, and he could now envision Kate as his partner in the priceless parenting business. Kate, who'd had a successful business career of her own before Noah was born, also saw value in the analogy of a businesslike partnership. Both understood that in order for a business to thrive, its partners needed to maintain a positive relationship, even if they did not enjoy a personal one. Why should they do any less in their roles as their son's parents?

Kate and Michael adopted a model of parallel parenting during that first year. They managed to be respectful toward each other but were in contact only when necessary, which minimized the opportunities for conflict. They communicated about Noah during brief phone calls, carefully adhering to a specific agenda about his needs and activities. Noah spent time in both their homes, with joint legal custody, and his grades and behavior began to improve. When Kate decided to go back to work, Michael helped her secure a good position in a successful company.

Three years after their divorce, we had a follow-up meeting. Both Kate and Michael were in new relationships, and they were able to be more cooperative, sometimes even sharing activities with their son. When I met with Noah, he expressed a wish that both his parents would come to his birthday party at a local skating rink. His drawing shows his delight at having this wish come true—quite a contrast from his earlier drawing of World War III.

The Story of Eric, Diana, and Their Three Daughters

Diana and Eric had been married eighteen years when Eric announced he was involved with someone else and wanted a divorce. The news came as a complete shock to Diana, who felt blindsided and betrayed. Their children, ages sixteen, thirteen, and ten, were stunned, too. They simply could not believe that their once happy family suddenly was breaking apart. The first year following the separation was a period of tremendous sadness and turmoil for everyone. Since all of the family members shared close relationships with one another, the changes were deeply troubling. Adjusting to them did not come easily for anyone.

The divorce was particularly difficult for the oldest daughter, Erika, who took on the role of caretaker for her parents and siblings. She grew up quickly, and in the process, missed out on some of the normal experiences of adolescence. She worried about her mother, who was deeply distraught and losing weight rapidly as she grieved the loss of her marriage. She worried about her dad, who initially withdrew and became somewhat tentative in his manner with her and her siblings. "At first I didn't see much of Dad," she said, "I think because he felt so guilty about the affair and unsure about how to interact with all of us." She also worried about her two younger sisters, who now cried and fought and showed their distress in many other ways.

Years later, with characteristic insight, Erika said she had felt mostly numb during the first year or so after her parents' separation. "Mom and Dad were both in such pain that I lived in some in-between space and did not know where to land. Taking care of other people was a kind of self-protection that kept me at a distance from my own pain."

Today, Erika and both of her sisters are thriving. Although each of them remembers the time following their parents' separation and divorce as a period of great sadness and turmoil, they are now able to put those times, emotions, and experiences in perspective and take charge of their own lives and futures with optimism.

How did they get to this point? "My parents were always my parents," says Erika. "They did not abdicate those roles, even when they were in total misery about their marriage and my dad was a little distant." Both parents remained committed to nurturing the bonds with their children and providing them with clear guidance, accountability, and abundant expressions of their love. What she described was a fundamental attachment to both parents that served as a safety net during shaky emotional times. During the early months while emotions ran very high, Diana and Eric found it helpful to be formal and businesslike, setting clear boundaries as they worked at their altered partnership in child-rearing. Over time, they were able to relax and develop an amicable, respectful coparenting relationship.

About two years elapsed before all the family members adjusted to the divorce, as they all worked their way through their emotions on different timetables. Ultimately, Diana and Eric were able to see again the qualities they had once liked in each other. These became part of their conversations with their children, who were reassured by the appreciation and respect their parents showed each other. Four years later, Diana's remarriage to a loving partner and nurturing stepfather helped to further stabilize family life.

Erika, now twenty-five, reflects on what helped her and her sisters through a difficult time. "Both of my parents acknowledged the importance of the other's presence in my life and, to the best of their ability, never asked me to choose between them. They never made us get involved in a legal process. We weren't kept in the dark, and it was okay to ask questions, which they almost always answered. We were encouraged to speak up without worrying about hurting our parents' feelings. Of course this was practically impossible (at least for me), but it meant something that they asked. They encouraged us to seek whatever help we needed and even insisted on my sisters and me seeing a therapist. None of us ended up staying in therapy (at least at that point), but it showed us that even in the midst of their own turmoil, they were still taking care of us.

"My dad sacrificed financially so that we didn't have to sell our house and my sisters and I didn't have to move, on top of all the other changes we were facing. We were never asked to change our social lives or give up any of our extracurricular activities. We never worried that we weren't going to be able to go to college.

"After the first few years, both my parents made a big effort to actually become friends again. That was—and still is—really important. Even though it was kind of weird at first, I much preferred looking up during my basketball games and seeing my parents sitting together instead of on opposite sides of the bleachers.

"Now it's not out of the question to think of us all being able to spend holidays together. It hasn't happened yet, but it could happen. Holidays continue to be one of the hardest times to have divorced parents, but since Mom and Dad are friends, it is easier for them to be flexible, understanding, and accommodating to each other, and especially to my sisters and me. I am incredibly lucky to have a family as loving and supportive as the one I do, and out of every variable, it is my parents' love and behavior that made the biggest differences in my adjustment to their divorce."

At this point, Erika can also talk about the emotions she suppressed for a long time and how she finally dealt with them. "My parents' divorce was one of the biggest changes in my life. In the midst of it, I felt like the bottom completely fell out of my life, leaving me with no place to land. Letting go of my anger and disappointment about all that had happened was a big step and required a huge amount of work. As long as I was angry, the past ruled my life. I'm not saying that I didn't have a right to those feelings, or that I should have had them for a shorter time. But developing an awareness of my feelings, allowing them in, and then letting them go was when it *finally* began to feel like my life was settling down. My parents had moved on with their lives and my sisters were doing their own thing, but I couldn't get comfortable with myself until I took responsibility for my own emotions."

Today, it is evident that Erika is comfortable with herself and confidently pursuing her career, deeply motivated to help make the world a better place. She is a remarkable young woman whose zest for life is reflected in a radiant smile and loving relationships with friends and family. I see her sisters less often, but she assures me they are doing well, too. This family's story is a powerful reminder that divorce does not automatically mean long-term problems and dysfunctional family relationships. Instead, this family's journey and Erika's resilience is a beacon of hope for what is possible.

How They Succeeded: Common Themes

These three stories share recurring themes that are active ingredients in the families' ultimate success. They are the same themes that have formed the foundation for this book. When parents focus on their children, listen to the feelings behind their words and actions, contain their own conflict, provide quality parenting—with *all* that implies—take care of themselves, and, if they enter into new romantic relationships do so slowly and carefully, they provide a foundation for their children's healthy adjustment. This is not to deny the pain or the difficulties that are part of divorce and its aftermath.

Adjusting to the multiple emotions and changes attached to the breakup of a family is not a quick fix, but an extended process, as the stories in this chapter reveal. Even though these parents ultimately achieved success in parenting children who developed resilience as they worked through the painful fallout from divorce, they—like all of us—made mistakes at times, had dark days, and struggled with problems. But they never gave up hope, and they never stopped trying, learning, and growing. They are not perfect parents; none of us are. What they did, though, was to learn and apply daily some of the skills and knowledge contained in these pages. Their hard work, willingness to search for the high points in each day, and positive outlook did bring about better days, for them and for their children.

And You . . .

As you've read this book, you may have been filled with a mixture of emotions—perhaps sadness and guilt about your marriage ending, anger and resentment about not wanting to be in this situation, and worry about how your children will fare over time. Collectively, the stories of the children told here reveal that divorce is unquestionably painful for them. It represents a major life change that many would erase from their lives if they could.

Yet they also recognize that some good things emerge from a "successful" divorce—an end to conflict and angry exchanges, and the opportunity for new beginnings and positive changes for their family, often in ways they had never before imagined. Samantha's words in chapter 1 acknowledge the difficulties, but also offer hope. "Divorce is like a kidney stone. It's painful, but when it's treated right, it passes." The vast majority of the research on children and divorce is consistent with this view of divorce from the eyes of this child.

What is your vision for the future for yourself and your children? I hope you can foresee one in which all of you are thriving. I hope you will all someday be able to look back and say, "Those surely were some tough times we faced, but we never gave up. We worked hard and got through them, and just look at us now!" Finally, I hope this book has given you some of the knowledge and tools you need to get there. May you find ways for your heart and your children's hearts to heal and soar with hope and love—just like Meg's.

NOTES

TO BEGIN . . .

Page 1 Eight-year-old "Jessica": In order to protect fully the confidentiality of my clients, I never use their real names, situations, or circumstances. Like all the children and parents I portray in this book, Jessica is a fictionalized character. Yet their experiences are very real, and the feelings conveyed through their words are repeated with remarkable consistency.

Page 8 Some researchers and clinicians: Paul R. Amato, "Children of Divorce in the 1990s: An Update of the Amato and Keith (1991) Meta-analysis," *Journal of Family Psychology* 15, no. 3 (2001): 355–370; N. Zill, D. Ruane Morrison, and M. J. Coiro, "Long-Term Effects of Parental Divorce on Parent-Child Relationships, Adjustment and Achievement in Young Adulthood," *Journal of Family Psychology* 7, no. 1 (1993): 91–103; Frank F. Furstenberg, Jr. and Andrew J. Cherlin, *Divided Families: What Happens to Children When Parents Part* (Cambridge, MA: Harvard University Press, 1991).

Page 8 In a study my colleagues and I undertook: Lynn A. Hoyt, Emory L. Cowen, JoAnne L. Pedro-Carroll, and Linda J. Alpert-Gillis, "Anxiety and Depression in Young Children of Divorce," *Journal of Clinical Child Psychology* 19, no. 1 (1990): 26–32.

Page 8 This perspective: E. Mavis Hetherington and John Kelly, *For Better or for Worse: Divorce Reconsidered* (New York: W. W. Norton, 2002).

Page 8 As some researchers have noted: Lisa Laumann-Billings and Robert E. Emery, "Distress Among Young Adults from Divorced Families," *Journal of Family Psychology* 14, no. 4 (2000): 671–687.

Page 9 When divorce results in: Paul R. Amato and Alan Booth, "The Legacy of Parents' Marital Discord Consequences for Children's Marital Quality," *Journal of Personality and Social Psychology* 81, no. 4 (2001): 627–638; Paul R. Amato and A. Booth, *A Generation* *at Risk: Growing Up in an Era of Family Upheaval* (Cambridge, MA: Harvard University Press, 1997).

Page 9 It has consistently been shown: Robert E. Emery, *The Truth About Children and Divorce: Dealing with the Emotions So You and Your Children Can Thrive* (New York: Viking, 2004).

Page 9 We know that divorce is second: T. H. Holmes and R. H. Rahe, "The Social Readjustment Rating Scale," *Journal of Psychosomatic Research* 11, no. 2 (1967): 213–218.

Page 10 In her "Virginia Longitudinal Study": Hetherington and Kelly, 2002.

Page 11 it is low-conflict divorces: Alan Booth and Paul R. Amato, "Parental Predivorce Relations and Offspring Postdivorce Well-Being," *Journal of Marriage and Family* (February 2001): 197–212.

Page 11 one of the major challenges to intervening early: John Mordechai Gottman and Julie Schwartz Gottman, "The Marriage Survival Kit: A Research-Based Marital Therapy," in Roni Berger and Mo Therese Hannah, eds., *Preventive Approaches in Couples Therapy* (New York: Routledge, 1999): 304–330.

Page 11 Couples who realize that their marriage is in trouble: C. Notarius and J. Buongiorno, *Wait Time Until Professional Treatment in Marital Therapy.* Unpublished manuscript, 1999.

CHAPTER ONE. "MY DIVORCE": WHAT CHILDREN SAY AND WHAT THEY MEAN

Page 19 reveal higher levels of anxiety: Lynn A. Hoyt, Emory L. Cowen, JoAnne L. Pedro-Carroll, and Linda J. Alpert-Gillis, "Anxiety and Depression in Early Latency Aged Children of Divorce," *Journal of Clinical Child Psychology* 19 (1990): 26–32.

Page 27 Elizabeth Marquardt: *Between Two Worlds: The Inner Lives of Children of Divorce* (New York: Crown, 2005).

Page 30 "I believed in you": This poem conveys the sentiments of those written by children with whom I have worked, but altered to protect confidentiality.

Page 32 Studies show that children: Lawrence A. Kurdek and Berthod Berg, "Correlates of Children's Adjustments to Their Parents' Divorces," in L.A. Kurdek, ed., *New Directions for Child and Adolescent Development: Children and Divorce* 19 (San Francisco: Josie Bass, 1983): 47–60.

Page 35 when children have realistic positive expectations: Peter A. Wyman, Emory L. Cowen, William C. Work, and J. H. Kerley, "The Role of Children's Future Expectations in Self-System Functioning and Adjustment to Life Stress: A Prospective Study of Urban At-Risk Children," *Development and Psychopathology* 5, no. 4 (1993): 649–661.

Page 36 The late Mr. Rogers's wise words: Fred Rogers (1928–2003), educator, songwriter, ordained Presbyterian minister, and children's television producer, was known to millions of children and their parents as the host of *Mr. Rogers' Neighborhood.*

Page 39 Abundant behavioral research: J. David Creswell, Baldwin M. Way, Naomi I. Eisenberger, and Matthew D. Leiberman, "Neural Correlates of Dispositional Mindfulness during Affect Labeling," *Psychosomatic Medicine* 69 (2007): 560–565.

Page 39 Recently, using functional magnetic resonance imaging: Matthew D. Leiberman, Naomi I. Eisenberger, Molly J. Crockett, Sabrina M. Tom, Jennifer H. Pfeifer, and Baldwin M. Way, "Putting Feelings into Words: Affect Labeling Disrupts Amygdala Activity in Response to Affective Stimuli," *Psychological Science* 18, no. 5 (2007): 421–428.

Page 40 The goal: These concepts are similar to those described in *How to Talk So Kids Will Listen & Listen So Kids Will Talk* by Adele Faber and Elaine Mazlish (New York: Avon, 1980).

CHAPTER TWO. RISK AND RESILIENCE: THE POTENTIAL IMPACT OF DIVORCE OVER TIME

Page 49 Considerable evidence from numerous studies: Paul R. Amato, "The Consequences of Divorce for Adults and Children," *Journal of Marriage and the Family* 62 (2000): 1269–1287; Paul R. Amato, "Children of Divorce in the 1990s: An Update of the Amato and Keith (1991) Meta-Analysis," *Journal of Family Psychology* 15 (1998): 355–370; Andrew J. Cherlin, P. L. Chase-Lansdale, and C. McRae, "Effects of Divorce on Mental Health Throughout the Life Course," *American Sociological Review* 63 (1998): 239–249; Robert E. Emery, *Marriage, Divorce and Children's Adjustment,* 2nd ed. (Thousand Oaks, CA: Sage, 1999); E. Mavis Hetherington, M. Bridges, and Glenda M. Insabella, "What Matters? What Does Not? Five Perspectives on the Association between Marital Transition and Children's Adjustment," *American Psychologist* 53 (1998): 167–184; S. McLanahan and G. Sandefur, *Growing Up with a Single Parent: What Hurts, What Helps* (Cambridge, MA: Harvard University Press, 1994).

Page 49 One such meta-analysis: Paul R. Amato and B. Keith, "Parental Divorce and the Well-Being of Children: A Meta-Analysis," *Psychological Bulletin* 110 (1991): 26–46.

Page 50 Children and adolescents: Amato and Keith, 1991; Amato, 2000; Paul R. Amato, "The Consequences of Divorce for Adults and Children," *Journal of Marriage and the Family* 62 (2000): 1269–1287; Emery, 1999; Joan B. Kelly, "Children's Adjustment in Conflicted Marriage and Divorce: A Decade of Review Research," *Journal of Child and Adolescent Psychiatry* 39 (2000): 963–973; E. Mavis Hetherington, "Should We Stay Together for the Sake of the Children?" in E. M. Hetherington, ed., *Coping with Divorce, Single Parenting and Remarriage* (Mahwah, NJ: Erlbaum, 1999): 93–116.

Page 50 One study found that: Nicholas Zill, Donna R. Morrison, and Mary J. Coiro, "Long-Term Effects of Parental Divorce on Parent-Child Relationships, Adjustment, and Achievement in Young Adulthood," *Journal of Family Psychology* 7 (1993): 91–103.

Page 50 Other large-scale studies: E. Mavis Hetherington and John Kelly, *For Better or for Worse: Divorce Reconsidered* (New York: W. W. Norton, 2002).

Page 50 The greatest number of serious problems: Amato, 2001; Emery, 1999; Hetherington et al., 1999; E. Mavis Hetherington and W. G. Clingempeel, "Coping with Marital Transitions," *Monographs for the Society for Research in Child Development* 57 (1992): 1–299.

Page 50 Although not as common: Amato, 2001; Hetherington and Kelly, 2002.

Page 50 These reactions begin to diminish: E. Mavis Hetherington and M. Stanley-Hagan, "Parenting in Divorced and Remarried Families," in M. Bornstein, ed., *Handbook of Parenting,* 2nd ed. (Mahwah, NJ: Erlbaum, 2002).

Page 51 Children from divorced families: Sara McLanahan, "Father Absence and the Welfare of Children," in E. M. Hetherington, ed., *Coping with Divorce, Single Parenting and Remarriage: A Risk and Resiliency Perspective* (Mahwah, NJ: Erlbaum, 1999): 117–146.

Page 51 Young adults from divorced families: Paul R. Amato, "The Consequences of Divorce for Adults and Children," *Journal of Marriage and the Family* 62 (2000): 1269–1287; P. L. Chase-Lansdale, A. J. Cherlin, and K. E. Kierman, "Effects of Divorce on Mental Health Throughout the Life Course," *American Sociological Review* 63 (1995): 239–249.

Page 51 Studies reveal that adults: Amato, 2000; Paul R. Amato and A. Booth, *A Generation at Risk: Growing Up in an Era of Family Upheaval* (Cambridge, MA: Harvard University Press, 1997); Larry Bumpass, Teresa C. Martin, and James A. Sweet, "The Impact of Family Background and Early Marital Factors on Marital Disruption," *Journal of Family Issues* 12 (1991): 22–42; McLanahan and Sandefur, 1994.

Page 51 One study explores: Paul Amato and Juliana M. Sobolewski, "The Effects of Divorce and Marital Discord on Adult Children's Psychological Well-Being," *American Sociological Review* 66, no. 6 (2001): 900–922; Patrick Davies and Mark Cummings, "Marital Conflict and Child Adjustment: An Emotional Security Hypothesis," *Psychological Bulletin* 116 (1994): 387–411; E. Mavis Hetherington and Glenn Clingempeel, "Coping with Marital Transitions: A Family Systems Perspective," *Monographs of the Society for Child Development,* Serial No. 227, 57, nos. 2–3, 1992; Rex Forehand, A. M. Thomas, A. M. Wierson, and R. Fauber, "Role of Maternal Functioning and Parenting Skills in Adolescent Functioning Following Divorce," *Journal of Abnormal Psychology* 99 (1990): 278–283.

Page 52 children's emotional ties: Amato and Sobolewski, 2001; Rosalind C. Barnett, Nazli Kabria, Grace K. Baruch, and Joseph H. Pleck, "Adult Daughter-Parent Relationships and Their Associations with Daughters' Subjective Well-Being and Psychological Distress," *Journal of Marriage and the Family* 53 (1991): 29–42.

Page 52 children's psychological adjustment: Amato and Sobolewski, 2001.

Page 52 The number of stressful life transitions: N. H. Wolfinger, "Beyond the Intergenerational Transmission of Divorce: Do People Replicate the Patterns of Marital Instability They Grew Up With?" *Journal of Family Issues* 21 (2000): 1061–1086.

Page 58 Nonaggressive conflicts: E. M. Cummings, M. Ballard, M. El-Sheikh, and M. Lake, "Resolutions and Children's Responses to Interadult Anger," *Developmental Psychology* 27 (1991): 462–470; E. M. Cummings, Paul R. Amato, and Alan Booth, *A Generation at Risk: Growing Up in an Era of Family Upheaval* (Cambridge, MA: Harvard University Press: 1997).

Page 61 High rates of parental discord: Amato and Booth, 1997.

Page 61 Adults who recall high levels: Paul R. Amato and Alan Booth, "The Legacy of Parents' Marital Discord Consequences for Children's Marital Quality," *Journal of Personality and Social Psychology* 81, no. 4 (2001): 627–638.

Page 61 Research links children's exposure: Mona E. El-Sheikh, Mark Cummings, Chrystyna D. Kouros, Lori Elmore-Staton, and Joseph Buckhalt, "Marital Psychological and Physical Aggression and Children's Mental and Physical Health: Direct, Mediated and Moderated Effects," *Journal of Consulting and Clinical Psychology* 76, no. 1 (2008): 138–148.

Page 61 Recent studies add: P. T. Davies, M. L. Sturge-Apple, Dante Cicchetti, and E. M. Cummings, "Adrenocortical Underpinnings of Children's Psychological Reactivity to Interparental Conflict," *Child Development* 79, no 6 (2008).

Page 61 Children with significant stress: Kamila S. White and Robert D. Farrell, "Anxiety and Psychosocial Stress as Predictors of Headache and Abdominal Pain in Urban Early Adolescents," *Journal of Pediatric Psychology* 31 no. 6 (2006): 582–596.

Page 61 After exposure to: Mark V. Flinn and Barry G. England, "Childhood Stress and Family Environment," *Current Anthropology* 36, no. 5 (December 1995): 854–866.

Page 61 Another study suggests: Scott Montgomery, Mel Bartley, and Richard Wilkinson, "Family Conflict and Slow Growth," *Archives of Disease in Childhood* 77 (1997): 326–330.

Page 61 divorce has positive consequences: Alan Booth and Paul R. Amato, "Parental Predivorce Relations and Offspring Postdivorce Well-Being," *Journal of Marriage and Family* 63 (2001): 197–212; Amato and Booth, 1997.

Page 61 children of parents in high-conflict: Booth and Amato, 2001; Amato and Booth, 1997.

Page 62 One of the best predictors: Joan B. Kelly and Robert Emery, "Children's Adjustment Following Divorce: Risk and Resilience Perspectives," *Family Relations* 52, no. 4 (2003): 352–362.

Page 63 The power of effective parenting: Sharlene A. Wolchik, Irwin Sandler, R. E. Millsap, B. A. Plummer, S. M. Greene, and E. R. Anderson, "Six Year Follow-Up of a Randomized Controlled Trial of Preventive Interventions for Children of Divorce," *Journal of the American Medical Association,* 288 (2002): 1–8.

Page 63 Unfortunately, studies show that: Nicholas Zill, Donna R. Morrison, and Mary J. Coiro, "Long-Term Effects of Parental Divorce on Parent-Child Relationships, Adjustment, and Achievement in Young Adulthood," *Journal of Family Psychology* 7 (1993): 91–103.

Page 64 Several studies of mothers: Hetherington, 1999; Patrick. T. Davies and E. Mark Cummings, "Marital Conflict and Child Adjustment: An Emotional Security Hypothesis," *Psychology Bulletin* 116 (1994): 387–411; A. Krishnakamur and C. Buehler, "Interparental Conflict and Parenting Behaviors: A Meta-Analytic Review," *Family Relations* 49 (2000): 25–44.

Page 64 Problems in parenting: E. Mavis Hetherington, M. Cox, and R. Cox, "Effects of Divorce on Parents and Children," in M. Lamb, ed., *Nontraditional Families* (Hillsdale, NJ: Erlbaum, 1982): 233–288.

Page 64 A significant negative effect: Nicholas Zill, Donna R. Morrison, and Mary J. Coiro, "Long-Term Effects of Parental Divorce on Parent-Child Relationships, Adjustment, and Achievement in Young Adulthood," *Journal of Family Psychology* 7 (1993): 91–103.

Page 64 Studies using direct observation: Hetherington and Kelly, 2002.

Page 65 Increasing numbers of studies: Amato, 2000; Krishnakamur and Buehler, 2000; Irwin Sandler, J. Miles, J. Cookston, and S. Braver, "Effects of Father and Mother Parenting on Children's Mental Health in High and Low Conflict Divorces," *Family Court Review* 46 (2008): 282–296.

Page 65 In a study my colleague Aaron Black: Aaron E. Black and JoAnne L. Pedro-Carroll, "The Role of Parent-Child Relationships in Mediating the Effects of Marital

Disruption," *Journal of the American Academy of Child and Adolescent Psychiatry* 32 (1993), 1019–1027.

Page 65 Research shows that, compared with young adults: Booth and Amato, 2001.

Page 65 In a meta-analysis: Amato and Gilbreth, 1999; Black and Pedro-Carroll, 1993; C. M. Buchanan, E. E. Maccoby, and S. M. Dornbusch, "Caught Between Parents: Adolescents' Experience in Divorced Homes," *Child Development* 6 (1991): 1008–1029.

Page 66 The consensus from studies: Amato and Gilbreth, 1999; Black and Pedro-Carroll, 1993; C. M. Buchanan, E. E. Maccoby, and S. M. Dornbusch, "Caught Between Parents: Adolescents' Experience in Divorced Homes," *Child Development* 6 (1991): 1008–1029.

Page 67 Ten years after their parents' divorce: L. Laumann-Billings and Robert E. Emery, "Distress Among Young Adults from Divorced Familes," *Journal of Family Psychology* 14 (2000): 671–687.

Page 68 Reports of emotional pain: Ibid.

Page 68 So much depends: Ibid.

Page 68 Children of Divorce Intervention Program: See more about this program in chapter 6; JoAnne Pedro-Carroll, "Fostering Resilience in the Aftermath of Divorce: The Role of Evidence-Based Programs for Children," *Family Court Review* (2005): 52–64.

Page 69 For young adults, the sense: Kelly and Emery, 2003.

Page 69 The majority of children and adolescents: J. Dunn, L. Davies, T. O'Connor, and W. Sturgess, "Family Lives and Friendships: The Perspectives of Children in Step, Single-Parent, and Nonstep Families," *Journal of Family Psychology* 15 (2001): 272–287.

Page 69 Even when it comes to planning: Joan B. Kelly, "Psychological and Legal Interventions for Parents and Children in Custody and Access Disputes: Current Research and Practice," *Virginia Journal of Social Policy and Law* 10 (2002): 129–163.

Page 69 Studies have found a link: Dunn et al., 2001.

CHAPTER THREE. TELLING THE CHILDREN AND PREPARING THEM FOR CHANGES

Page 76 In one study of parent-child communication: J. Dunn, L. Davies, T. O'Connor, and W. Sturgess, "Family Lives and Friendships: The Perspectives of Children in Step, Single-Parent, and Nonstep Families," *Journal of Family Psychology* 15 (2001): 272–287.

Page 79 best to tell the children after your decision to separate is final: There is one exception to this. When there is very little conflict, parents may need to prepare their children for the possibility of a divorce. Guidance on this appears on pages 89 and 90.

Page 86 Ultimately, it is children who suffer most: Robert E. Emery, *The Truth About Children and Divorce: Dealing with the Emotions So You and Your Children Can Thrive* (New York: Viking, 2004).

Page 87 Research has shown that children who maintain: Paul R. Amato, "Children of Divorce in the 1990s: An Update of the Amato and Keith (1991) Meta-analysis," *Journal of Family Psychology* 15, no. 3 (2001): 355–370.

Page 89 Studies reveal that children in high-conflict marriages: Booth and Amato, 2001.

Page 109 Functional MRI studies show: Deborah Yurgelun-Todd, PBS *Frontline* interview "Inside the Teen Brain," www.pbs.org/wgbh/pages/frontline/shows/teenbrain/interviews/todd.html.

Page 110 At the same time that teens: Giedd, 1999.

Page 110 Research suggests that: A. Brown, S. Tapert, E. Granholm, and D. Delis, "Neurocognitive Functioning of Adolescents: Effects of Protracted Alcohol Use," *Alcoholism: Clinical and Experimental Research* 24 (2000): 164–171; Aaron M. White and H. Scott Swartzwelder, "Age-Related Effects of Alcohol on Memory and Memory-Related Brain Function in Adolescents and Adults," in Marc Galanter, ed., *Recent Developments in Alcoholism* 17 (New York: Springer U.S., 2006): 161–176.

Page 110 One recent study found: Ralph W. Hingson, Timothy Heeren, and Michael R. Winter, "Age at Drinking Onset and Alcohol Dependence: Age at Onset, Duration, and Severity," *Archives of Pediatrics and Adolescent Medicine* 160 (2006): 739–746.

Page 110 A 2007 MTV and Associated Press survey: "Youths Find Happiness in Family," AP-MTV Poll, as reported in *Rochester Democrat and Chronicle*, August 20, 2007.

Page 110 Yet another survey: David Walsh, *WHY Do They Act That Way? A Survival Guide to the Adolescent Brain for You and Your Teen* (New York: Free Press, 2004).

Page 117 the average time: E. Mavis Hetherington and John Kelly, *For Better or for Worse: Divorce Reconsidered* (New York: W. W. Norton, 2002).

CHAPTER FOUR. PARENTING PLANS:
POSITIVE APPROACHES TO DIFFICULT DECISIONS

Page 122 Although aggressive representation: Andrew Schepard and Peter Salem, "Special Issue: The Family Law Education Reform Project," *Family Court Review* 44, Issue 4 (2006): 513–521.

Page 122 The Virginia Mediation Study: Robert E. Emery, L. Laumann-Billings, M. C. Waldron, D. A. Sbarra, and P. Dillon, "Child Custody Mediation and Litigation: Custody, Contact, and Coparenting 12 Years after Initial Dispute Resolution," *Journal of Consulting and Clinical Psychology* 69, 2 (2001): 323–332; Robert E. Emery and Melissa M. Wyer, "Child Custody Mediation and Litigation: An Experimental Evaluation of the Experience of Parents," *Journal of Consulting and Clinical Psychology*, 55 (1987): 179–186; Robert E. Emery, *The Truth About Children and Divorce: Dealing with the Emotions So You and Your Children Can Thrive* (New York: Viking, 2004).

Page 123 This study found: Robert E. Emery, *The Truth About Children and Divorce: Dealing with the Emotions So You and Your Children Can Thrive* (New York: Viking, 2004).

Page 127 In a study that asked what words: Patrician's 1984 work is discussed in M. K. Pruett and R. Barker, "Joint Custody: A Judicious Choice for Families—But How, When, and Why?" In R. M. Galatzer-Levy and L. Kraus, eds., *The Scientific Basis of Custody Decisions,* 2nd ed. (New York: Wiley, 2009).

Page 127 Increasingly, legal and mental health professionals: A. I. Schepard, *Children, Courts and Custody: Interdisciplinary Models for Divorcing Families* (New York: Cambridge University Press, 2004).

Page 128 Fortunately, many states: Honorable Sondra Miller, *NYS Matrimonial Commission Report*, February 2006.

Page 129 The American Psychological Association: American Academy of Child and Adolescent Psychiatry, "Practice Parameters for Child Custody Evaluations," *Journal of the American Academy of Child and Adolescent Psychiatry* 36 (1997); 57S–68S; American Psychological Association, "Guidelines for Child Custody Evaluations in Divorce Proceedings," *American Psychologist* 49 (1994): 677–680; Association of Family and Conciliation Courts, *Model Standards for Child Custody Evaluation* (Madison, WI: Association of Family and Conciliation Courts, 1995).

Page 130 Studies have shown that parents who use mediation: Robert E. Emery and Melissa Wyer, "Child Custody Mediation and Litigation: An Experimental Evaluation of the Experience of Parents," *Journal of Consulting and Clinical Psychology* 55 (1987): 179–186.

Page 130 used in 50 to 90 percent of post-divorce decrees: Joan B. Kelly, "Children's Living Arrangements Following Separation and Divorce: Insights from Clinical and Empirical Research," *Family Process* 46 (2007): 35–52.

Page 130 This represents a dramatic increase: C. W. Nord and N. Zill, *Noncustodial Parents' Participation in Their Children's Lives: Evidence from the Survey of Income and Program Participation* (Washington, DC: U.S. Department of Health and Human Services, 1996).

Page 131 Studies show that parents who share legal custody: Robert E. Emery, *The Truth About Children and Divorce: Dealing with the Emotions So You and Your Children Can Thrive* (New York: Viking, 2004).

Page 131 Legal scholars point out that this shared-time: A. I. Schepard, *Children, Courts and Custody: Interdisciplinary Models for Divorcing Families* (New York, Cambridge University Press, 2004).

Page 131 some estimates show only 5 to 10 percent: Nord and Zill, 1996; Marjorie L. Gunnoe and Sanford L. Braver, "The Effects of Joint Legal Custody on Mothers, Fathers, and Children: Controlling for Factors that Predispose a Sole Maternal versus Joint Legal Award," *Law and Human Behavior* 25, no. 1 (February 2001).

Page 131 Even in states such as California: E. E. Maccoby and R. H. Mnookin, *Dividing the Child: Social and Legal Dilemmas of Custody* (Cambridge, MA: Harvard University Press, 1992); S. L. Braver and D. O'Connell, *Divorced Dads: Shattering the Myths* (New York: Tarcher, 1998); Schepard, 2004.

Page 131 A meta-analysis of thirty-three studies: R. Bauserman, "Child Adjustment in Sole Custody Versus Joint Custody Arrangements: A Meta-Analytic Review," *Journal of Family Psychology* 16 (2002): 91–102.

Page 132 Research shows that children: J. R. Johnston, M. Kline, and J. Tschann, "Ongoing Post Divorce Conflict in Families Contesting Custody: Effects on Children of Joint Custody and Frequent Access," *American Journal of Orthopsychiatry* 59 (1989): 576–592; J. R. Johnston, "Research Update: Children's Adjustment in Sole Custody Compared to Joint Custody Families and Principles for Custody Decision Making," *Family and Conciliation Courts Review* 3 (1995): 415–425.

Page 132 Children do not benefit from frequent contact: Joan B. Kelly, 2007.

Page 132 Above all, when domestic violence is present: Schepard, 2004.

Page 133 Research provides additional information about characteristics: M. K. Pruett, 2009; S. B. Steinman, S. E. Zemmelman, and T. M. Knoblauch, "A Study of Parents Who Sought Joint Custody Following Divorce: Who Reaches Agreement and Sustains Joint Custody and Who Returns to Court," *Journal of the American Academy of Child Psychiatry* 24 (1985): 554–562.

Page 133 The parents who make shared residence agreements: M. K. Pruett, 2009.

Page 134 Studies have shown that over the long term: Joan B. Kelly, 2007; Pruett and Barker, 2009.

Page 139 The quality of parenting: Paul R. Amato and J. M. Sobolewski, "The Effects of Divorce and Marital Discord on Adult Children's Psychological Well-Being," *American Sociological Review* 66 (2001): 900–921.

Page 143 Studies show that 40 to 50 percent of parents: M. K. Pruett, 2009.

Page 145 Recent studies show that nearly half of children and teens: Joan Kelly, 2007.

Page 145 Fewer than 10 percent of youths: W. V. Fabricius and J. Hall, "Young Adults' Perspectives on Divorce: Living Arrangements," *Family and Conciliation Courts Review* 38, no. 4 (2000): 446–461.

Page 145 More than half of surveyed college students: W. V. Fabricius, "Listening to the Children of Divorce: New Findings That Diverge from Wallerstein, Lewis and Blakeslee," *Family Relations* 52 (2000): 385–396.

Page 145 children who have regular weekly contact: Kelly, 2007.

Page 146 An analysis of data from 1976 through 2002: Paul R. Amato, C. E. Meyers, and Robert E. Emery, "Changes in Nonresident Father-Child Contact from 1976 to 2002," *Family Process* 58, no. 1 (2009): 41–53.

Page 146 research has shown that reduced conflict: Joan B. Kelly and Michael E. Lamb, "Using Child Development Research to Make Appropriate Custody and Access Decisions for Young Children," *Family and Conciliation Courts Review* 39 (2000): 297–311; M. K. Pruett, "Applications of Attachment Theory and Child Development Research to Young Children's Overnights in Separated and Divorced Families," *Overnights and Young Children: Essays from the Family Court Review* (2005): 5–12; R. Warshak, "Who Will Be There When I Cry in the Night?" *Family Court Review* 40 (2002): 208–219.

Page 147 considerable evidence to suggest that most infants: Kelly and Lamb, 2000.

Page 147 recent research based on attachment theory: Joan B. Kelly and Michael E. Lamb, "Using Child Development Research to Make Appropriate Custody and Access Decisions for Young Children," *Family and Conciliation Courts Review* 39 (2000): 297–311.

Page 151 Having one or more overnights a week with the nonresidential parent: M. K. Pruett, R. Ebling, and G. Insabella, "Critical Aspects of Parenting Plans for Young Children: Interjecting Data into Debate about Overnights," *Family Court Review* 42 (2004): 39–59.

Page 156 In a large study of adolescents: C. M. Buchanan, E. E. Maccoby, and S. Dornbusch, *Adolescents after Divorce* (Cambridge, MA: Harvard University Press, 1996).

Page 156 Yet teens who spent time in both parents' homes: Buchanan et al., 1996.

Page 157 Regardless of the living arrangements: Ibid.

Page 157 High school and college students whose parents: Fabricius, 2003.

CHAPTER FIVE. TAKING CONTROL OF
CONFLICT AND TAKING CARE OF YOURSELF

Page 174 Studies show that parents often underestimate: "What Grown-Ups Understand about Child Development: A National Benchmark Study," *Zero to Three* 21, no. 2 (2000): 56–60.

Page 176 A long-term study of divorce: Judith S. Wallerstein and Sandra Blakeslee, *Second Chances: Men, Women and Children a Decade After Divorce* (New York: Ticknor & Fields, 1989); Judith S. Wallerstein, Julia M. Lewis, and Sandra Blakeslee, *The Unexpected Legacy of Divorce: The 25 Year Landmark Study* (New York: Hyperion, 2000).

Page 179 the effects of purposeful aerobic laughter: Heidi Beckman, Nathan Regier, and Judy Young, "Effect of Workplace Laughter Groups on Personal Efficacy Beliefs," *The Journal of Primary Prevention* 28, no. 2 (2007): 167–182.

Page 181 The chart below: This chart is adapted from the original developed by E. Wilson and J. McBride. With their permission, I have modified it to reflect current research and practice. Original appeared in E. Wilson and J. McBride, "Programs for High Conflict Separated/Divorced Parents: Lessons from the Front," presented at Pre-Institute, Addressing Needs of High Conflict Families, 4th International Congress on Parent Education, AFCC Kiawah, SC, November 2002.

Page 182 The concept of parallel parenting: Philip Michael Stahl, *Parenting After Divorce: A Guide to Resolving Conflicts and Meeting Your Children's Needs* (Atascadero, CA: Impact Publishers, 2000).

Page 185 Higher levels of cooperation: M. F. Whiteside and B. J. Becker, "Parental Factors and Young Children's Post Divorce Adjustment: A Meta-Analysis with Implications for Parenting Arrangements," *Journal of Family Psychology* 14 (2000): 5–26.

Page 185 children can be well-adjusted: E. Mavis Hetherington and John Kelly, *For Better or for Worse: Divorce Reconsidered* (New York: W. W. Norton, 2002); E. E. Maccoby and R. H. Mnookin, *Dividing the Child: Social and Legal Dilemmas of Custody* (Cambridge, MA: Harvard University Press, 1992); Joan B. Kelly, "Children's Living Arrangements Following Separation and Divorce: Insights from Clinical and Empirical Research," *Family Process* 46 (2007): 35–52.

Page 187 Parallel parenting affords these individuals: Evelyn Frazee, "Sensitizing Parent Education Programs to Domestic Violence Concerns: The Perspective of the New York State Parent Education Advisory Board," *Family Court Review* 43, no. 1 (2005): 124–135.

Page 187 nearly every parent education program nationwide: Susan L. Pollet and Melissa Lombreglia, "A nationwide survey of mandatory parent education," *Family Court Review* 46, no. 2 (2008): 375–394; Joan B. Kelly, "Children's Living Arrangements Following Separation and Divorce: Insights from Clinical and Empirical Research," *Family Process* 46 (2007): 35–52.

Page 188 Early research on this program: A.C.T. for the Children (Assisting Children through Transition) is a parent education program that I developed with the Honorable Evelyn Frazee, Justice, New York State Supreme Court, and colleagues in Rochester, New York. JoAnne Pedro-Carroll, Ellen Nakhnikian, and Guillermo Montes, "A.C.T.

for the Children: Helping Parents Protect Their Children from the Toxic Effects of On-going Conflict in the Aftermath of Divorce," *Family Court Review* 39, no. 4 (2001): 377–392.

Page 188 A follow-up study: Pedro-Carroll and Frazee, 2001

Page 191 In their classic text: Bruce M. Patton, William L. Ury, and Roger Fisher, *Getting to Yes: Negotiating Agreement Without Giving In*, 2nd ed. (New York: Houghton Mifflin Harcourt, 1992).

Page 207 The new study shows that women: Rick Nauert, "Spirituality Linked to Mental Health," *Psych Central*, January 2, 2009.

Page 207 In his book *Forgiveness Is a Choice*: Robert D. Enright, *Forgiveness Is a Choice: A Step-By-Step Process for Resolving Anger and Restoring Hope* (Washington, DC: American Psychological Association, 2001).

Page 208 Another study of parents of children aged ten to thirteen: K. Ashelman, "Forgiveness as a Resiliency Factor in Divorced or Permanently Separated Families," Unpublished master's thesis, University of Wisconsin-Madison (1996).

CHAPTER SIX. BUILDING CHILDREN'S RESILIENCE SKILLS

Page 213 The skills they learn: JoAnne L. Pedro-Carroll, "Fostering resilience in the aftermath of divorce: The role of evidence-based programs for children," *Family Court Review* 43 (2005), 52–64; JoAnne L. Pedro-Carroll, Sara E. Sutton, and Peter A. Wyman, "A two year follow-up evaluation of a preventive intervention program for young children of divorce," *School Psychology Review* 28 (1999), 467–476; JoAnne Pedro-Carroll and Sheryl. H. Jones, "A Preventive Play Intervention to Foster Children's Resilience in the Aftermath of Divorce," in L. A. Reddy, C. E. Schaeffer, and T. M. Hall, eds., *Empirically Based Play Interventions for Children* (Washington, DC: American Psychological Association, 2005); Stolberg and Garrison, 1985; Arnold Stolberg and J. Mahler, "Enhancing Treatment Gains in a School-Based Intervention for Children of Divorce Through Skill Training, Parental Involvement, and Transfer Procedures," *Journal of Consulting and Clinical Psychology* 62 (1994): 147–156; R. L. Fischer, "Children in Changing Families: Results of a Pilot Study of a Program for Children of Separation and Divorce," *Family and Conciliation Courts Review* 37 (1999): 240–245.

Page 215 The Children of Divorce Intervention Program: Special thanks to my colleagues Drs. Linda Alpert-Gillis, Sharon Sterling, Sara Sutton, and Aaron Black for their valuable contributions to the development of CODIP for different age groups. For more information about CODIP, contact the Children's Institute, Rochester, New York, or see www.childrensinstitute.net.

Page 215 In CODIP: JoAnne Pedro-Carroll and Sheryl. H. Jones, "A Preventive Play Intervention to Foster Children's Resilience in the Aftermath of Divorce," in L. A. Reddy, C. E. Schaeffer, and T. M. Hall, eds., *Empirically Based Play Interventions for Children* (Washington, DC: American Psychological Association, 2005).

Page 216 Skills That Promote Resilience and Emotional Intelligence: Daniel Goleman, *Emotional Intelligence: Why It Can Matter More Than IQ* (New York: Bloomsbury, 1995).

Page 225 In our children's groups and other evidence-based programs: Special thanks to Dr. Arnold Stolberg and colleagues for their pioneering work on the Divorce Adjustment Project, which provided a model for my doctoral dissertation and early work developing CODIP. See Arnold. L. Stolberg and Kathleen M. Garrison, "Evaluating a Primary Prevention Program for Children of Divorce: The Divorce Adjustment Project," *American Journal of Community Psychology* 13 (1985): 111–124.

Page 225 Help children understand what they can realistically control: Judith S. Wallerstein, "Children of Divorce: Stress and Developmental Tasks," in Norman Garmezy and M. Rutter, eds., *Stress, Coping and Development in Children* (New York: McGraw-Hill, 1983): 265–302.

Page 227 Studies of learned helplessness: L. Y. Abrahamson, M. E. P. Seligman, and J. D. Teasdale, "Learned Helplessness in Humans: Critique and Reformulation," *Journal of Abnormal Psychology* 87 (1978): 49–74.

Page 235 But research has proven that children benefit: Irwin N. Sandler, J. Y. Tein, P. Mehta, Sharlene A. Wolchik, and T. Ayers, "Perceived Coping Efficacy and Psychological Problems of Children of Divorce," *Child Development* 74, no. 4 (2000): 1097–1118; I. N. Sandler, J. Y. Tein, and S. G. West, "Coping, Stress and Psychological Symptoms of Children of Divorce: A Cross Sectional and Longitudinal Study," *Child Development* 65 (1994): 1744–1763; Sharon E. Sterling, "School-Based Intervention Program for Early Latency-Aged Children of Divorce," unpublished Ph.D. dissertation, University of Rochester, 1986.

CHAPTER SEVEN. EMOTIONALLY INTELLIGENT PARENTING BEFORE, DURING, AND AFTER DIVORCE

Page 249 Quality parenting is one of the best predictors: Paul R. Amato, "The Consequences of Divorce for Adults and Children," *Journal of Marriage and the Family* 62 (2000): 1269–1287; E. E. Maccoby and R. H. Mnookin, *Dividing the Child: Social and Legal Dilemmas of Custody* (Cambridge, MA: Harvard University Press, 1992); E. Mavis Hetherington, Margaret Bridges, and Glendessa M. Insabella, "Five Perspectives on the Association Between Marital Transitions and Children's Adjustment," in Margaret E. Hertzig and Ellen A. Farber, eds., *Annual Progress in Child Psychology and Development 1999* (New York: Psychology Press/Routledge, 2001).

Page 249 child development researchers typically define: Robert E. Emery, *The Truth About Children and Divorce: Dealing with the Emotions So You and Your Children Can Thrive* (New York: Viking, 2004); Maccoby and Martin, 1983.

Page 250 Current research shows that weak emotional bonds: Paul R. Amato and J. M. Sobolewski, "The Effects of Divorce and Marital Discord on Adult Children's Psychological Well-Being," *American Sociological Review* 66 (2001): 900–921.

Page 250 Children who suffer: Irwin Sandler, J. Miles, J. Cookston, and S. Braver, "Effects of Father and Mother Parenting on Children's Mental Health in High and Low Conflict Divorces," *Family Court Review* 46 (2008): 282–296.

Page 257 appreciations that stick like Velcro: Special appreciation to Joyce and Tom DeVoge for sharing this concept from their work promoting healthy marriages. See J. Thomas DeVoge and Joyce B. DeVoge, "Communication and Conflict Resolution," in

Rita DeMaria and Mo Therese Hannah, eds., *Building Healthy Relationships* (New York: Brunner-Routledge: 2003).

Page 258 Along with effective discipline: Wolchik et al., 2002.

Page 259 It is important to convey to your children: This is half of an important concept: All feelings are acceptable, but all behaviors are not necessarily acceptable. This concept will be discussed in greater depth in the section titled "Love and Limits: Creating Structure and Effective Discipline," beginning on page 264.

Page 260 An empathetic, nonjudgmental response: This approach is adapted from noted child psychologist Haim Ginott and his students Adele Faber and Elaine Mazlish in their book *How to Talk So Kids Will Listen & Listen So Kids Will Talk.*

Page 260 Appropriate, regular bedtimes: John Guidubaldi et al., "The Impact of Parental Divorce on Children: Report of the Nationwide NASP Study," *School Psychology Review* 12, no. 3 (1983): 300–323.

Page 263 The link between social connectedness: K. K. Kline, *Report of the Commission on Children at Risk* (Hanover, NH: Dartmouth Medical School, 2003).

Page 271 In *Between Two Worlds:* Elizabeth Marquardt, *Between Two Worlds: The Inner Lives of Children of Divorce* (New York: Crown, 2006).

CHAPTER EIGHT. NEW RELATIONSHIPS, DATING, AND REMARRIAGE: HOW THE CHILDREN SEE THEM

Page 281 In *For Better or for Worse:* E. Mavis Hetherington and John Kelly, *For Better or for Worse: Divorce Reconsidered* (New York: W. W. Norton, 2002).

Page 282 stepfamilies typically experience important positive changes: Hetherington and Kelly, 2002.

Page 282 divorce rates are higher in remarriage: Ibid.

Page 285 Although many children are wary: Ibid.

Page 286 Research shows that good relationships between stepmothers and stepchildren: Ibid.

Page 287 One of the most pervasive and unproductive beliefs: E. B. Visher and J. S. Visher, *Old Loyalties, New Ties: Therapeutic Strategies with Stepfamilies* (New York: Brunner/Mazel, 1988).

Page 287 For some children, especially girls: Hetherington and Kelly, 2002.

Page 287 it takes a substantial amount of time: S. C. Clarke and B. F. Wilson, "The Relative Stability of Remarriages: A Cohort Approach Using Vital Statistics," *Family Relations* 43 (1994): 305–310.

Page 287 The general course of family life: Hetherington and Kelly, 2002.

Page 287 children in stepfamilies are more likely: A. J. Cherlin and F. F. Furstenberg, "Stepfamilies in the United States: A Reconsideration," *Annual Review of Sociology* 20, no. 1 (1994): 359–381; M. Coleman, L. Ganong, and M. A. Fine, "Reinvestigating Remarriage: Another Decade of Progress," *Journal of Marriage and the Family* 62 (2000): 1288–1307; H. L. Ganong and M. Coleman, *Stepfamily Relationships: Development, Dynamics, and Interventions* (New York: Kluwer, 2004).

Page 289 In recognition of the importance of supporting: F. Adler-Baeder and B. Higginbotham, "Implications of Remarriage and Stepfamily Formation for Marriage

Education," *Family Relations* 53 (2004): 448–458; F. Adler-Baeder, B. Higginbotham, and L. Lamke, "Putting Empirical Knowledge to Work: Linking Research and Programming on Marital Quality," *Family Relations* 53 (2004): 537–546.

Page 290 *Communication*: The marital skills described in this section, beginning with "Communication," are discussed in the technical report by A. Robertson, F. Adler-Baeder, A. Collins, D. DeMarco, D. Fein, and D. Schramm, *Meeting the Needs of Low-Income Stepfamily Couples in Marriage Education Services* (Washington, DC: Administration for Children and Families, U.S. Department of Health and Human Services, 2007). As part of the *Healthy Marriage Initiative,* a team of experts proposed recommendations for Marriage Education Programs for Stepfamilies that is based on substantive research. Their recommendations include approaches to new stepfamily relationships that are helpful for all families, regardless of income.

Page 290 Couples in successful remarriages: H. J. Markman, S. M. Stanley, and S. L. Blumber, *Fighting for Your Marriage: Positive Steps for a Loving and Lasting Relationship* (San Francisco: Jossey-Bass, 1994); John Mordechai Gottman and Julie Schwartz Gottman, "The Marriage Survival Kit: A Research-Based Marital Therapy," in Roni Berger and Mo Therese Hannah, eds., *Preventive Approaches in Couples Therapy* (New York: Routledge, 1999): 304–330.

Page 290 With the added stresses of stepchildren: J. Thomas DeVoge and Joyce B. DeVoge, "Communication and Conflict Resolution," in Rita DeMaria and Mo Therese Hannah, eds., *Building Healthy Relationships* (New York: Brunner-Routledge, 2003).

Page 291 understanding the importance of the stepchild-stepparent relationship: Robertson et al., 2007.

Page 291 The younger the children are: M. A. Fine, M. Coleman, and L. H. Ganong, "Consistency in Perceptions of the Step-Parent Role Among Step-Parents, Parents and Stepchildren," *Journal of Social and Personal Relationships* 15 (1998): 810–828.

Page 291 much more difficult for adolescents: J. H. Bray and S. H. Berger, "Developmental Issues in Stepfamilies Research Project: Family Relationships and Parent-Child Interactions," *Journal of Family Psychology* 7 (1993): 76–90.

Page 291 Some research suggests: Hetherington and Kelly, 2002.

Page 293 Negotiating parenting roles: Longitudinal studies of stepfamilies highlight further the specific qualities and practices that relate to successful and enduring remarriages. Hetherington and Kelly, 2002; J. Bray and J. Kelly, *Stepfamilies: Love, Marriage, and Parenting in the First Decade* (New York: Broadway, 1998).

Page 293 Tensions between and among stepchildren: Ganong and Coleman, 2004.

Page 293 Remarriages fare better: Longitudinal studies of stepfamilies highlight further the specific qualities and practices that relate to successful and enduring remarriages. Hetherington and Kelly, 2002; Bray and Kelly, 1998.

Page 294 relationships between stepparents: Longitudinal studies of stepfamilies highlight further the specific qualities and practices that relate to successful and enduring remarriages. Hetherington and Kelly, 2002; Bray and Kelly, 1998.

INDEX

Arizona
  joint custody in, 131
  safety-based parenting plans in, 132
Assisting Children through Transition
        (A.C.T.), 188
Associated Press, 110
Association of Family and Conciliation
        Courts (AFCC), 126, 129
Attachment, 24, 65
  developmental stages and, 91–94, 147–50
  enduring power of, 10, 33
  negative, 59, 176
  in stepfamilies, 287, 292
Attorneys. *See* Lawyers
Australia, 53
  preventive intervention in, 215
Authoritarian parenting, 249
Authoritative parenting, 54, 56, 60, 62,
        65–67, 82, 189, 249
  limit-setting in, 265, 306
  parenting plans and, 139, 146
  in stepfamilies, 286
Awareness, emotional, 216, 221–23

Bedtime routines, 168, 253, 260–61
  developmental stages and, 147, 151
  structured choices in, 268
Behavior problems, 104, 267
  risk of, 50, 58, 63
  See also Acting-out behaviors
Behavioral research, 8, 39
Betrayal, feelings of, 23, 29–31, 58, 74, 85
  rumors and, 84
Between Two Worlds (Marquardt), 27, 271
Biopsychosocial wellness, 61
Birthdays, 164, 166, 167
Blame, 86, 104, 176
Blended families. *See* Stepfamilies
Brain research, 8, 39–40, 109
Bronfenbrenner, Urie, 294
Buddhism, 39, 208

California, joint physical custody in, 131
Canada, 53
  preventive intervention in, 215
Certified financial planners (CFPs), 202
Certified public accountants (CPAs), 202
Change, planning for, 140–42
Changing Families Groups, 215
Chanukah, 166
Child support payments, 131
Children of Divorce Intervention Program
        (CODIP), 68–69
"Childrenese," 16–19
Choices, structured, setting limits with,
        267–71

Christmas, 166
Clinginess, 21, 22, 28
Coaches, collaborative practice, 125
Cognitive behavior therapy, 228
Collaborative law, 124–26, 201, 209–10
Collaborative problem-solving, 197–201
Communication, 74–75
  in collaborative law, 125
  about decision to divorce. *See* Decision to
        divorce, telling children about
  in effective coparenting, 272
  of emotions, 16–19, 36–46, 178
  lack of, impact of, 70
  in parenting plans, 135, 136, 144–45, 162–63
  to reduce conflict, 60, 175, 188–89,
        191–96
  in stepfamilies, 290
  therapy and, 204–5
  withdrawal from, 3
Community, engagement in, 263
Conduct disorders, 50
Conflict, 8, 25–26, 51, 111, 169–75
  containing, 57–61, 64, 94, 162, 167
  custody and, 128, 132
  guilt over, 31
  ineffective parenting and, 64
  legal options and, 121–23, 126
  levels of, before divorce, 9–11, 89
  lingering painful memories of, 67–68
  managing and resolving, 187–201, 290,
        293–94
  parenting plans and, 134, 135, 143–44
  and telling children about decision to
        divorce, 76–77, 85, 86, 89
  unresolved, perils of, 170–72
  worries magnified by, 23
Context, creating, 43–44
Control, realistic perceptions of, 225–29
Cooperative parenting, 56, 57, 120, 126,
        172–75, 181–82, 184–87, 191
Coparenting, effective, 271–74
  remarriage and, 293
Coping, 32–35
  silence as means of, 15
  See also Resilience
Cortisol, 61
Cosby, Bill, 179
Couples therapy, 73
Cowen, Emory, 5
Creative writing, 220–21
Crying, excessive, 29, 43, 90, 92, 140, 173–74
Custody, 1, 58–59, 67–68
  court's role in, 128–29
  legal definitions of, 129–33
  See also Parenting plans
Cyprus, preventive intervention in, 215